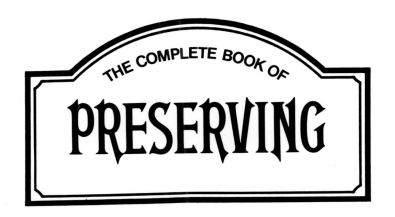

THE COMPLETE BOOK OF
PRESERVING

THE COMPLETE BOOK OF PRESERVING

Marye Cameron-Smith

Marshall Cavendish

Edited by Nicky Hayden

Designed and illustrated by Caroline Austin

Published by
Marshall Cavendish Books Limited
58 Old Compton Street
London W1V 5PA

© Marshall Cavendish Limited 1976, 1977, 1982

First printed 1976
Reprinted 1977
This printing 1982

ISBN 0 85685 174 4

Printed in Hong Kong

Introduction

Preserving used to be one of those kitchen skills which was almost second nature to cooks up to a couple of generations ago. Then came the development of convenience foods which seemed to save so much time. Now preserving is coming back into its own, not because food needs to be processed to make it keep for long periods – modern refrigeration has changed that – but for equally important reasons: quality, economy and variety.

There are many ways of preserving different foodstuffs. The techniques may take a little time, but this is amply rewarded by the superior quality of the finished product. If fresh produce is preserved in your own home, you know that the quality is as good as you can make it. As for economy, if you use this book wisely, it really will help you save money. Seasonal foods can be bought at their cheapest and best, or better still gathered from your own kitchen garden. There are methods to preserve almost any type of produce: jams and jellies, bottling, making chutneys and pickles, candying fruit, home freezing, and lesser known techniques such as drying or curing – information enough to keep any household well-stocked all year round for minimum cost. And finally, *The Complete Book of Preserving* can bring variety into your kitchen by supplying many different recipes either for making the preserves themselves or for using preserved produce in exciting ways. Of course there are thousands of recipes which could have been chosen – those included represent a wide selection which will inspire any cook to get into the kitchen at once and start preserving.

Contents

Metrication Chart

Guide to Metric and Imperial equivalent measures

Solid measures

Metric	Imperial
grams (g)	ounces (oz)
25g	1oz
50g	2oz
75g	3oz
100-125g	4oz ($\frac{1}{4}$lb)
150g	5oz
175g	6oz
200g	7oz
225g	8oz ($\frac{1}{2}$lb)
250g	9oz
275g	10oz
300g	11oz
350g	12oz ($\frac{3}{4}$lb)
375g	13oz
400g	14oz
425g	15oz
450g	16oz (1lb)
1,000g = 1 kilogram (kg)	

Note : The above metric weights are approximate equivalents. For ease of multiplying when converting Imperial to Metric the grams are rounded down to the nearest 25g (28.32g is the exact conversion of 1oz). They are sufficiently accurate when weighing quantities up to 1kg.

When scaled-up for larger quantities the conversion error becomes more important. For this reason when using weights more than 3lb the following conversions are more accurate. However, since it is important to 'think metric', a reasonable approximation is given as well. The important thing to remember is to adjust the proportions of liquid and solid ingredients equally.

1kg 360g (Approx 1.35kg)			3lb
1kg 815g (	,,	1.75kg)	4lb
2kg 270g (	,,	2.25kg)	5lb
2kg 720g (	,,	2.75kg)	6lb
3kg 175g (	,,	3.20kg)	7lb
3kg 630g (	,,	3.35kg)	8lb
4kg 80g (	,,	4.75kg)	9lb
4kg 535g (	,,	4.50kg)	10lb

Liquid measures

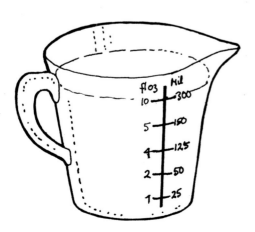

Millilitres	Fluid ounces
25ml	1fl oz

50ml	2fl oz
125ml	4fl oz
150ml	5fl oz ($\frac{1}{4}$ pint)
300ml	10fl oz ($\frac{1}{2}$ pint)
400ml	15fl oz ($\frac{3}{4}$ pint)
600ml	20fl oz (1 pint)
1,000ml = 1 litre	35fl oz ($1\frac{3}{4}$ pints)
4 litres	8 pints (1 gallon)

Spoon measures

1 tablespoon	15ml approx
2 teaspoons	10ml ,,
1 teaspoon	5ml ,,
$\frac{1}{2}$ teaspoon	2.5ml ,,

Linear measures

Millimetres (mm) and Centimetres (cm)	Inches (in) and Feet (ft)
5mm	$\frac{1}{4}$in
10mm (1cm)	$\frac{1}{2}$in
25mm (2.5cm)	1in
50mm (5cm)	2in
75mm (7.5cm)	3in
100mm (10cm)	4in
12.5cm	5in
15cm	6in
17.5cm	7in
20cm	8in
22.5cm	9in
25cm	10in
27.5cm	11in
30cm	12in (1ft)
1 metre (1m)	39in (3ft 3in)

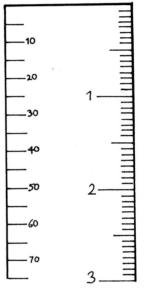

Temperature measures

Temperature Guide	Celsius (°C)	Fahrenheit (°F)	Gas Mark
	70°C	150°F	
	80°C	175°F	
	100°C	200°F	
Very cool	110°C	225°F	$\frac{1}{4}$
	120°C	250°F	$\frac{1}{2}$
	140°C	275°F	1
Cool	150°C	300°F	2
Warm	160°C	325°F	3
Moderate	180°C	350°F	4
Fairly hot	190°C	375°F	5
	200°C	400°F	6
Hot	220°C	425°F	7
	230°C	450°F	8
Very hot	240°C	475°F	9
	260°C	500°F	9

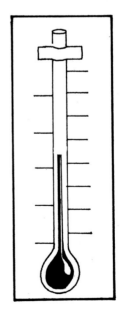

A note for North American cooks

New metric spoon measures are exactly right for
North America (ie. 1 teaspoon = 5ml, 1 tablespoon = 15ml).
However, cup and liquid measurements cannot be metricated exactly:
1 American cup = 0.24 litres
1 American pint (16fl oz) = 0.47 litres
1 American quart (32fl oz) = 0.95 litres

The practice of preserving

Preserving, to many people, conjures up nostalgic visions of country kitchens full of bubbling pans of fruity jam or gleaming jars of crunchy pickles. Yet the scope of food preservation is much, much wider, stemming as it did from the centuries before modern refrigeration. The legacy of these practical and literally vital techniques is a wealth of excitingly different tastes and textures from many different raw materials – some of them very commonplace. And curiously enough, in this latter part of the twentieth century, one of its greatest advantages is coming back into its own – that of economy.

There are many methods of preserving, depending on the food to be stored and many are almost as old as civilization itself. But they all have one thing in common – to make seasonal foods available at a time when they are normally difficult to come by. It is no coincidence that preserving is a tradition of many north and east European countries which has been 'exported' to America and kept alive especially in the colder East Coast areas. Some of the methods are known to be very old – sun drying and salting for instance have been in existence for at least two thousand years, and probably originated in pre-historic times. The object of preserving then – and indeed until the early part of the twentieth century – was often a life or death matter: to store away as much food as possible during a plentiful harvest or animal slaughter to last the community over the harsh months of winter or, in hot climates, periods of prolonged drought. Fish and meat were habitually preserved in salt for long sea voyages, though by all accounts the results were often pretty unpalatable.

Nowadays preserving is no longer a matter of survival, though in some inaccessible and primitive cultures some of the oldest methods are still in general use for this reason. But in more highly developed regions such as ours, preserving has several quite distinct advantages – economy, quality, variety and that indefinable sense of personal satisfaction that any sort of 'do-it-yourself' brings.

Economy may not be at the top of everyone's list, but nobody can deny that it *is* an advantage today. And there is certainly nothing more pleasing than to know that by preserving you have made a real saving simply by using a little forethought and setting aside some time and energy. Most methods of preserving take time – candying fruit (though a simple enough procedure) can actually take as much as two weeks to complete! However, if you can obtain fresh produce in season, either by growing it yourself or buying at a local market when it is plentiful and cheap, there are usually several ways – some

11

Below: A well-stocked store cupboard will always contain some preserved foods such as bottled fruit, dried herbs and vegetables, cured meats, pickles, sauces and chutneys, jams and jellies.

Opposite: Fresh vegetables can be preserved in a number of ways, such as drying or pickling, but undoubtedly the best way to preserve their true texture and flavour is by home freezing. Full instructions are given from page 146.

long, some short – of making preserves, while it is in peak condition and relatively cheap. In this way you can fill your store cupboard to bursting with delicious and useful foodstuffs, which can be used in countless ways and in thousands of recipes. Fruit can be preserved by bottling or drying, in jams and jellies, in pickles and chutneys, in marmalades. Vegetables can be turned into juicy chutneys or crisp pickles, some can be bottled, dried or salted, or used in sauces. Fish can be salted and smoked with especially interesting results, and for the real enthusiast, some meats – particularly pork – can be cured and smoked with success if care is taken in the preparation. And almost all foods, cooked and uncooked, can be preserved by the most recent technique – home freezing.

In technical terms, the object of preserving is to slow down or stop the inevitable process of decay inherent in all organic matter, whether

it is caused by bacteria, yeasts, moulds, enzymes, oxidation or dehydration. The first is based on sterilization by heat (as in bottling). Naturally for this method the containers have to be sealed to prevent recontamination during storage. The second category includes methods which reduce the activity of water in food, and this is done by drying, salting, adding sugar or vinegar, or by freezing. Whichever method is used, there will generally be a change of flavour or texture – but one which is just as palatable as the natural flavour – and in some cases, such as smoked salmon, actually preferred.

Of course, for anyone with a good kitchen garden or allotment, preserving is the first – or perhaps second – step to self-sufficiency. But even if you don't have the opportunity to indulge in domestic husbandry on this scale, almost anyone can grow surplus tomatoes for chutney, or enough herbs to dry a plentiful supply, or pick enough windfalls for bottled apple purée. There's another readily available source of supply as well – and it's by far the cheapest! A day's wandering along a hedgerow or thicket in late summer might supply the diligent picker with blackberries, elderberries, rose hips, sloes, crab apples – even wild pears or field mushrooms – and produce the most economical preserves of all – for nothing.
(A word of warning here, however: make sure your preserves don't end up as a false economy. Sugar is no longer particularly cheap, so jam making should be geared to your family's needs *and* likes. Work out the yield in advance and don't gather more than you really need for the year. Even the best preserved foods have a limited life span – and endless pots of bramble jelly or green tomato chutney can pall if there's nothing else for teatime toast or cold cuts.)

Freezing and curing require a slightly different treatment. Freezers involve a substantial capital outlay and become, far more than other methods of preserving, a matter of day-to-day home management. But if minimum changes in taste, texture and nutritional value are what you want, freezing is certainly the best way to achieve them – and a freezer will also save you time and money if it is used properly. Curing is another matter. Curing fish and meat can be a risky business, and commercially cured products of a very high standard are readily available. But the flavour of home-cured foods is quite different from any other, and, if you have the facilities, you can smoke foods as well, producing delicious and unusual foods by traditional methods. For both freezing and curing it is wise to befriend a fishmonger and a butcher so that you can get really fresh produce – if you can't catch it yourself!

In the end, the reasons for home preserving must be personal. 'Self-sufficiency' may be far from your thoughts as you stir the chutney or spread the apple rings to dry in your airing cupboard. A love of good things cooked and prepared in your own kitchen using natural and wholesome ingredients may be the only motivation needed to set you off. Whether you opt for a few jars of marmalade when Seville oranges are in season, or whether you're anxious not to waste surplus produce from the kitchen garden or orchard, the following chapters will give you plenty of scope to learn new skills, perfect old ones, and give you a supply of different and inviting treats throughout the year, regardless of season.

Though some varieties of apple have been developed which are suitable for storing throughout the winter, most are strictly seasonal and can only be kept for eating fresh for a relatively short time. Over the centuries several ways of preserving apples have evolved. They can be dried, sliced into rings then strung together to save space in the kitchen or larder; they can be bottled either in slices or as apple pulp or purée; (for instance, Bramley cooking apples do not bottle well in pieces – pulp or purée them for best results). Apples can be combined with sugar and spices to make apple butter; and their high pectin content makes them an ideal addition to jams and jellies made with low pectin fruits such as blackberries. Finally, they can be pressed to make drinks ranging from simple apple juice, through rough 'scrumpy' cider, to the refined apple brandy of France known as Calvados.

Bottling

Bottled fruits are a delicious and practical addition to a store cupboard. They can be used to liven up desserts and pies at times when seasonal fruits are not available.

Bottling is one of the methods of preserving food by heat, and will only be successful if the processing is efficiently and correctly carried out and the bottles are completely sealed for storage. Home bottling of vegetables is not recommended unless a pressure cooker with a very accurate pressure control is available. The reason for this is that

vegetables are low in acid and may contain forms of bacteria which are resistant to heat. They may also contain a toxin which develops during storage that could cause fatal food poisoning. It is possible that this would not be destroyed during normal processing unless the sterilization temperature is higher than the boiling point of water; this must be at least 115°C (240°F) which can only be achieved in a reliable pressure cooker. Brief details are given for bottling vegetables in this way later. However, it is inadvisable to try unless you are really experienced in using a pressure cooker.

On the other hand food that contains a high percentage of acid – like fruit and tomatoes – are ideal for bottling as the acid inhibits the growth of bacteria and prevents formation of toxin. Different fruits of course vary in the amount of acid they contain, and those with a lower content require to be processed for a longer time – these times are given in the Bottling Chart, page 28.

Equipment
There are two types of bottles specially made for this purpose, one with a spring-clip top and the other with a screw band. These are

Bottling jars come in various sizes and types, with clip or screw tops. Screw top jars are probably the most familiar type. Lightly grease the screw bands before use so that they are easier to remove after storage. Most fruits can be bottled successfully; shown here (left to right) are blackberries, cherries, apples, peaches, pears, strawberries, raspberries, gooseberries and apricots.

Left: Peaches are best bottled in a heavy syrup. They can also be preserved in brandy, which is combined with sugar syrup (see page 32 for method). Far left: A selection of fruits suitable for bottling.

available in various sizes and are obtainable from hardware, kitchen equipment or department stores. Jam jars can also be used in most methods but *not* in a pressure cooker. Whichever type of bottle is used, it must not be chipped or cracked and should be scrupulously clean. If glass lids are used these should not be chipped. Metal lids should not be scratched or damaged in any way.

Clip-sealed bottles have a rubber ring between the lid and rim of the bottle. These help to form a complete seal when the bottle has been processed. During the processing the lid is kept on by a spring-clip which allows any air and steam to escape. When the bottle is cooling the clip holds the lid in position while a vacuum is forming inside the bottle. These are removed when the bottles are stored.

Screw-band bottles either have glass lids and separate rubber rings or, more generally, a metal lid fitted with a rubber ring, kept in place by a band which screws on. During processing (except during the oven methods) this band should be loosely screwed on and then tightened while the bottle is cooling.

If you are using separate rubber rings make sure they are the correct size. Always use new rings; once they have been used they stretch and will not form a satisfactory seal the second time around. Before using rubber rings, soak them in warm water for about ten minutes, then quickly dip into boiling water immediately before using.

A large container for processing the bottles is another essential. If the processing is done on top of the cooker then the container must have a false bottom – a wooden or wire rack is ideal – so that the bottles do not come into direct contact with the container. If they do they will crack. The container also must be deep enough to hold sufficient water to cover the bottles completely. Special bottling pans are available and one of these is a good investment if a lot of bottling is done each year. However, if you use the oven method, (see page 22), a large asbestos mat is necessary to stand the bottles on.

Other useful items of equipment are a thermometer, a long handled spoon, a pair of tongs and a heat-proof jug.

Preparation of fruit

Fruit used for bottling must be fresh, firm and clean. Wash the fruit in cold water and leave to drain in a colander. Soft fruits – raspberries, blackberries and loganberries – can be soaked for a few minutes in salted water to remove any grubs or insects, rinsed in fresh cold water and left to drain. Hull fruits such as raspberries and strawberries, 'top and tail' gooseberries and blackcurrants. Remove the peel and pith from citrus fruits, cut the segments away from the tissues and remove any pips. Pears and apples are best peeled, cored and cut into slices or quarters. Apricots, peaches and plums may be bottled whole or halved with the stones removed.

Fruit may be bottled in plain fresh water or syrup. Syrup is preferable as it helps to preserve the colour and flavour. The strength of the syrup depends on the sweetness of the fruit and also how it is packed. The proportions are generally 225g (8oz) to 600ml (1 pint) water.

To make the syrup dissolve the sugar in the water over a moderate heat and when the sugar is dissolved boil for one minute. If the syrup is cloudy, strain it through muslin as clear syrup gives a better finish to the fruit. The sugar used for syrup may be granulated or loaf or, for a different flavour, honey or golden syrup could be used instead. The syrup is used either cold or very hot, depending on the processing method.

A brine solution is best for tomatoes. Make it with 1 tablespoon ($\frac{1}{2}$oz) of salt to 1 litre ($1\frac{3}{4}$ pints) water. If they are packed solidly no water is necessary but 1 teaspoon of salt should be added to each 450g (1lb) tomatoes.

Packing the bottles

Rinse the clean bottles in cold water, drain them but do not dry them – it is much simpler to pack the fruit into wet bottles as it slips down more easily. Fill with the prepared fruit and press down with

Right: Adding the sugar to the water to make bottling syrup. Far right: Using a pressure cooker for bottling. The bottles should not touch each other or the sides of the cooker (this applies to all processing methods).

the handle of a wooden spoon. Make sure the fruit is tightly packed but be careful not to bruise it. Fill the bottles to within 10-25mm ($\frac{1}{2}$-1in) of the rim then pour the syrup or water over the fruit a little at a time. Twist the bottle from side to side after each addition to remove any air bubbles.

Methods of processing

Processing the bottles may be done on top of the cooker or in the oven; the former is known as the water-bath method, the latter the oven method. There are three variations on the water-bath method, and two for the oven method. The advantages of the water-bath methods are reliability and economy of fuel, but they can only be done in a container large and deep enough to allow the bottles to be completely immersed. It is more difficult to control the temperature with the oven method and the processing time is longer. Times and temperatures for different fruits and methods are given in the chart on page 28.

Method 1: Slow water-bath

Pack the bottles with fruit and pour in enough *cold* syrup (or brine) to come to the top of the bottle. This is best done slowly to allow the syrup to penetrate to the bottom of the bottle. Place the lid on top and secure it with a spring clip or screw-band (see Equipment). Place the bottles in a deep container, making sure they do not touch each other or the sides of the container. Completely cover them with cold water, cover the container with a lid. (If no lid is available a pastry board is a good substitute.) Bring the water slowly to the boil. The temperature of the water should be raised gradually from cold to 55°C (130°F) in one hour and up to the required temperature (see chart page 28) in up to another half hour. If the water is heated too quickly the fruit may rise in the bottles and more time may be needed at the maximum temperature to enable heat to penetrate the fruit in the centre of the bottle.

When the processing time is finished remove the bottles from the container using a pair of tongs and place them on a wooden table or board. Tighten bands on the screw-topped bottles and leave for 24 hours before testing that the seal is complete (see page 21).

Method 2: Quick water-bath

This method is similar to method 1 and is recommended when no thermometer is available. However, temperatures are given for those who have a thermometer in order to achieve the best results. The main difference between methods 1 and 2 is that hot syrup at 60°C (140°F) is poured into the packed bottles and these are then placed in the container and covered with warm water at 38°C (100°F). 25 to 30 minutes after the processing starts the water should reach simmering point, 88°C (190°F), and should be kept simmering throughout the whole process. If the bottles are over 1kg (approx 2lb) capacity extra time will be required. Remove and finish the jars as in method 1.

Method 3: Pressure cooker

This is a quick method of bottling fruit, as the temperature of boiling point is raised when under pressure, so reducing the processing time and saving energy. The pressure to use should be L or 5lb for

Top: Packing the bottles. Centre: Filling the bottle with syrup. Above: Testing the seal (see overleaf).

bottling. (Pressure cookers are fitted with a weight gauge which is measured either by the appropriate weight or by the letters L, M or H. When using a pressure cooker for bottling it is always advisable to follow the manufacturer's instruction booklet.) However the basic principles are the same as other water-bath methods: the cooker must be deep enough to hold the bottles and have a trivet or rack in the bottom. There should be 850ml (1½ pints) of water in the cooker before the trivet or rack and bottles are put in, and it should be at boiling point before the filled bottles are inserted.

The fruit is packed into warm bottles and boiling syrup poured on top leaving 25mm (1in) headspace. Cover the bottles and place them in the cooker making sure they do not touch each other or the sides. Cover the pan and bring up to L or 5lb pressure over moderate heat and process for the times given in the chart on page 28. Leave the bottles in the cooker and allow pressure to reduce at room temperature. Remove the bottles and finish as in the previous methods.

Method 4: Slow oven

This method is not suitable for light coloured fruits which discolour in air – apples, pears, peaches etc – or for solid pack tomatoes. The fruit will go brown, and the temperature is not high enough to penetrate a solid pack. It is, however, suitable for gooseberries and dark coloured fruit such as Victoria plums, black cherries, blackberries or blackcurrants.

Pre-heat the oven to 120°C (250°F, Gas Mark ½). Pack the bottles with the fruit but do not pour over the syrup or liquid. Place the lids on top, but without clips or screw-bands. Place the bottles on an asbestos mat or a piece of thick cardboard (it is easier if these are placed on the centre oven shelf first), allowing at least 50mm (2in) between each bottle and the sides of the oven. After the processing time (see chart, page 28), remove the bottles one by one and fill quickly to the top with boiling syrup, securing the lids with clips or screw-bands immediately. Sometimes the fruit may shrink down in the bottles in which case add fruit from another bottle before pouring over the syrup. The secret of success with this method is in the quick filling and sealing of the bottles as soon as they are removed from the oven. Leave overnight and test for seal.

Method 5: Moderate oven

This method can be used for all types of fruit and also for solid pack tomatoes. Pre-heat the oven to 150°C (300°F, Gas Mark 2).

Pack warm bottles with the fruit and pour in boiling syrup or brine leaving 25mm (1in) head space. Place the lids on top but not the clips or screw-bands. Put the bottles 50mm (2in) apart on a baking tray lined with newspaper and place in the centre of the oven. After the processing time (see chart page 28), secure the lids with clips or screw-bands. Leave for 24 hours and test for seal.

Testing the seal

This is necessary to ensure that a complete vacuum has been formed during the processing and there is no air in the bottles which would quickly cause mould to grow on the fruit.

After the bottles have been left for 24 hours and are completely cool, remove the clips or screw-bands. Lift the bottles carefully by the lids. If these are tight and secure the seal is complete. The clips

should be washed, dried and set aside for future use. The screw-bands may be replaced after being washed, dried and greased on the inside with a little oil – be careful not to screw them back on too tightly as they may be difficult to remove after the bottles have been stored. If the lids are loose the fruit should be reprocessed – the liquid should be poured off and re-heated separately except when using Method 1 – or used within two days.

Label each bottle with the name of fruit, date processed and whether with water, light or heavy syrup, or brine.

Storing bottled fruit
The bottles should be stored in a cool, dry, dark place and if a lot of bottling is done throughout the year use them on a 'first bottled, first used' principle.

Bottling pulped fruit
This is a convenient and simple way of bottling fruit and is ideal for uneven sized fruits and those that may be slightly bruised – providing the bruised parts are discarded. Stew the fruit in a little water and add sugar to taste; for tomatoes add a little salt and sugar. When the fruit is soft and pulped pour it into hot jars, cover with lids and seal with clips or screw-bands. Process the bottles as in Method 1.

Using bottled fruit
Bottled fruit may be used straight from the bottle and served cold as a dessert or as part of many hot or cold baked desserts. Citrus fruit such as oranges (particularly Seville), lemons and grapefruit are useful for making marmalade. If the fruit has been bottled in syrup take note of how much sugar has been used and subtract this amount (and the liquid) before adding the required amounts for marmalade making (see page 66).

Bottling vegetables
As already emphasised, the bottling of vegetables should only be

Freshly picked peas and beans may be bottled in brine to give a constant supply of vegetables regardless of season.

done in a reliable pressure cooker – if you are in any doubt it is wise to check with the manufacturer of the cooker.

As the processing is rather lengthy, it is sensible to bottle the more expensive vegetables and those with a short season such as asparagus, sweetcorn, red and green peppers, peas or beans.

Vegetables should be young and very fresh and processed as soon after gathering as possible. After preparation – peas podded, sweetcorn kernels removed from the cob, and asparagus trimmed – they should be washed in cold running water.

Vegetables need to be blanched before bottling. This is done by plunging them into boiling water for two to five minutes, depending on the vegetables, then dropping them in cold water. Drain them well before packing into sterilized, warm bottles. This helps to retain the colour of the vegetables and causes them to shrink slightly, making it easier to pack into the bottles. Do not pack them tightly or press them down. Fill the bottles with boiling brine made with 25g (1oz) of salt to 1 litre (2 pints) of water leaving 10mm ($\frac{1}{2}$in) headspace. Green food colouring may be added to the brine to retain the colour of vegetables like peas and beans.

Cover the bottles in the same way as for fruit. Follow Method 3 for the processing *except* for the pressure and length of time. Place the covered cooker over medium heat and reduce it to low when steam starts to escape through the vent. Bring up to M (10lb) pressure and maintain this for the required time – between 30 to 50 minutes. This may vary according to the type of pressure cooker, so check in your instruction manual first.

When the bottles have been sterilized, the seal should be tested. If it is not tight the bottles may be re-sterilized, although there will be a loss of quality. Otherwise, use the contents at once.

Red or green peppers
Peppers can also be bottled using a pressure cooker, though the method is slightly different from the other vegetables as no brine is required. Blanch the peppers (the younger the better) for three to four minutes in boiling water. Remove the outer skin, then halve them and scrape out the seeds and white pith. Pack in tight layers in sterilized jars. Prepare the jars as for other bottled vegetables and cook under M (10lb) pressure for 40 minutes.

Canning
Canning was first introduced as a form of food preservation in 1809. In 1795 the French were in the middle of war and revolution and the government were worried about feeding the army and navy. It was at this time that Napoleon was reputed to have coined the well-known saying 'An army marches on its stomach'. A prize of 12,000 francs was offered to anyone who could invent a method of preserving fresh food that would remain wholesome for long periods of time and also be easy to transport. It was some years before a Frenchman, Nicolas Appert, after lengthy experiments, produced a satisfactory method and in 1809 he collected the prize money from Napoleon himself.

Appert's methods were not far removed from today's sophisticated commercial process, except he thought it was only air that destroyed the food and that by heating the containers it would be removed. Appert used glass jars which were sealed with a cork; it was another year before an Englishman, Peter Durand, thought of putting food into metal containers. These were based on the design of the old tea canisters – hence the word 'can'. Like Appert, he had little knowledge of the scientific processes involved; the cans often burst and it was an uneconomic process. 50 years later Louis Pasteur discovered it was not air but bacteria that destroyed the food, and they could only be eliminated if the cans were correctly sealed and then sterilized in water that was at, or above, 100°C (212°F).

Canning food at home
As in bottling the object of canning is to preserve fruits by killing the yeasts and moulds in the fruit and to prevent their re-entry. This is achieved by correct processing and canning at a high temperature. Domestic canning of food is an expensive and time-consuming method of preserving and can only be carried out if the right equipment is available and enough care is taken. On the other hand it could be useful if there is a large amount of produce available because, if correctly processed, the canned food will keep for relatively long periods. Home canning was carried out on quite a large scale before and immediately after the war, but has declined in recent years since domestic sealing machines, essential for successful canning, are no longer manufactured. In addition, if the canning process is not carried out absolutely efficiently, the risk of food spoilage or even food poisoning is very high. Commercially canned produce is so freely available and still so relatively cheap that it is best to stick to bottling as a reliable method of fruit and vegetable preservation.

Peppers come from the Capsicum family of plants and are native to South America, although they are now cultivated extensively throughout the world. Shown here is the most common pepper, the sweet or bell pepper, which has a mild, slightly sweet taste. These peppers are used unripe, when green or ripe, when they turn yellow or red. They can be served on their own or used in stews, casseroles or salads. The red pepper, also known as the pimiento, is sometimes dried to make the spice paprika. Bottled peppers are a useful addition to any store cupboard as, once again, they have a relatively short season so can be bought at their best and cheapest and bottled for long storage. Also shown here are dried red chillis, a much hotter variety of pepper which is an essential ingredient of many of the pickles described later. Their seeds are particularly hot and should be removed if a milder taste is preferred.

Bottling Chart

Preparation, methods and processing times

FRUIT	PREPARATION	Method 1 Temp	*Time maintained minutes	Method 2 Temp	*Time maintained minutes	Method 3 Time maintained at L (5lb) pressure in minutes	Method 4 Time 450g-1.75kg (1-4lb) minutes	2.25kg-4.5kg (5-10lb) minutes	Method 5 Time 450g-1.75kg (1-4lb) minutes	2.25kg-4.5kg (5-10lb) minutes
Apples (in syrup)	Peel, core and quarter or slice. Keep under salted water (1 teaspoon salt to 1 litre (2 pints) water). Drain and rinse before bottling.	74°C (165°F)	10	88°C (190°F)	2	1	Not recommended		30-40	45-60
Apples (solid pack)	Prepare as above. Blanch in boiling water for 2 to 3 minutes or steam over boiling water until just tender. Pack warm.	83°C (180°F)	15	88°C (190°F)	20	3-4	Not recommended		50-60	65-80
Apricots	Remove stalks. Pack whole or cut in half and remove stones.	83°C (180°F)	15	88°C (190°F)	10	1	Not recommended		40-50	55-70
Blackberries	Remove stalks and leaves.	74°C (165°F)	10	88°C (190°F)	2	1	45-55	60-75	30-40	45-60
Cherries	Remove stalks.	83°C (180°F)	15	88°C (190°F)	10	1	55-70	75-90	40-50	55-70
Citrus fruits (Oranges, lemons, grapefruit etc).	Remove peel and white pith. Divide into segments and discard pips.	83°C (180°F)	15	88°C (190°F)	10	1	Not recommended		40-50	55-70
(For marmalades)	Wash and cut the fruit into pieces. No liquid is required for Method 3.	83°C (180°F)	15	88°C (190°F)	20	15	Not recommended		50-60	65-80
Currants (Black, red, white)	Remove stems and broken fruit.	83°C (180°F)	15	88°C (190°F)	10	1	55-70	75-90	40-50	55-70
Damsons	Remove stems.	83°C (180°F)	15	88°C (190°F)	10	1	55-70	75-90	40-50	55-70
Gooseberries (for cooking)	Top and tail. If using syrup, nick the ends to prevent shrivelling.	74°C (165°F)	10	88°C (190°F)	2	1	45-55	60-75	30-40	45-60
(for use uncooked)		83°C (180°F)	15	88°C (190°F)	10	1	55-70	75-90	40-50	55-70
Greengages	Remove stalks. This fruit is often cloudy when bottled.	83°C (180°F)	15	88°C (190°F)	10	1	Not recommended		40-50	55-70
Loganberries	Remove stalks. This fruit attracts maggots so pick carefully.	74°C (165°F)	10	88°C (190°F)	2	1	45-55	60-75	30-40	45-60
Peaches	Peel (see Tomatoes). Pack in halves or whole.	83°C (180°F)	15	88°C (190°F)	20	3-4	Not recommended		50-60	65-80
Pears	Prepare as for apples in syrup. Pack and process as quickly as possible after preparing. Cooking pears should be stewed until tender.	88°C (190°F)	30	88°C (190°F)	40	4	Not recommended		60-70	75-90
Pineapples	Remove peel and centre core. Cut into rings or cubes.	83°C (180°F)	15	88°C (190°F)	20	3	Not recommended		50-60	65-80

	PREPARATION									
Plums	Remove stalks. Pack whole, or cut in half and remove stones. Replace a few kernels if liked.	83°C (180°F)	15	88°C (190°F)	10	1	Not recommended		40-50	55-70
Raspberries	See Loganberries.									
Rhubarb (for cooking)	Best bottled when young so no need to peel. Wipe and cut stalks.	74°C (165°F)	10	88°C (190°C)	2	1	45-55	60-75	30-40	45-60
(for use uncooked)		83°C (180°F)	15	88°C (190°F)	10	1	55-70	75-90	40-50	55-70
Strawberries	Remove hulls. This fruit loses colour and may rise when bottled. A few drops of red food colouring may be added if liked.	74°C (165°F)	10	88°C (190°F)	2	1	Not recommended		30-40	45-60
Tomatoes (whole)	Remove calyx. Pack with or without skins. The skins can easily be peeled off if the tomatoes are put into boiling water for 5 to 15 seconds and then dipped in cold water.	88°C (190°F)	30	88°C (190°F)	40	5	80-100	105-125	60-70	75-90
Tomatoes (solid pack)	Peel, cut in halves or quarters. Pack tightly in the jars, sprinkling salt on each layer – 2 teaspoons to every 1kg (2lb) of tomatoes. A teaspoon of sugar added to each jar will improve the flavour. Press the tomatoes well down in the jars but do not add any liquid.	88°C (190°F)	40	88°C (190°F)	50	7	Not recommended		70-80	85-100

*Increase process time for large jars when using Methods 1 and 2.
2kg (3-4lb) size by 5 minutes all packs except Tomatoes Solid Pack 10 minutes
3kg (5-6lb) size by 10 minutes all packs except Tomatoes Solid Pack 10 minutes
4kg (7-8lb) size by 15 minutes all packs except Tomatoes Solid Pack 30 minutes

VEGETABLES	PREPARATION	Blanching Times (minutes)	Time maintained at M (10lb) pressure
Asparagus	Peel or scrape the stalks and trim to equal lengths. Tie in bundles (about 6 in each). Pack into bottles with stalks uppermost.	2–3	35
Beans, broad	Remove and discard pods. (Note: Broad beans may turn brown during sterilization.)	3	40
Beans, French	Trim ends and remove string if necessary. Wash and pack whole.	3	35
Beans, runner	Wash, string and slice.	3	35
Peas	Remove and discard pods. Ideally select peas of even size for each bottle.	2	45
Pimientos (Green and red peppers)	Blanch in boiling water for 3-5 minutes. Drain and remove peel. Dip into cold water. Halve and remove seeds and white pith. Cut into quarters. Pack in layers.		40
Sweetcorn	Remove and discard the husks and silk thread. Cut the corn kernels from the cob, making sure the kernels are not damaged.	3	50

Note: It is advisable to use bottles of 500ml to 1 litre (1-2 pints) capacity to ensure the sterilizing process is complete. The above times are based on these sizes. If larger bottles are used an extra 5-10 minutes should be added. Bottles larger than 4 litres (8 pints) capacity must not be used for bottling vegetables.

Recipes for bottled fruit and vegetables

Bottled fruits can of course be served just as they are, with cream, ice cream or custard. Alternatively they can be used as the basis of some delicious and surprising desserts. Similarly, bottled vegetables can be used for savoury dishes like flans and soups.

Apple and Cinnamon Pie
4-6 servings

75g (3oz) butter or margarine
150g (6oz) flour
4 teaspoons castor sugar
Cold water
675g (1½lb) apples, drained and syrup reserved
1 teaspoon ground cinnamon

Below: Preparing the apple and cinnamon pie. Once the strip of pastry has been cut for the edge of the pie dish, lift the pastry cover round a rolling pin and roll it gently across the dish. Fold the two dampened edges of pastry together and press them down firmly with your fingers or with a fork. Opposite: The finished pie can be sprinkled with sugar or glazed with some of the bottling syrup. For added spiciness, add three or four whole cloves to the juice and serve with a good helping of vanilla ice-cream. Alternatively thicken the syrup left over from the recipe with a little arrowroot or cornflour and add it to custard to serve with the pie.

Rub the butter or margarine into the flour until it resembles fine breadcrumbs. Mix in the sugar. Add sufficient cold water, a little at a time, until a firm dough is formed. Lightly knead the dough and set aside in the refrigerator for 10 minutes. Preheat the oven to 200°C (400°F, Gas Mark 6).

Place the apples in a medium-sized pie dish and stir in the cinnamon. Roll out the pastry about 25mm (1in) larger than the top of the pie dish. Cut off a strip of pastry wide enough to cover the rim of the dish, dampen the rim with water and press the pastry strip over the rim. Dampen the pastry and place the remaining piece of pastry on top, taking care not to stretch it. Trim the edges and press the two layers of pastry together with a fork or fingertips. Brush the top with a little of the reserved syrup. Bake for 30-35 minutes until the pastry is crisp and light gold in colour. Serve hot.

Right: Cherry Jubilee is a colourful, flamboyant dessert that takes only a few minutes to prepare. Bottled black cherries are ideal for this recipe, but Brandied Cherries would be even more exotic. These are very simple to preserve: simply dissolve 450g (1lb) sugar in a litre (2 pints) of water over moderate heat, then add washed cherries, a few at a time and boil for 1 minute. Remove them and set aside. Measure 600ml (1 pint) of the syrup and put it in a pan with the remaining 900gc 2lb) sugar. Dissolve over low heat, then boil rapidly until the liquid is clear or reaches 100°C (212°F) on a sugar thermometer. Cool slightly then strain. Measure the strained liquid and mix in an equal quantity of brandy. Pack the cherries into sterilized preserving jars and cover with the syrup, seal, label and store for 4-6 months before use. Far right: Blackberry Fluff is another quick but luscious dessert for a dinner party. Make it in advance and transfer to individual serving dishes so that it is ready to bring to the table straight from the refrigerator.

Cherry Jubilee

4 servings

**450g (1lb) cherries, drained and
syrup reserved**
25mm (1in) piece cinnamon stick
Strip of lemon rind
4 teaspoons arrowroot
50ml (2fl oz) brandy
Castor sugar, to taste

If necessary make the syrup up to
250ml (8fl oz) with water and pour into
a saucepan. Add the cinnamon stick
and lemon rind and bring to the boil.
Remove the cinnamon stick and lemon
rind. Blend the arrowroot with a little
water and stir it into the cherry syrup.
Place the pan over low heat and,
stirring all the time, cook until the
mixture is clear and slightly thickened.
Stir in the cherries and cook for a
further minute or two so that the
cherries are warmed through. Add
sugar to taste if liked.

Pour the cherries and juice into a
serving dish. Heat the brandy and pour
it over the cherries, set it alight and
serve as soon as the flames have died
down, with ice-cream.

Blackberry Fluff

4-6 servings

450g (1lb) blackberries, drained
300ml (10fl oz) double cream
1 egg white
50g (2oz) castor sugar
Pieces of angelica

With the back of a wooden spoon
push the blackberries through a nylon
sieve placed over a bowl and discard
the small pips in the sieve.

Whip the cream until it is fairly
thick and stir it into the blackberry
purée. Beat the egg white until it begins
to thicken and add half the sugar.
Continue beating until the egg white is
stiff and stir in the remaining sugar.
Gently fold the egg white into the
blackberry and cream mixture. Spoon
into individual serving glasses. Decorate
with pieces of angelica and serve at
once with sponge finger biscuits.

Most bottled fruits can successfully be used in crumbles. Gooseberries are recommended in the recipe given here, but apples, rhubarb, apricots or blackberries are just as suitable.

Gooseberry Crumble
4 servings

1 teaspoon butter
675g (1½lb) gooseberries, drained
125g (4oz) sugar
2 tablespoons water
100g (4oz) flour
75g (3oz) butter, cut into small pieces
50g (2oz) brown sugar

Preheat the oven to moderate 180°C (350°F, Gas Mark 4). Lightly grease a medium-sized baking dish with butter.

Arrange the gooseberries in the dish and sprinkle them with the sugar and water.

Sift the flour into a medium-sized mixing bowl. With your fingertips, rub

the butter into the flour until the mixture resembles fine breadcrumbs. Stir in the brown sugar.

Cover the gooseberries with the crumble mixture and place the dish in

Peach Brulée is a rich dessert which looks stunning. White peaches add subtlety of taste and delicacy of texture, but for a really special treat use Peaches in Brandy. These can be prepared in the same way as Brandied Cherries (see page 32), though it is best to peel, halve and stone the peaches as for ordinary bottling.

the oven. Bake for 45 minutes, or until the crumble is golden brown. Remove the dish from the oven and serve at once with cream.

Peach Brulée
4 servings

5 egg yolks
50g (2oz) castor sugar
475ml (16fl oz) double cream
1 teaspoon vanilla essence
8 peach halves, drained
50g (2oz) soft brown sugar

Beat the egg yolks and castor sugar until they are smooth and thick. Gradually beat in the cream. Pour the mixture into a saucepan and cook over low heat, stirring frequently, until the mixture is thick enough to coat the back of a wooden spoon. Remove the pan from the heat and beat the custard for 1 to 2 minutes. Stir in the vanilla essence. Pour the custard into a heatproof serving dish and when cool arrange the peach halves, cut side down, on top of the custard. Chill in the refrigerator for 1 hour.

Sprinkle the soft brown sugar over the peaches and place the dish under a hot grill. When the sugar melts and starts to caramelize, remove the dish from the grill and serve at once.

Pineapple Trifle
6-8 servings

6 small sponge cakes
Raspberry or strawberry jam
450g (1lb) pineapple, drained and syrup reserved
3 tablespoons sherry
300ml (10fl oz) milk
100g (4oz) sugar
4 egg yolks
300ml (10fl oz) double cream
25g (1oz) castor sugar
Browned, blanched almonds

Halve the sponge cakes and spread with jam. Sandwich them together again and cut each one into quarters. Arrange the sponge cakes in a glass serving bowl. Mix the reserved syrup and sherry to make 150ml (5fl oz). Pour

Opposite: Pear Condé is another of the great classic French desserts. It looks complicated but is really quite simple to prepare, and can be made well in advance for a dinner party. This is a recipe which could make good use of home-prepared vanilla sugar (see page 241).

this over the sponge cakes. Chop half of the pineapple into small pieces and place on top of the sponge cakes. Set aside and make the custard.

Pour the milk into a saucepan and add the sugar. Bring the liquid to the boil and remove the pan from the heat. Beat the egg yolks and pour a little of the sweetened milk into them. Stir well to mix. Return the egg mixture to the remaining milk and cook over low heat, stirring frequently until it thickens. Remove from the heat and pour on to the pineapple and sponge cakes. Set aside and when cool place in the refrigerator to chill for at least 30 minutes.

Whip the cream and sugar until it is thick enough to coat the back of a spoon. Arrange the remaining pineapple on top of the custard and spoon half of the cream on top. Whip the remaining cream until very thick and pipe rosettes around the side of the dish. (If preferred all the cream can be whipped until thick and then spread over the pineapple.) Sprinkle the almonds over the top and serve.

Pear Condé
4 servings

100g (4oz) round grain rice
900ml (1½ pints) milk
50g (2oz) sugar
25g (1oz) butter
½ teaspoon vanilla essence
6 egg yolks
675g (1½lb) pears, drained
125g (5oz) raspberry jam
Finely grated rind of ½ lemon
Pinch of nutmeg
3 tablespoons water
2 tablespoons brandy
Glacé cherries

Cook the rice over very low heat in the milk, sugar, butter and vanilla essence until the liquid is absorbed. Stir in the egg yolks and cook gently, stirring often, for 2-3 minutes. Set aside.

Slice the pears if they were bottled whole or in halves. Spoon one third of the rice mixture into a serving dish, cover with one third of pear slices and continue making layers ending up with a layer of pears on top. Decorate with the glacé cherries. Cover the dish and chill in the refrigerator for 1 to 2 hours.

Meanwhile make the sauce. Sieve the jam into a saucepan and discard the small pips. Add the lemon rind, nutmeg and water. Heat gently for 2 minutes. Add the brandy and cook for another minute, allow to cool. Pour the sauce into a serving dish and chill.

Gooseberry Charlotte
4 servings

75g (3oz) fresh white breadcrumbs
25g (1oz) ground almonds
Finely grated rind of 1 small lemon
50g (2oz) sugar
450g (1lb) gooseberries, drained
50g (2oz) butter

Preheat the oven to 180°C (350°F, Gas Mark 4).

Mix the breadcrumbs, ground almonds, lemon rind and sugar together in a mixing bowl.

Arrange the gooseberries and breadcrumb mixture in layers in an ovenproof dish, ending with a layer of crumbs. Cut the butter into small pieces and place on top of the crumbs. Bake for ¾ to 1 hour until the top is crisp and golden brown. Serve hot or cold with custard or cream.

Clafoutis
6 servings

300ml (10fl oz) milk
2 eggs
2 tablespoons brandy
125g (4oz) castor sugar
125g (4oz) flour
Pinch of salt
25g (1oz) butter, melted
450g (1lb) cherries, well drained
Icing sugar

Grease a medium-sized shallow baking

dish with a little butter. Preheat the oven to 180°C (350°F, Gas Mark 4).

Place the milk, eggs and brandy in a large mixing bowl, and beat with a wire whisk until the mixture is smooth and frothy. Add the castor sugar a little at a time and beat well until the sugar is dissolved. Add the flour in the same way and add the salt with the last spoonful. Beat in the melted butter. The mixture should be very smooth and the consistency of light batter.

Pour half of the batter into the prepared dish and spread the cherries over it. Pour the remaining batter over the top.

Bake for 40-50 minutes or until the pudding is firm in the centre. Sprinkle with a little icing sugar and serve hot.

Apricot and Cream Cheese Dessert
6-8 servings

125g (4oz) butter, melted
225g (8oz) brandy snaps, crushed
½ teaspoon ground ginger
450g (1lb) full-fat cream cheese
50g (2oz) castor sugar
125ml (4fl oz) single cream
2 tablespoons lemon juice
1 tablespoon gelatine dissolved in
2 tablespoons hot water
450g (1lb) apricot halves, drained

50g (2oz) preserved ginger, drained and chopped
400ml (15fl oz) double cream
50g (2oz) soft brown sugar

Grease a 23cm (9in) loose-bottomed cake tin with a little butter. Place the butter, brandy snaps and ground ginger in a mixing bowl and stir well to mix. Spoon the mixture into the base of the cake tin and press it down with the back of the spoon. Set aside.

Place the cream cheese and castor sugar in a mixing bowl and beat well with a wooden spoon until the mixture is smooth and creamy. Stir in the single cream, lemon juice and gelatine. Beat well until the ingredients are thoroughly blended.

Spoon the mixture into the tin and set aside in the refrigerator for 30-40 minutes until the filling has set. Preheat the grill to high. Remove the tin

Below: Bottled cherries are ideal for use in Clafoutis, a well-known French pudding. Opposite: Apricot and Cream Cheese Dessert is a really superb and unusual cheesecake which can be served for tea or at a dinner party. It would also be an excellent substitute for the conventional gâteau generally served at a buffet luncheon.

from the refrigerator. Arrange the apricot halves on top of the filling and sprinkle over the preserved ginger. Spread the double cream over the top and sprinkle with the soft brown sugar.

Place the tin under the grill for 2 to 3 minutes until the sugar has caramelized. Remove the dessert from the tin and serve.

Raspberry Cream Mousse
6 servings

450g (1lb) raspberries, drained and syrup reserved
Finely grated rind of ½ orange
350ml (12fl oz) double cream
4 eggs, separated
1 tablespoon gelatine dissolved in 3 tablespoons hot reserved syrup

Grease a 1 litre (approx 3 pint) mould with a little vegetable oil.

Place the raspberry syrup and orange rind in a saucepan and boil for 1 minute. Add the raspberries and cook for 2 minutes.

Remove the pan from the heat and pour the mixture into a nylon sieve placed over a mixing bowl. With the back of a wooden spoon press the raspberries through the sieve until only the small pips and orange rind are left. Discard these and set the raspberry purée aside.

Place the cream and egg yolks into a heatproof bowl and put this on top of a saucepan half filled with boiling water. Place the pan over moderate heat and cook the mixture, stirring frequently, until it forms a custard consistency thick enough to coat the back of a wooden spoon. Beat the

custard into the raspberry purée and stir in the dissolved gelatine. Set aside to cool, stirring occasionally.

Meanwhile, beat the egg whites until they are stiff, then gently fold into the raspberry mixture. Pour the mixture into the prepared dish and chill in the refrigerator for 2 to 3 hours. Serve the mousse from the mould or if preferred, turn it out on to a serving dish. (To help the mousse to slide out easily, dip the base of the dish into hot water for a few seconds, place the serving dish inverted on top, reverse and give the mould a sharp shake.)

Decorate with whipped cream, blanched almonds and a few glacé cherries if liked.

Pineapple Upside-Down Cake
6-8 servings

150g (5oz) butter or margarine
50g (2oz) soft brown sugar
9 pineapple rings, drained
9 glacé cherries
100g (4oz) castor sugar
3 eggs
150g (6oz) self-raising flour
Pieces of angelica (optional)

Grease a 20cm (8in) square cake tin with a little butter. Preheat the oven to 180°C (350°F, Gas Mark 4).

Melt 25g (1oz) of the butter and pour into the prepared cake tin. Sprinkle the soft brown sugar over the butter and arrange the pineapple rings over the sugar. Place a cherry in the centre of each ring and set aside. Place the remaining butter and castor sugar in a mixing bowl and beat with a wooden spoon, until they are soft and creamy. Add the eggs, one at a time, beating well until the mixture is light and fluffy. Stir in the flour and if necessary add a little milk to give the mixture a soft dropping consistency. Carefully spoon the cake mixture into the tin and level the top.

Bake for 40 to 50 minutes until the cake is golden brown and a skewer inserted into the centre comes out dry.

Leave the cake to cool in the tin for 5 minutes then turn out on to a serving dish if serving it hot, or on to a wire rack to cool. Decorate with pieces of angelica if liked.

The cake may be served hot with whipped cream as a dessert or cold with tea or coffee.

Right: Raspberries are usually expensive to buy as they are difficult to harvest on a commercial scale. If you have a garden, growing your own is undoubtedly the solution and you can bottle or freeze the surplus fruit for use in many different recipes, including Raspberry Cream Mousse.
Far right: Pineapple Upside-Down Cake is a versatile recipe, as it can be served with tea or coffee or, as a pudding, with whipped cream. It is generally decorated with glacé cherries, and is even more attractive if pieces of angelica are used as well. Both glacé cherries and candied angelica can be made at home, although it is a lengthy process (see page 104).

Opposite: Pea Soup with Bacon is a perfect combination of taste and texture. It could be served as a first course, or would make a sustaining and economical lunch or supper, accompanied by wholemeal bread and butter, and followed by cheese and fruit.

Pea Soup with Bacon
4 servings

1 bacon hock, soaked overnight in cold water and drained
2 litres (4 pints) water
1 bouquet garni
1 teaspoon pepper
450g (1lb) peas with liquid reserved
25g (1oz) butter
1 large onion, peeled and chopped
1 clove garlic, crushed
1 large potato, peeled and chopped

Place the bacon hock in a large saucepan and add the water, bouquet garni and pepper. Bring to the boil, reduce the heat to low, cover the pan and simmer for about 2 hours or until the bacon is falling off the bone. Place the bacon on a plate, cover and set aside.

Strain the cooking liquid into a mixing bowl, cool then chill in the refrigerator for 2 hours. Remove the fat that will have risen to the surface. Melt the butter in a large saucepan and fry the onion, garlic and potato for 2-3 minutes. Add the peas with their liquid and the reserved bacon liquid. Bring to the boil, then reduce the heat to low and simmer for 5 minutes. Allow to cool slightly then purée the mixture in a food mill or electric blender. Return the soup to the pan.

Remove all the bacon from the hock bone and cut it into small pieces. Add the bacon pieces to the soup and return the pan to the heat to cook until the soup is really hot. Serve at once with croûtons or toast.

Corn Chowder
4-6 servings

2 tablespoons butter
1 medium-sized onion, finely chopped
1 tablespoon flour
2 medium-sized potatoes, parboiled for 10 minutes in boiling salted water and finely chopped
450g (1lb) sweetcorn, drained
250ml (8fl oz) chicken stock
300ml (10fl oz) milk
1 teaspoon salt
½ teaspoon pepper
250ml (8fl oz) double cream
2 tablespoons chopped pimiento

In a small frying-pan melt the butter

over moderate heat. When the foam subsides, add the onion. Reduce the heat to low and cook, stirring continuously, for 5 to 6 minutes, or until the onion is transparent but not brown. Remove the frying-pan from the heat, stir in the flour and set aside.

Put the potatoes, corn, chicken stock and milk in a large saucepan and, over moderate heat, bring the mixture to the boil, stirring occasionally until all the ingredients are blended. Pour a little of the liquid on to the onion and flour mixture. Stir to form a smooth, thick liquid and stir into the potato mixture. Cover the saucepan, reduce the heat to very low and simmer for 20 minutes.

Season with salt and pepper and add the cream, stirring to blend it thoroughly into the mixture. Heat for

a further 2 minutes over very low heat. Stir in the chopped pimiento and serve immediately.

Corn with Red Peppers

35g (1½oz) butter
450g (1lb) red peppers, drained and diced
450g (1lb) sweetcorn, drained
½ teaspoon salt
½ teaspoon freshly ground black pepper

In a medium-sized saucepan melt the butter over moderate heat. Add the red peppers to the pan and cook them for 3 minutes, stirring occasionally.

Left: Drained bottled peas are ideal for Pea Soup with Bacon, but fresh or frozen peas could be substituted.

Stir in the corn, salt and pepper and cook for 5 minutes. Transfer the vegetables to a warmed serving dish and serve immediately.
Note: This vegetable mixture goes particularly well with turkey.

43

Above: Kidneys with Sweetcorn is a tasty way to serve tender lambs' kidneys. There is no need to prepare a heavy accompaniment to this dish like rice or potatoes, simply serve a green vegetable, like French beans, and slices of toast.

Asparagus Flan
4 servings

175g (6oz) flour
Pinch of salt
37g (1½oz) butter
37g (1½oz) margarine
Cold water to mix
225g (8oz) lean bacon rashers, rinds removed, chopped and fried until crisp
125ml (4fl oz) single cream
75ml (3fl oz) milk
3 eggs
25g (1oz) grated Parmesan cheese
Pinch of salt and pepper
12 asparagus tips, drained

Place the flour and salt in a mixing bowl and rub in the butter and margarine. Add cold water, a little at a time, until a firm dough is formed. Lightly knead the dough and roll it out into a circle large enough to line a 23cm (9in) flan dish. Set aside in the refrigerator. Preheat the oven to 200°C (400°F, Gas Mark 6).

To make the filling, allow the fried bacon to cool and set aside. In a mixing bowl combine the cream, milk, eggs, cheese, salt and pepper and mix well.

Sprinkle the bacon over the bottom of the flan case and pour the egg mixture on top. Arrange the asparagus

tips over the top.

Place the flan dish on a baking sheet and bake for 35-40 minutes until the filling is firm and the top golden brown. Serve hot or cold.

Kidneys with Sweetcorn
4 servings

350g (12oz) sweetcorn, drained
150ml (5fl oz) single cream

Left: Asparagus Flan looks very tempting when the asparagus tips are arranged like the spokes of a wheel on the flan. It can be served as a supper dish, and is particularly suitable as party fare.

2 teaspoons chopped fresh chives
1 teaspoon chopped fresh parsley
½ teaspoon salt
½ teaspoon black pepper
25g (1oz) butter
12 lambs' kidneys, cleaned, prepared and cut into slices

Purée the sweetcorn in an electric blender with the cream. Alternatively, put the corn through a food mill and mix in the cream. Put the corn purée into a small saucepan. Stir in the chives, parsley, salt and pepper. Place the pan over low heat and cook for 5 minutes or until the mixture is very hot. Do not allow it to boil. Remove the pan from the heat and keep the purée hot while you fry the kidneys.

In a large frying-pan, melt the butter over moderate heat. When the foam subsides, add the kidney slices and, turning them frequently, cook for 5 minutes or until they are cooked through.

Spread the sweetcorn purée on a heated serving dish and arrange the kidneys beside or on top of it.

45

Whitsun Lamb
4 servings

1kg (2lb 2oz) asparagus
1kg (2lb 2oz) leg of lamb, cut into
50mm (2in) cubes
50g (2oz) seasoned flour, made with
50g (2oz) flour, 1 teaspoon salt and ½
teaspoon black pepper
50g (2oz) butter
2 medium-sized onions, thinly sliced
300ml (10fl oz) chicken stock
150ml (5fl oz) double cream
1 teaspoon salt
1 teaspoon black pepper
Juice of ½ lemon

Heat the asparagus in salted water. Cut off the asparagus tips and set them aside. Keep hot.

Place the stems in the jar of an electric blender and blend until they form a smooth purée. Set aside.

Roll the lamb cubes in the seasoned flour, shaking off any excess. In a large flameproof casserole, melt the butter over moderate heat. When the foam subsides, add the onions and fry, stirring occasionally, for 5 to 7 minutes or until they are soft and translucent but not brown.

Add the lamb cubes and fry, stirring and turning occasionally, for 5 to 8 minutes or until they are lightly and evenly browned. Stir in the stock and bring the liquid to the boil. Reduce the heat to low and simmer the mixture for 50 minutes to 1 hour or until the meat is tender when pierced with the point of a sharp knife.

Remove the casserole from the heat and, with a slotted spoon, transfer the

Corn is a very versatile vegetable with a limited season so it is a good idea to bottle a good supply of fresh corn while it is available. This American recipe, Vermont Corn Bake, is a filling side dish to accompany chops, steak or hamburgers. It could also be served on its own as a light meal.

lamb cubes to a plate. Keep hot.

Stir the puréed asparagus and cream into the sauce in the casserole. Add the salt, pepper and lemon juice and cook, stirring frequently, for 3 to 5 minutes or until the sauce is thick and smooth.

Place the meat on a serving dish and pour the sauce around the meat. Garnish with the reserved asparagus tips and serve immediately.

Vermont Corn Bake
4 servings

50g (2oz) plus 1 teaspoon butter
4 eggs
25g (1oz) flour
350ml (12fl oz) single cream

1 teaspoon salt
½ teaspoon black pepper
450g (1lb) sweetcorn, drained

Preheat the oven to moderate, 180°C (Gas Mark 4, 350°F). Using the teaspoon of butter, grease a large, fairly shallow baking dish and set aside.

In a large mixing bowl, using a wire whisk or rotary beater, beat the eggs until they are light and frothy. Stir in the flour, cream and the remaining melted butter. Add the salt, pepper and sweetcorn and stir well for 1 minute.

Pour the mixture into the prepared baking dish. Place the dish in the oven and bake for 1 to 1½ hours or until the top is golden brown and a skewer inserted into the centre of the mixture comes out clean.

Serve at once, straight from the dish.

Fruit syrups, juices & liqueurs

Almost any fruit can be used to make syrups, juices and liqueurs. Autumn is a very good time to prepare them as a number of fruits reach maturity then, many of which can simply be gathered from the hedgerows and woodlands. In addition, fruit liqueurs made in the autumn will be ready just in time for Christmas, as most need about three months to mature.

It is useful to make your own supply of fruit drinks, both soft and alcoholic. Not only do they taste delicious, but they are economical and health giving. And of course, children love the syrups and juices and it is a useful way to make sure they get essential Vitamin C. Fruit syrups differ slightly from juices in as much as the latter have some of the fruit pulp added. They are less sweet than syrups and are generally drunk undiluted. Fruit syrups are best made with soft berry fruits. Citrus fruits may also be used for syrups although they require a slightly different method of preparation. Fruit liqueurs are more extravagant as they have an alcoholic base but they are fun to make and are particularly palatable.

Fruit syrups

Bilberries, blackberries, blackcurrants, loganberries or mulberries are all ideal for making into syrups. The fruit should be fresh and ripe – in fact it is an excellent way to use fruit that is too ripe for bottling or jam making. Unripe fruit should not be used as it is too acid and the juice yield will be insufficient. Rose hips make an excellent syrup and are rich in Vitamin C. They require a slightly different method preparation and this is given in the recipe (page 54).

Wash the fruit in cold water and drain. Place the fruit in a basin that will fit over a large saucepan, or use a double boiler. Some fruits require a little water – blackberries and blackcurrants especially – but the minimum should be used, depending on the juiciness of the fruit. Half fill the saucepan with water and bring to the boil, reduce to simmering point. Place the bowl on top of the saucepan or the top of the double boiler over the water and heat the fruit until the juices flow out. Press the fruit with a wooden spoon while it is heating. The time taken again depends on the fruit but generally 2.75kg (6lb) fruit will take one hour. Make sure that the water in the lower pan is replenished when necessary. When the juice is flowing freely crush it with a potato masher. When all the juice has been extracted pour it into a jelly bag with a bowl underneath it and allow the juice to drain through for 24 hours. Press the pulp thoroughly to extract any remaining juice. The amount of sugar used depends on the sweetness of the fruit but generally 350g (12oz) sugar to 600ml (1 pint) of liquid is sufficient.

Add the sugar to the juice and stir without heating until the sugar dissolves. Strain again through muslin or a fine meshed nylon sieve. Pour into clean dry bottles and cover them. Bottles with screw tops are the most convenient, but if ordinary bottles are used corks which have been boiled can be used. They will have to be secured with fine wire or string to stop them from blowing out during processing. Leave 25mm (1in) headspace for screw tops and 35mm (1½in) for corks.

Processing the bottles

Lightly seal the bottles and place them in a pan with a false bottom or rack deep enough for the water to come to the lower level of the corks. To keep the bottles upright, folds of newspaper can be put between them, but make sure the bottles are not too close together otherwise the water will not circulate freely. Bring the water up to simmering point, 88°C (190°F) and simmer for 20 minutes.

Remove the bottles and tighten the screw caps or push the corks well in as soon as possible. When the syrup is cool and the corks are dry dip the tops of the bottles into melted paraffin wax to make a completely air-tight seal. The wax should cover the screw caps or corks and come down over about 10mm (¾in) of the neck of the bottle. Label and store in a cool, dry place.

When making syrups from citrus fruits only use part of the peel, otherwise the flavour will be too strong. The rest can be finely grated or pared but none of the white pith should be used as it makes the syrup bitter and unpleasant. The juice is used with added water, more than is used for berry fruits, and the proportion of sugar is higher. Extra citric acid is usually added to these syrups to improve the flavour but it is not essential in lemon syrups.

Bottling and processing are the same as for syrups made with berry fruits. Syrups made from citrus fruits do not keep as long, as the flavour and colour will deteriorate after about two months.

Fruit juices

The same types of fruit are suitable for juices. This is a useful way of using over-ripe fruit when there is not enough sugar available to make syrups. An average amount of sugar is 75g (3oz) to each 600ml (1 pint) of juice.

The bottling and processing is the same as for syrups but once a bottle is opened it should be kept in the refrigerator and used within two or three days.

Above: Syrups and juices must be properly sealed after sterilization. Dip the necks of the bottles in paraffin wax once corks or caps are in place.

Below: Syrups can be made from almost any fruit, although citrus fruits need a little care. Syrups are generally drunk diluted with water, while juices are usually served undiluted.

Recipes for fruit syrups, juices and liqueurs

Using the basic methods already given, refreshing fruit drinks and exciting liqueurs can be made from garden produce or wild fruit from the hedgerows, for use all year round.

Blackcurrant Syrup

Blackcurrants
Water
Sugar

Wash the fruit, 'top and tail' it and then weigh it. Place the fruit in a large bowl over a saucepan of boiling water or top of a double boiler. Press with a wooden spoon to extract some of the juice. Add 300ml (10fl oz) water for every 450g (1lb) of fruit. Heat the fruit

gently and continue as method on page 48.

Measure the juice and allow 350g (12oz) sugar to 600ml (1 pint) of juice. **Blackberry syrup** is made in the same way but less water is required. For 2.75kg (6lb) fruit, 300ml (10fl oz) of water is generally sufficient.

Raspberry or strawberry syrups: No water is required with these fruits. For the best results hull the fruit, weigh and place in a large mixing bowl with an equal amount of sugar. Leave overnight then continue with the basic method.

Lemon Syrup

Quartered rind of 6 lemons
1 litre (1¾ pints) water
1.35kg (3lb) sugar
600ml (1 pint) lemon juice

Blackcurrant Syrup, diluted with water or soda and served with lots of ice and slices of lemon makes a refreshingly different and nutritious summertime drink.

You can brighten up Lemon Syrup by diluting it with soda water and adding freshly squeezed lemon juice just before serving. This would be a welcome change at a children's party, indoors or out.

Place lemon rind, water and sugar in a large saucepan. Heat gently until the sugar has dissolved, stirring frequently. Strain into a mixing bowl, then add the lemon juice. Bottle and process as given on page 48.

Orange syrup is made in the same way as lemon syrup, except less sugar is required – 900g (2lb) – and the addition of 25g (1oz) citric acid gives extra flavour. Add the citric acid when adding the orange juice to the strained sugar and water mixture.

Rosehip Syrup

4.50 litres (9 pints) water
1.75kg (4lb) ripe rose hips
1kg (2lb 2oz) sugar

Pour 3 litres (6 pints) of the water into an aluminium preserving pan or large saucepan. Bring to the boil.

Wash and mince the rosehips and add to the boiling water. Bring back to the boil then remove from the heat. Set aside to cool slightly for about 15 minutes.

When cooled, pour into a jelly bag placed over a large mixing bowl. (See jelly making page 65).

When the juice is drained through, return the pulp in the jelly bag to the pan and add the remaining water. Bring the mixture back to the boil and pour into a clean jelly bag. Allow to drain until all the juice has dripped through.

Pour the two bowls of juice into a clean pan. Bring it to the boil and boil until the juice reduces in quantity to about 1.5 litres (3 pints). Reduce the heat to low, add the sugar and simmer until it has dissolved, stirring frequently. Bring to the boil and boil for a further 5 minutes.

Pour the syrup into clean, hot bottles, cover and process as for other syrups. Once opened, rose hip syrup will not keep for more than one or two weeks so it is advisable to use small bottles.

Lime Juice Cordial

225g (8oz) sugar
300ml (10fl oz) water
Finely pared rind of 6 limes
Juice of 12 limes

Place the sugar and water in a medium sized saucepan over moderate heat. Stir constantly until the sugar has dissolved.

When the sugar has dissolved, add the lime rind. Increase the heat to high and boil the syrup for 5 minutes, then set aside to cool.

When the syrup is cool, stir in the juice of the limes and strain the cordial into a clean bottle. Cover and set aside in a cool dark place until ready for use, as a soft drink with soda and ice, or as an accompaniment to vodka or gin.

Note: This cordial should be made in small quantities as it will only keep for a few days.

One of the advantages of making your own fruit syrups is that they are a very good source of Vitamin C. Even if children are fussy about fruit, they will not be able to resist the tempting drinks given here. Rosehip Syrup is particularly good for small babies (well diluted of course), as it is not too acid for their immature stomachs.

Fruit liqueurs keep well and are perfect for serving with coffee after dinner. Apricot Liqueur requires a certain amount of preparation to soften the fruit before infusing. The same method could be used for other firm fruits such as pears (using crushed or ground ginger instead of allspice) or apples (using cinnamon).

Apricot Liqueur

**450g (1lb) fresh apricots, halved and
 stones reserved**
1 teaspoon ground allspice
450g (1lb) sugar
900ml (1½ pints) dry white wine
625ml (16fl oz) gin

Place the apricots in a large saucepan and stir in the allspice, sugar and wine. Bring to the boil, stirring frequently until the sugar has dissolved. Remove from the heat and stir in the gin.

Crack the apricot stones and remove the inside kernels. Skin them and add the kernels to the apricot mixture.

Pour into a crock or jug and cover the top tightly. Set aside for 5 to 6 days to infuse.

Sterilize and dry 2 or 3 bottles.

Strain the liqueur through a piece of muslin placed over a large jug or mixing bowl, squeeze as much liquid out as possible. Pour the liquid into the bottles and seal with new corks.

Allow at least 1 month for the liqueur to mature before serving. As with all home-made liqueurs the longer they are kept the better they will taste!

Note : Peach, Nectarine or Plum Liqueur can be made in the same way.

Peach Brandy

450g (1lb) fresh peaches, sliced and stones reserved
225g (8oz) sugar
625ml (16fl oz) brandy
½ teaspoon grated nutmeg

Place the peaches in a mixing bowl. Add the sugar, brandy and nutmeg and stir well to mix. Crack the peach stones and remove the inside kernels, remove the skin and add the kernels to the peach mixture.

Pour into a crock or jug and cover the top tightly. Set aside for 1 to 2 weeks to infuse.

Sterilize and dry 1 or 2 bottles.

Strain the liqueur through a piece of muslin placed over a jug or mixing bowl, squeeze as much liquid out as possible. Pour the liquid into the bottles and seal with new corks.

Allow at least 1 month for the liqueur to mature before serving.

Blackberry Liqueur

2 litres (4 pints) blackberry juice
900g (2lb) sugar
1 tablespoon grated nutmeg
2 tablespoons whole cloves
400ml (15fl oz) brandy

Place the blackberry juice and sugar in a preserving pan or large saucepan. Bring to the boil and if necessary remove the scum from the top.

Add the nutmeg and cloves and simmer for 15 minutes. Remove from the heat and add the brandy.

Pour into a crock or jug and cover the top tightly. Set aside for 3 days.

Sterilize and dry 2 or 3 bottles.

Strain the liqueur through a piece of muslin, placed over a jug or mixing bowl. Pour the liqueur into the bottles and seal with new corks.

Allow at least 1 month for the liqueur to mature before serving.

Sloe Gin

450g (1lb) sloes, trimmed and washed
1 litre (2 pints) gin
125g (4oz) sugar
Few drops almond essence

Using a large needle, prick the sloes all over and place them in a large mixing bowl. Pour over the gin and mix well. Add the sugar and almond essence and stir well to blend.

Pour the mixture into a large jug or crock and cork it tightly. Set the jug or crock aside in a dark place and allow the mixture to infuse for 3 months, shaking it occasionally.

Sterilize and dry two bottles. Pour the mixture through a funnel lined with very fine cheesecloth into the bottles, squeezing any pulp remaining in the cheesecloth with your hands to extract the liquid. Discard the pulp that is left over.

Seal the bottles and set them aside for at least 6 months before drinking.
Note : Blackcurrant gin can be made in the same way, substituting 8 fresh or dried verbena leaves for the almond essence.

Sloes, the bitter fruits of the common blackthorn, are freely available in hedges and woods, often by the roadside, in the later part of autumn. Providing there is not a late spring frost, you should be able to predict whether there will be a good crop of sloes by the amount of snow white blossom which precedes the leaves in spring.

Jams, jellies & marmalades

Jams, jellies and marmalades are probably the most popular and widely used forms of fruit preservation. They must be about the best way of using up surplus fruit and, despite the excellence of some commercially produced jams, there is nothing to beat really good home-made ones.

General information

Although different methods are used for jams, jellies and marmalades the basic principles are the same. The fruit must be fresh, firm and under-ripe rather than over-ripe. Over-ripe fruit will not make successful jam as it will not set. Fruit sets when boiled with sugar because it contains a natural substance in its cells called pectin. The acid in fruit helps to extract the pectin thus ensuring a good set and a bright, clear colour, which helps to prevent the sugar from crystallizing when the jam is stored.

Equipment

The preserving pan. The most essential requirement is a suitable pan. This must be large as jam tends to be made in substantial quantities. However it should only be half full when the sugar is added to the fruit so that when the jam boils up quickly, it does not rise over the side during cooking. It is best to use a special preserving pan made from good quality aluminium, stainless steel or unchipped enamel. If jam is made in a metal pan it must not be left to stand in it longer than necessary. If the second stage (when the sugar is added) has to be delayed for some reason, the fruit should be transferred to a mixing bowl and returned to a clean pan when the process is ready to be completed. A little glycerine or butter rubbed over the bottom of the pan will help to prevent sticking and lessen the amount of scum.

Jam jars. Any type of jar is suitable, providing it is unchipped, clean and dry. Jars should be warmed slightly in the oven to prevent them cracking when the jam is poured into them.

Jam covers can be bought in most stationers: they consist of waxed discs which are put on top of the jam when it is hot (they should exactly fit the surface and not overlap the edge of the jar); and parchment or cellophane circles which are placed on top of the jar, when the jam is cold, and secured with an elastic band. Commercial jam jars often have screw tops which provide an airtight seal. If the metal cover is lined with a thin piece of card this should be removed and the cover washed and dried. Place a wax disc on the surface of the jam before the lid is screwed on. Plastic push-on lids are available to fit standard-sized jars and although they cost more thay can be used time and time again. If metal or plastic lids are used they must

Of all the fruit preserves, jams and jellies are probably the most associated with the months of summer. Luscious fruits available in profusion can be gathered or bought and preserved with sugar. It is a relatively simple process which is also particularly rewarding, as home-made jams generally taste much fruitier than commercial ones.

Above: A jelly bag can be improvised by tying a large piece of muslin to the legs of an upturned stool, with the bowl resting on the base. Right: Jams and marmalades are an essential part of a good traditional breakfast or tea. Shown here (clockwise from the top) are Apricot Jam, Damson Jam, Orange Jelly Marmalade, Plum and Apple Jam, and Pineapple Jam. Recipes for these and many others can be found from page 70.

be put on while the jam is hot – if the jam is warm, or actually cold, then mould may form after a short period of storage.

A heat-proof jug is useful for pouring the jam into the jars, together with a long-handled wooden spoon for stirring the jam, and a slotted one for removing scum.

A large bowl and jelly bag are required for jelly making, although the latter may be an improvised one made by tying a large square of cheesecloth or linen over the top of an upturned stool.

A sugar thermometer is a useful item if large quantities of jam are made as it is the most accurate way to test that setting point has been reached.

Labels. All jams, jellies and marmalades need labelling with the type of fruit and date on which it was made. Labels are often included with packets of jam covers or may be bought separately.

The fruits to use

Most fruits may be used for jam making but, as mentioned previously, they must be fresh, dry and slightly under-ripe. After preparation, the first stage for jam, jelly and marmalade is to soften the fruit. This must be done before adding sugar or any other ingredients. The fruit should be cooked slowly with a little water so that the skins soften and the pectin is released. The amount of water and length of this cooking time depends on the juiciness and ripeness of the fruit and also the quantity – the more fruit, the less water. Soft fruits such as blackberries, raspberries, and strawberries do not require any water and the softening time will be much shorter. Fruits which are most easily made into jam are those which are high in pectin, although these low in pectin can be successfully made with the addition of high pectin fruits or substitutes.

High pectin fruits: Citrus fruits (oranges, lemons, grapefruits etc.); cooking apples, crab apples, cranberries, damsons, gooseberries, plums and quinces.

Medium pectin fruits: Apricots, blackberries, greengages, loganberries and raspberries.

Low pectin fruits: Cherries, figs, grapes, marrows, pears, pineapple, rhubarb and strawberries.

Measuring pectin content

If you are using a vegetable such as marrow to make jam, it will require extra acid (lemon juice or citric acid) to give it a good set. The pectin and acid contents of fruit can vary according to weather conditions, variety of fruit, season and ripeness, so to be sure of a good set the pectin quantity can be measured in the following way.

Simmer a little of the fruit until it is soft and the juice runs out. Strain off one teaspoon of the juice into a small bowl or cup. When it is cool add three teaspoons of methylated spirits. Shake the mixture and leave it for one or two minutes. If a large, transparent, jelly-like clot forms the fruit is high in pectin; if it forms into two or three lumps the pectin content is medium; and if it breaks into small pieces the pectin content is low.

To make successful jam from low pectin and acid fruit extra pectin should be added and this can be done in one of the following ways.

1. Mix the low or medium pectin fruit with a high pectin one, for example, apple and blackberry or rhubarb and plum.

Above: The most accurate way to test that setting point has been reached is to use a sugar thermometer. If large quantities of jam are to be made each year it is well worth investing in one.

2. Add a pectin stock made from fruits such as apples, gooseberries or redcurrants.

3. Add commercially-made pectin, which is generally available in liquid, or sometimes powdered, form.

4. Add lemon juice or citric acid.

When adding extra pectin to the fruit, it must be very well softened before the pectin and sugar are added. The amount of pectin to add can vary according to the fruit used but a general guide is 150ml (5fl oz) pectin stock to 2kg (4lb) fruit; alternatively 50-125ml (2-4fl oz) of commercial liquid pectin, or 2 teaspoons dried pectin, to each 450g (1lb) fruit. If using lemon juice 2 tablespoons to 2kg (4lb) fruit is generally sufficient.

Pectin stock

Apple, redcurrant, gooseberry and damson juice, all of which have a high pectin content may be used to add to jams and jellies made from fruits low in pectin.

Prepare and strain the juice as for jelly making. When the juice has been strained, bring it to the boil and pour it quickly into hot preserving jars or heatproof bottles. Immerse these in a deep pan of hot water and boil for five minutes. Cover and label.

Sugar

Granulated, preserving or cube sugar, made from either cane or beet, can be used for jam, jelly or marmalade making. The advantage of using preserving sugar, although slightly more expensive, is that less scum is formed and the jam generally has a clearer appearance. Brown sugar may be used but as it gives a dark colour it is best to keep it for something like a chunky marmalade or black cherry jam.

The amount of sugar required to give a good set depends on the pectin quantity of the fruit and should represent 60 per cent of the final weight of jam; therefore if a recipe uses 2.75kg (6lb) sugar the final yield should be about 4.50kg (10lb) jam. The following is an approximate guide to the quantity of sugar needed for the different types of fruit, depending on their pectin content:

High pectin fruits – 575-675g (1¼-1½lb) sugar to 450g (1lb) fruit
Medium pectin fruits – 450g (1lb) sugar to 450g (1lb) fruit
Low pectin fruits – 350g (12oz) sugar to 450g (1lb) fruit

If too much sugar is used the jam may crystallize with storing and if too little is used it may result in fermentation. However, if a less sweet jam is preferred, less sugar can be used – although it will not keep for so long and there will be a smaller yield. The one advantage is that the jam will have a much more fruity flavour.

On a final note of economy, if the sugar is warmed before adding it to the fruit, it dissolves more quickly, thereby using less energy in the process.

Tests for setting

A test that setting point has been reached should be made after the jam, jelly or marmalade has been cooked for the suggested time in the recipe you are following. Care should be taken not to boil beyond setting point otherwise the colour, texture and flavour will be spoiled, so the pan should always be removed from the heat during testing. Testing the setting point can be done in several ways.
1. The easiest and simplest way is to put a teaspoon of the hot mixture on a saucer and leave it to cool. If you have a freezer this can be done in a few seconds. When cool, the surface should be set and the jam should crinkle when pushed with a finger. If it is still runny, return the pan to the cooker and continue boiling and testing until set.
2. Dip a wooden spoon into the jam, remove it, and after a second or

two tilt the spoon so that the jam drips. If the jam is almost set and the drops run together in large flakes then setting point has been reached.

3. A sugar thermometer is the most accurate way of testing the set. Place the thermometer in a jug of hot water before and after testing. Stir the jam, then immerse the thermometer into it – do not allow the bulb to touch the bottom of the pan otherwise it may break and the whole batch would be ruined! If the temperature is between 104°C (220°F) and 107°C (222°F) the jam is at setting point.

Finishing off

When the jam, jelly or marmalade is ready, remove any scum from the surface with a slotted spoon. If the jam contains whole fruit, such as strawberries, or peel, as in marmalade, leave it to cool slightly until a thin skin forms on top (this prevents the fruit from rising to the top). Stir the jam gently and pour it into the warm jars. Place a waxed disc on the surface and press it down gently to exclude any air. Wipe the rims of the jars with a damp cloth if they are sticky, then cover when either hot or cold depending on the covering used. Label and store the jars in a cool, dark place.

Jam making

Prepare the fruit by rinsing in cold water if necessary. Remove any stalks or leaves. Fruit with stones such as cherries, peaches, plums and greengages may be left whole or stoned. The latter is preferable as it makes for easier use, particularly if the jam is used in tarts and cake fillings. For apricot and plum jam the stones can be cracked and the inner white kernel added to the fruit to give a pleasant flavour.

Cook the fruit, with or without water, over low heat until it is completely softened and broken down. Add the sugar and pectin, if necessary, cook slowly and stir frequently until the sugar is dissolved. Then raise the heat and boil the jam rapidly without stirring. Take care that the jam does not rise to the top of the pan – if it does, give it a gentle stir to cook it down a fraction. Providing the initial cooking of the fruit has been sufficient the jam should reach setting point within 5 to 20 minutes. Then pour the jam into the jars leaving 10mm (½in) headspace, cover and label.

Jelly making

The difference between jelly and jam is that the fruit for jelly is cooked until very soft then strained through a jelly bag, piece of cheesecloth or double muslin. Only the juice is then cooked with sugar.

The basic principles are the same as for jam making, and to achieve the required consistency the same substances – pectin, acid and sugar – are needed. The low pectin fruits – cherries, pears, strawberries and marrow – are not really suitable on their own for jelly making, as the amount of pectin required to give a good set will disguise the flavour of the fruit. However, a mixture of high and low pectin fruit can be used.

As the yield is not as large as in jam making, cheap or wild fruit are often used in jellies. Blackberries, sloes, elderberries, bilberries and crab apples are all suitable, the currants (red, white and black), cooking apples, gooseberries and quinces also make delicious jellies.

The fruit should be just ripe and if there are any bruised parts

Opposite: Many different types of jar can be used to contain jam, ranging from conventional pots needing cellophane covers secured with rubber bands, to special glass storage jars. Home-made jams make very acceptable gifts; decorate the jars with pretty labels for a change. Below: Jam is a standard ingredient of many sweet pastries, of which jam tarts are probably a general favourite.

65

these should be discarded. There is no necessity to peel or remove stems but the fruit should be washed and the large ones cut into pieces.

Cooking the fruit for jelly
Like jam, the amount of water required depends on the type and juiciness of the fruit. Hard fruit and fruit with tough skins – such as apples, damsons or sloes – should be covered with water and will take a longer time to cook. The fruit should be gently simmered for about an hour; press it occasionally with a wooden spoon.

Straining the fruit
When the fruit is really soft pour it into the jelly bag with a large bowl underneath. The jelly bag or cloth should first be scalded by pouring boiling water through it.

Allow the juice to drain through the jelly bag and leave it for several hours or overnight. Do not be tempted to push the pulp through with a spoon or squeeze the bag as this will make the juice cloudy. If there is any doubt about the amount of pectin in the juice, it can be tested in the same way as for jam (page 63); but it is worth noting that if the juice is thick and sticky it is a sign that there is sufficient pectin. If the pectin content is low the pulp and juice can be re-cooked. Alternatively return the juice only to the pan and simmer it to allow some of the water to evaporate.

Sugar for jelly
Measure the juice and pour it into a preserving pan or large saucepan and bring to the boil before adding the sugar.

The amount of sugar used depends on the pectin quantity of the juice. For every 600ml (1 pint) of juice rich in pectin add 450-575g ($1-1\frac{1}{4}$lb) sugar and for medium pectin quantity add 300g (12oz) sugar.

After adding the sugar cook the mixture slowly until it dissolves, then bring it to the boil and boil rapidly for ten minutes. Remove the pan from the heat and test for setting (page 63).

Finishing the process
When setting point has been reached, remove any scum from the surface of the jelly then pour it into the prepared jars. Cover and store in the same way as for jam. It is not possible to give accurate yields in recipes for jellies as these will vary according to the ripeness and quality of the fruit, and also the amount of pulp lost in straining. An approximate yield is 2.25kg (5lb) jelly to every 1.35kg (3lb) sugar used.

Marmalade
Marmalade is a preserve made with citrus fruits and is traditionally British. The name is said to be derived from the Portuguese word *marmelada*, a jam made with quinces. This connection with the Iberian peninsula is strengthened by the fact that the bitter Seville oranges are popularly used to make marmalade.

Marmalade can, in fact, be made with oranges, lemons, limes, grapefruit or tangerines, each imparting its own tangy flavour. On the other hand citrus fruit may be mixed with other fruits – apples, pears or pineapples – to make a pleasant combination, or flavoured with ginger or other spices if wished. The best time of year for

Above: A jelly bag stand is important for large quantities. Opposite: Sugar is an essential ingredient of any jam, jelly or marmalade. Normally it is best to use preserving sugar (shown here in the top left compartment) as it is specifically refined to reduce to a minimum the amount of scum formed during the jam making process. However, granulated (top right) or cube (bottom centre) are both suitable, and granulated sugar is certainly the most economical. For special flavours and textures you could also use one of the brown sugars: shown here top to bottom are light soft brown sugar, dark soft brown or Barbados sugar and Demerara sugar. Other sugars are coffee crystals, icing and castor.

marmalade making is during January and February. This is the season for the genuine Seville orange, and it is very short. If you have a freezer, Seville oranges and other citrus fruits with a short season can be frozen, meaning that marmalade can be made at any time of the year. To freeze citrus fruit put them whole in a freezer bag and store until required. Alternatively the fruit can be cut up, cooked and packed into wax cartons. When using whole fruit cook them while they are still frozen, as this prevents discoloration. If the fruit has been cooked before freezing, allow it to thaw before the final cooking with sugar. As there may be some pectin loss in Seville oranges and tangerines during storage it is advisable to add extra weight of fruit – about one eighth – to the amount stated in the recipe.

The main difference between marmalade and jam making is that citrus fruit skin requires long slow cooking in a larger amount of water to soften it before adding the sugar. However, the length of cooking time can be shortened considerably with the use of a pressure cooker.

There are two types of marmalade: thick marmalade and jelly marmalade – the yield from the latter is less than that of thick marmalade.

Preparation of fruit
The fruit must be fresh and just ripe. It should be washed and if necessary scrubbed with a clean brush.

There are three methods of preparing thick marmalade, and whichever method is used remember that the pectin content is in the pulp, white pith and pips, *not* in the peel, so it is important to add these to the fruit while cooking.

In some recipes lemon juice or citric acid is added. This is because the acid content of the fruit may be lowered owing to the high proportion of water and sugar used in making marmalade. There is no necessity to add extra acid to marmalade made with two or more fruits, or to lemon and lime marmalades.

Method 1
This is the most usual method, and the simplest.

Scrub and scald the fruit in boiling water (this makes it easier to remove the peel). Remove the peel as thinly as possible and cut into thick or thin shreds. Place the peel, acid (if used) and half the quantity of water in a preserving pan. Bring to the boil, then simmer for one-and-a-half to two hours until the peel is soft.

Meanwhile cut the fruit and pith into pieces and simmer in another pan for an hour and a half. Strain the mixture through a colander placed over a bowl, then discard the pips, coarse tissue and pith and add the pulp to the peel. If a thicker marmalade is required the pulp can be pressed through a fine nylon sieve. Add the sugar and cook over low heat stirring frequently until the sugar dissolves. Bring to the boil and cook rapidly until setting point is reached (see page 63). Remove any scum from the top, allow the marmalade to cool slightly and finish off as for jam making.

Method 2
Wash the fruit and cut each one in half. Squeeze out the juice and pips and strain the juice into the preserving pan. Tie the pips and

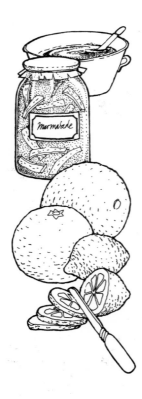

pulp in a piece of muslin. Cut the peel and pith into thick or thin pieces, depending on choice, and add the bag of pips, peel, acid and water to the juice in the pan. Simmer for two hours or until the peel is soft. Remove and squeeze any liquid from the bag of pips into the fruit and discard the bag. Add the sugar and cook over low heat, stirring frequently until the sugar has dissolved. Bring to the boil and cook until setting point has been reached. Finish as in Method 1.

Method 3

Wash the fruit and put it whole into the preserving pan with the water. Cover the pan and simmer for at least two hours or until the fruit is soft – test by piercing with a thin skewer or knitting needle.

Lift the fruit out of the water and chop it – use a knife and fork as the fruit will be hot. Remove the pips and tie them in a piece of muslin and return to the cooking liquid. Boil for five minutes then squeeze the bag to extract any juice. Discard the pips and add the fruit to the pan. Add the sugar and finish the marmalade as in Method 1.

Jelly marmalade

Wash the fruit and remove the peel very thinly. Cut the peel into fine strips and tie in a piece of muslin. Cut the remaining fruit and pith into pieces and place in the preserving pan with the acid and water. Simmer for two hours. Place the bag of peel in another pan with sufficient water. Cover and simmer for at least an hour and a half. Remove the peel and set aside. Pour the cooking water into the pulp mixture. Pour the contents of the pan into a jelly bag placed over a large bowl and leave to drain overnight. (See Jelly Making page 65). Measure the juice and pour it into the preserving pan, bring to the boil and add 450g (1lb) sugar to every 600ml (1 pint) juice. Add acid, if required, and the reserved peel. Finish as in Marmalade Method 1.

Making jams and marmalades in a pressure cooker

Normally the temperature of the boiling point of liquids is 100°C (212°F) and is controlled by atmospheric pressure and cannot be raised by the length of boiling time. If the atmospheric pressure can be raised, the temperatures can be increased accordingly but this can only be achieved by cooking in a pressure cooker.

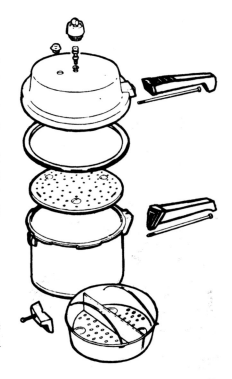

The cooking times of jams and marmalades can be reduced by using a pressure cooker. Ideally it should be one with a pressure control with three temperatures:
L (5lb) – Boiling Point 108.5°C (228°F); M (10lb) – Boiling point 115.3°C (239.8°F); H (15lb) – Boiling point 122°C (252°F). It is always advisable to follow the manufacturer's instructions as they may vary according to the cooker, but generally the following method is similar.
1. Remove the rack or trivet from the pan.
2. Never fill the pan more than half-full.
3. Pre-cook the fruit at M (10lb) pressure.
4. Use only half the amount of liquid in the recipe.
5. Finish cooking with the sugar in the pan without the pressure lid.

Generally the pre-cooking time of the fruit is about a third of the time taken by cooking in the usual way. However this may vary from cooker to cooker, so follow the manufacturer's instructions.

Recipes for jams, jellies and marmalades

Enough classic and unusual recipes are given here to stock your store cupboard for a year with tempting breakfast and teatime treats! There are fourteen different jams, twelve jellies – including several which make good accompaniments to meat – eight marmalades, and also some outsiders: three delicious curds, and homemade mincemeat.

Apricot Jam

2.75kg (6lb) apricots
600ml (1 pint) water
2.75kg (6lb) sugar

Wash the fruit, cut into halves and remove the stones. Place the fruit in a preserving pan. Split a few of the stones and remove the white kernels. Blanch these in boiling water, drain and chop, and add them to the apricots. Add the water and cook gently until the apricots are soft. Add the sugar and stir until it has dissolved. Bring to the boil and boil for 15 minutes. Test for setting and if necessary boil again until setting point has been reached. Bottle, cover and label. The approximate yield will be 4.5kg (10lb) of jam.

Dried Apricot Jam

450g (1lb) dried apricots
1.75 litres (3 pints) water
Juice of 1 lemon
1.35kg (3lb) sugar
50g (2oz) blanched almonds

Wash the apricots and cut into pieces. Place them in a large bowl with the water, making sure they are completely covered, and set aside for 24 hours.

Transfer the apricots and water to a preserving pan and simmer for 30 minutes or until the apricots are very soft. Add the lemon juice and sugar and stir until the sugar has dissolved. Add the almonds and bring the mixture to the boil. Boil rapidly for 15 minutes and test for setting point.

Bottle, cover and label. Yield will be about 2.25kg (5lb).
Note: If preferred, slivered almonds could be substituted for whole ones.

Below: An apricot tree will grow quite well in a sheltered spot which faces the sun. Most small gardens could accommodate one trained against a wall, which in a good year will yield enough surplus fruit for jam. Opposite: Dried apricot jam (including blanched almonds which complement the flavour of the fruit) is an unusual variation. To blanch almonds, plunge them into boiling water for a few seconds then slip the skin off with your fingers.

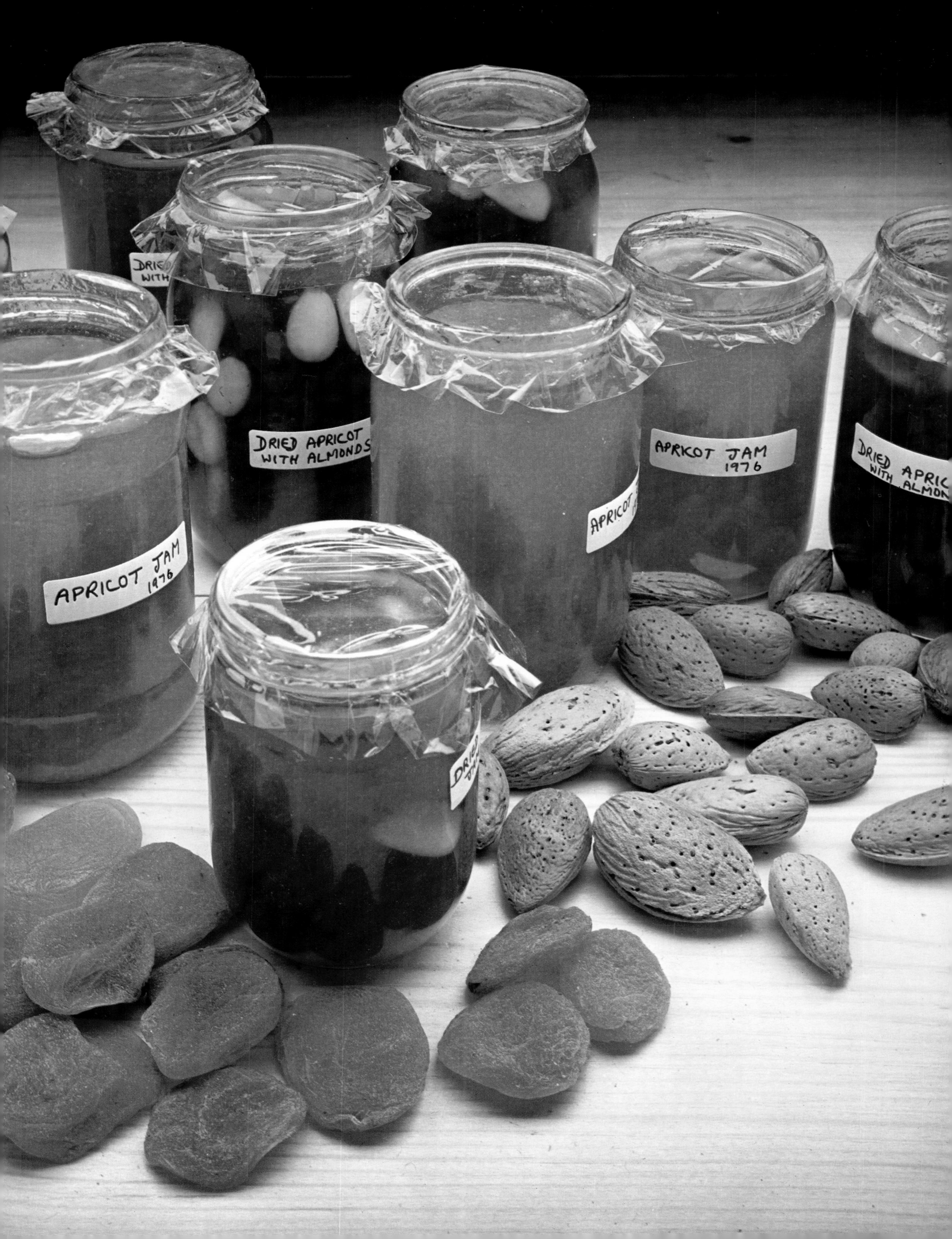
DRIED APRICOT
WITH ALMONDS
APRICOT JAM
1976
1976

Damson Jam

2kg (4lb) damsons, washed and stoned
600ml (1 pint) water
2-3kg (4-6lb) sugar

Preheat the oven to cool 150°C (300°F, Gas Mark 2).

Place the damsons and water in an ovenproof dish or pan. Cover the dish or pan and place it in the oven. Leave to cook for one hour only.

Remove the dish from the oven and measure the quantity of fruit and liquid. Pour the fruit and liquid into a preserving pan and add an equal quantity of sugar.

Place the pan over moderate heat and stir until the sugar dissolves.

Increase the heat to high and boil briskly for 2 minutes or until setting point is reached. With a metal spoon, skim any scum off the surface.

Remove the pan from the heat and pour the jam into clean, dry, warmed jam jars. Cover, label and store in a cool, dry place. Yield will be about 2.25kg (5lb).

Blackberry and Apple Jam

1.75kg (4lb) blackberries
300ml (10fl oz) water
1.75kg (4lb) cooking apples, peeled, cored and sliced
2.75kg (6lb) sugar

Place the blackberries and half the water in a preserving pan. Cook gently until the blackberries are soft. Cook

the apples in the remaining water until they are soft then combine the two fruits. (If a smooth jam is preferred the blackberries may be sieved and added to the apples in purée form.)

Add the sugar and when it has dissolved, boil the jam until setting point is reached.

Bottle, cover and label. The yield will be about 4.50kg (10lb).

Plum and Apple Jam

675g (1½lb) plums, halved and stoned
675g (1½lb) cooking apples, peeled, cored and sliced
1 tablespoon lemon juice
300ml (10fl oz) water
1.35kg (3lb) sugar

In a preserving pan or large saucepan, bring the plums, apples, lemon juice and water to the boil over high heat.

Reduce the heat to moderate and cook for 20 minutes or until the fruit is soft. Add the sugar and stir until it has dissolved. Bring the jam to the boil and boil until setting point is reached.

Remove the pan from the heat. With a slotted spoon, skim off the scum from the surface.

Pour the jam into clean, dry, warmed jam jars. Seal, label and store in a cool, dry place. Yield will be about 2.25kg (5lb).

Greengage Jam

2.75kg (6lb) greengages, washed, halved and stoned
600ml (1 pint) water
2.75kg (6lb) sugar

In a preserving pan or large saucepan, bring the greengages and water to the boil over high heat. Crack ten of the stones and add the kernels to the pan.

Reduce the heat to moderate and simmer for 20 minutes, or until the greengages are soft. Add the sugar and stir until it has dissolved.

Bring the jam to the boil and boil for about 15 minutes or until setting point is reached. Remove the pan from the heat. With a slotted spoon, skim off the scum from the surface of the jam.

Pour into clean, dry, warmed jam jars. Seal, label and store in a cool, dry place. Yield will be about 4.50kg (10lb).

Plum and apple jam is easy to make and uses fruit which is readily available and cheap during late summer. Plums do not keep well so make the jam as soon as possible after obtaining them.

73

Strawberry Jam

2.25kg (5lb) strawberries, hulled and washed
125ml (4fl oz) lemon juice
2kg (4½lb) sugar

Place the strawberries in a preserving pan and add the lemon juice. Simmer, stirring frequently, until the strawberries are soft.

Add the sugar and stir until the sugar has dissolved. Bring the mixture to the boil and boil rapidly for 15 to 20 minutes. Test for setting. When set, leave the jam for 10 minutes before pouring into the bottles. Cover, seal and label the jars.

Note: If the jam is preferred with whole fruit, then small strawberries should be used and pectin stock (page 62) added instead of the lemon juice. Also use equal quantity of sugar to fruit e.g. 2.75kg (6lb) strawberries, 2.75kg (6lb) sugar and 400ml (15fl oz) pectin stock. Add the pectin stock towards the end of cooking otherwise a good set may not occur. The approximate yield will be 3.2kg (7lb).

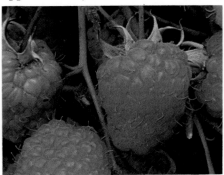

Right: Boiling the strawberries and sugar for Strawberry Jam. If whole strawberry jam is preferred, allow the jam to cool slightly before pouring it into the jars, so that the fruit is evenly distributed.

Raspberry Jam

1.75kg (4lb) raspberries, hulled and washed
2 tablespoons lemon juice
1.75kg (4lb) sugar

Place the raspberries in a preserving pan and cook very gently until some of the juice is extracted from the fruit. Add the lemon juice and simmer, stirring frequently until the fruit is soft. Add the sugar and stir until the sugar has dissolved.

Bring the mixture to the boil and boil rapidly for 10 minutes or until setting point is reached.

Bottle, cover and label. Approximate yield will be 2.75kg (6lb).

Peach jam is a preserve with a continental flavour, delicious served with croissants for breakfast.

Fig Preserve

900g (2lb) green figs, stalks removed
Hot water
900g (2lb) sugar
1 teaspoon finely grated lemon rind
3 tablespoons lemon juice

Put the figs into a large mixing bowl and pour over enough hot water to cover them completely. Leave the figs to soak for 2 to 3 minutes. Drain them into a colander and transfer them to a wooden board. With a sharp knife, chop them into small pieces.

Weigh the figs and put them into a large saucepan. Add the same amount of sugar to the saucepan with the lemon rind and juice.

Place the pan over low heat and cook, stirring occasionally, for 1¾ hours or until a thick clear syrup forms. Add a little water if the mixture becomes too thick.

Remove the saucepan from the heat and allow the preserve to become completely cold before pouring it into dry, clean jam jars.

Cover, label, and store in a dry, dark, cool place. Yield is about 1.35kg (3lb).

Peach Jam

1 medium-sized cooking apple, chopped
Thinly pared rind of 2 lemons
2 cloves
1.35kg (3lb) peaches, stoned and sliced
300ml (10fl oz) water
1 teaspoon ground allspice
1.35kg (3lb) sugar

Tie the apple, lemon rind and cloves in a double piece of muslin.

Place the peaches, water and muslin bag in a preserving pan. Bring the mixture to the boil then reduce the

Rhubarb Jam

1.75kg (4lb) rhubarb, washed, trimmed
and cut into 25mm (1in) pieces
250ml (8fl oz) water
Juice of 1 lemon
50mm (2in) piece fresh root ginger,
peeled and bruised
1.35kg (3lb) sugar
100g (4oz) crystallized ginger, finely
chopped

*Ginger complements many fruits
and is used either in crystallized or
preserved form. This recipe for
Rhubarb Jam uses crystallized
ginger for a contrast in texture and
flavour.*

heat and simmer, stirring frequently
until the peaches are just soft.

Remove the muslin bag and press it
against the side of the pan with a
wooden spoon to extract as much juice
as possible.

Add the allspice and sugar and stir
until the sugar has dissolved.

Bring the mixture to the boil and
boil rapidly for 15 to 20 minutes until
setting point is reached. Set aside for
10 minutes.

Bottle, cover and seal. Approximate
yield will be 2.25kg (5lb).

Place the rhubarb, water and lemon
juice in a preserving pan and bring to
the boil. Add the root ginger, reduce
the heat and simmer, stirring frequently,
until the rhubarb is soft. Remove the
piece of ginger.

Add the sugar and stir until it has
dissolved, add the crystallized ginger.

Bring the mixture to the boil and
boil rapidly for 10 to 15 minutes until
setting point is reached.

Bottle, cover and label. Approximate
yield will be 2.75kg (6lb).

Right: Juicy loganberries, said by some to be a cross between blackberries and raspberries, can be used as an interesting alternative to both.

Loganberry Jam

2.75kg (6lb) loganberries, washed and hulled
2.75kg (6lb) sugar

Put the fruit in a large preserving pan. Set the pan over low heat and cook, stirring frequently, until the fruit is soft.

Add the sugar and stir with a wooden spoon until it is completely dissolved. When the sugar has dissolved increase the heat to high and bring the mixture to the boil. Continue to boil for 15 to 20 minutes, or until setting point has been reached.

Skim the scum off the surface of the jam with a metal spoon. Fill clean, dry, warm jars to within 10mm (½in) of the tops. Cover, label and store. Yield is about 2.75kg (6lb).

Cherry Jam

4.50kg (10lb) stoned cherries (about 5kg (11lb) before stoning), stones reserved
Juice of 5 lemons
3kg (7lb) sugar

Put the cherries and lemon juice in a large preserving pan. Put the cherry stones in a cheesecloth bag and add it to the pan. Bring to the boil and simmer for 30 minutes, or until the cherries are tender. Remove the bag of stones from the pan and discard it.

Add the sugar to the pan and stir, over low heat, until it has dissolved. Increase the heat to moderate, bring to the boil and cook briskly until the mixture sets.

With a slotted spoon dipped in boiling water and dried, quickly remove the scum from the surface of the jam. Allow the jam to cool in the pan until a thin skin forms on the surface. Stir gently and pour it into clean, dry, warm jars. Cover, label and store them in a cool, dry, dark place until ready to use. Yield is about 6kg (12lb) of jam.

Note: Cherries contain little acid and pectin and so some people find that cherry jam is difficult to make. However, Duke cherries are considered best, though the acid Morello cherry is also successful. Halve the lemon juice if you use the latter.

Pear and Ginger Jam

3.20kg (7lb) pears
25mm (1in) piece fresh root ginger, peeled and bruised
Thinly pared rind and juice of 3 lemons
1 litre (2 pints) water
2.25kg (5lb) sugar

Peel, quarter and core the pears. Tie the pear peel and cores, the ginger and lemon rind in a large piece of cheese-cloth.

Place the pears, cheesecloth bag and water in a preserving pan. Bring the water to the boil, and simmer the pears for 30 minutes, or until they are soft. Remove the cheesecloth bag and, with the back of a wooden spoon, press it against the side of the pan to squeeze out as much juice as possible.

Add the sugar and stir until it has dissolved. Stir in the lemon juice. Increase the heat to moderately high and bring the jam to the boil. Boil it for 15 to 20 minutes or until setting point is reached.

Remove the pan from the heat. With a slotted spoon, skim off the scum from the surface. Let the jam stand for 5 minutes, then fill the jars, cover and

Vegetable marrow (left) and ginger (above) are combined in a subtle, spicy preserve which requires a slightly different method. Summer Squash could be substituted for marrow.

label, and store them in a cool, dry place. Yield is about 4.50kg (10lb).

Marrow and Ginger Jam

1.75kg (4lb) peeled and seeded vegetable marrow, cut into small cubes
Juice and very thinly pared rinds of 4 lemons
3 whole cloves
25mm (1in) piece fresh root ginger, peeled and bruised
1.35kg (3lb) sugar
100g (4oz) crystallized ginger, chopped

Put the marrow in the top part of a steamer. Half fill the bottom half with water and bring it to the boil over moderate heat. Place the top half in place, cover and steam the cubes for 20 to 25 minutes or until they are just tender.

Remove the pan from the heat. Transfer the marrow to a large mixing bowl and add the lemon juice. Put the lemon rind, cloves and bruised ginger in a muslin or cheesecloth bag and add it to the bowl. Add the sugar and mix it in thoroughly with a large spoon. Cover the bowl and leave the mixture for 24 hours.

Tip the contents of the bowl into a preserving pan or large saucepan. Put the pan over low heat and stir constantly until the sugar has dissolved. Then stir in the crystallized ginger. Increase the heat and boil the jam until the marrow is transparent, the syrup thick and setting point is reached.

Remove the pan from the heat. With a slotted spoon, lift out and discard the muslin or cheesecloth bag. Ladle the jam into warm jars, cover, label and store in a cool place. Yield will be approximately 2.75kg (6lb) of jam.

Pineapple Jam

3 lemons
1.35kg (3lb) fresh pineapple flesh
600ml (1 pint) water
1.75kg (3lb) sugar

Squeeze the juice from the lemons and set it aside. Tie the squeezed out lemons and the pips in a cheesecloth bag.

Place the pineapple, the reserved lemon juice, the cheesecloth bag and the water in a preserving pan or large saucepan. Bring the liquid to the boil. Reduce the heat to low, cover the pan and simmer until the pineapple pieces are tender. Remove the cheesecloth bag, squeezing it against the side of the pan with the back of a wooden spoon to extract as much juice as possible.

Add the sugar to the pan and cook the jam, stirring constantly, until the sugar has dissolved. Then boil without stirring for 15 minutes until setting point is reached. Remove the pan from the heat and let it stand for 5 minutes.

Ladle the jam into clean, warm, dry jam jars. Cover, label and store in a cool, dark, dry place. Yield is about 2.75kg (6lb).

Bramble Jelly

1.75kg (4lb) blackberries, washed
300ml (10fl oz) water
2 tablespoons lemon juice
Sugar

Place the blackberries, water and lemon juice in a preserving pan. Simmer until the fruit is soft. Wash well and pour the mixture into a jelly

Below: Bramble Jelly is one of the most popular of preserves, and it can be one of the cheapest if you take blackberry-picking seriously! Below right: Pineapples are very versatile: use them for jam (this page) or for liqueur (as for Apricot Liqueur, page 56).

bag. Leave for 24 hours, measure the juice and return it to a clean pan. Bring to the boil, then reduce the heat. Add 450g (1lb) sugar to each 600ml (1 pint) of juice and when the sugar has dissolved, boil rapidly for about 10 minutes until setting point is reached.

Bottle, cover and label. Yield will be about 2kg (4lb 4oz).

Gooseberry Jelly

1.75kg (4lb) gooseberries
1.75 litres (3 pints) water
Sugar

Wash the gooseberries and place in a preserving pan with the water. Bring to the boil, then reduce the heat and simmer for 45 minutes to an hour until the fruit is very soft. Wash well and

strain through a jelly bag. Measure the juice and add 450g (1lb) sugar to each 600ml (1 pint) juice. When the sugar has dissolved, boil rapidly for about 10 minutes until setting point is reached.

Bottle, cover and label. Yield will be about 1.75kg (4lb).

Guava Jelly

1.75kg (4lb) fresh guavas, washed and quartered
175ml (6fl oz) water
Lime juice
Sugar

Place the guavas in a preserving pan or large saucepan with the water. Bring to the boil over high heat. Reduce the heat and simmer the fruit for 30 minutes, or until it is quite tender,

The guava is a delicious aromatic fruit from the tropics, but is generally available elsewhere. It is well-suited to the making of jams and preserves, especially Guava Jelly.

Clear, crisp Sloe Jelly is another economical preserve if you have access to a blackthorn hedge or thicket.

occasionally mashing the fruit against the sides of the pan.

Pour the guava pulp into a jelly bag. Allow the juice to drain through for at least 12 hours. When the juice has completely drained through the jelly bag, discard the guava pulp.

Measure the juice before returning it to the rinsed preserving pan. And 450g (1lb) of sugar and 1 teaspoon of lime juice to every 600ml (1 pint) of liquid. Place the pan over low heat and stir to dissolve the sugar. When the sugar has completely dissolved, increase the heat to high and bring the mixture to the boil. Boil briskly, without stirring, for about 10 minutes, until setting point is reached.

Skim the foam off the surface of the jelly with a metal spoon. Ladle the jelly into hot, clean, dry jam jars,

leaving 10mm ($\frac{1}{2}$in) headspace. Wipe the jars with a damp cloth. Cover, label and store. Yield is approximately 1.75kg (4lb).

Note: Guava jelly is delicious served with venison or roast pork.

Sloe Jelly

1kg (2lb) sloes, trimmed and washed
500g (1lb) cooking apples, cut into quarters
Juice of 1 lemon
Sugar

Using a large needle, prick the sloes all over and place them, with the apples, in a large saucepan. Add enough cold water just to cover the fruit and add the lemon juice. Set the pan over moderate heat. Bring the mixture to the boil. Reduce the heat to low and simmer for 1 hour or until the fruit is tender. Mash the fruit occasionally against the side of the pan with the back of a wooden spoon.

Strain the sloe and apple pulp into a jelly bag or cloth for at least 12 hours or overnight. When the juice has dripped through, measure the juice and return it to the pan.

Add 450g (1lb) of sugar to every 600ml (1 pint) of juice. Set the pan over low heat and cook, stirring, until the sugar has dissolved. Increase the heat to high and bring the mixture to the boil. Boil briskly, without stirring, for about 10 minutes or until the jelly has reached setting point.

Ladle the jelly into hot, clean, dry jars. Cover, label and store in a cool, dark, dry place. Yield will be approximately 3.75kg (8lb).

Apple and Elderberry Jelly

2.75kg (6lb) cooking apples
1kg (2lb 2oz) elderberries
Water
Sugar

Wash the apples and cut into pieces. Strip the elderberries off the stems and place them with the apples in a preserving pan. Add sufficient cold water to cover the fruit. Bring the mixture to the boil then reduce the heat and simmer for 45 minutes or until the fruit is very soft and pulpy.

Strain through a jelly bag. Measure the juice and add 450g (1lb) sugar to each 600ml (1 pint) juice. When the sugar has dissolved boil rapidly until

setting point is reached.

Bottle, cover and label. Yield will be about 2.75kg (6lb).

Quince Jelly

1.75kg (4lb) ripe quinces, sliced
600ml (1 pint) water
6 allspice berries, bruised
Lemon juice
Sugar

Place the quinces in a preserving pan or large saucepan with the water and

allspice berries. Bring to the boil, then simmer for 40 to 50 minutes, until the fruit is tender.

Pour the quince pulp into a jelly bag. Allow the juice to drain through for at least 12 hours. Discard the pulp.

Measure the juice before returning it to the rinsed pan. Add 1 tablespoon of lemon juice and 400g (14oz) of sugar to every 600ml (1 pint) of liquid. Place the pan over low heat and stir until the sugar is dissolved. Bring the mixture to the boil, and boil briskly, without stirring, for 10 minutes or until the jelly reaches setting point. (Quinces are high in pectin so they set well.)

Skim the foam off the surface of the jelly with a metal spoon. Ladle the jelly into hot jars, leaving 25mm (1in) headspace. Cover, label and store in a cool place. Yield is about 1.2kg (2½lb).

Far left: The fruit of the elderberry tree makes an interesting alternative to blackberries in 'self-sufficient' preserving. They are low in pectin so need to be combined with apple to ensure a good set. Left: Quinces on the other hand are high in pectin, and only need a little lemon juice to set well. Quinces are very tart so this jelly makes a good condiment to serve with fatty meats such as roast pork, venison or goose.

Above: Japonica blossom. Right: The fruit of the mulberry tree.

Mulberry Jelly

450g (1lb) mulberries, stalks removed
1 large cooking apple, chopped
125ml (4fl oz) water
650-900g (1½-2lb) sugar

In a medium-sized saucepan, bring the mulberries, apple and water to the boil over moderate heat. Cover the pan, reduce the heat to low and cook the fruit for 20 minutes or until it is soft and pulpy. Remove the pan from the heat.

Pour the fruit mixture into a jelly bag and leave it to drain. Measure the quantity of juice. For each 600ml (1 pint) of juice you will need 450g (1lb) of sugar. Add the sugar to the juice. Place the pan over moderate heat and stir until the sugar has dissolved. Increase the heat to moderately high and bring the mixture to the boil. Boil briskly, without stirring, for about 10 minutes, or until the jelly has reached setting point.

With a metal spoon, skim the scum off the surface. Ladle the jelly into hot, dry jam jars, leaving 25mm (1in) headspace. Cover, label and store them in a cool, dark, dry place. Yield will be about 1.35kg (3lb).

Note: Mulberries are low in pectin, and this jelly, which contains only a small portion of apple to assist setting, has a very light set.

Japonica Jelly

1.35kg (3lb) japonica fruit
450g (1lb) tart cooking apples or windfalls
2.50 litres (4 pints) water
Juice of 1 lemon
Sugar

Cut the fruit in quarters and place in a large preserving pan or saucepan. Add the water and lemon juice.

Set the pan over moderate heat. Slowly bring the mixture to the boil. Reduce the heat to low and simmer for 1 hour, or until the fruit is quite tender. Mash the fruit occasionally against the sides of the pan with a wooden spoon.

Pour the japonica and apple pulp into a jelly bag. Allow the juice to strain for at least 12 hours. When the juice has completely strained through,

measure and return it to the pan. Discard the pulp.

Add 450g (1lb) of sugar to every 600ml (1 pint) of juice. Stir to dissolve the sugar over low heat. When the sugar has completely dissolved, increase the heat to high and bring the mixture to the boil. Boil briskly, without stirring, for about 10 minutes, or until the jelly has reached setting point.

Ladle the jelly into hot, clean, dry jars. Cover, label, and store them in a cool, dark, dry place. Yield is about 3.5kg (7½lb).

Note: Japonica is not available in shops and markets but this unusual jelly is delightful to make if the shrub grows in your garden.

Wine Jelly

1.35kg (3lb) ripe green grapes, crushed
300ml (10fl oz) dry white wine
675g (1½lb) cooking apples, sliced
1 lemon, thinly sliced
6 cardamom seeds
Sugar
175ml (6fl oz) brandy

Place the grapes and wine in a preserving pan or large saucepan. Bring to the boil over high heat. Reduce the heat to low and simmer the fruit for 20 to 30 minutes or until it is soft and pulpy. Add the apples, lemon and cardamom and continue to simmer for 20 to 30 minutes or until the apples are pulpy.

Pour the contents of the pan into a jelly bag or cloth and allow the juice to drip through the cheesecloth or bag for at least 12 hours or overnight. When the juice has completely drained through, discard the pulp. Rinse out the preserving pan or saucepan.

Measure the juice and pour it into the preserving pan or saucepan. Add 450g (1lb) of sugar to every 600ml (1 pint) of juice. Place the pan over low heat and stir until the sugar has dissolved. Increase the heat to high and bring the mixture to the boil. Boil briskly, without stirring, for about 10 minutes or until the jelly has reached setting point.

Ladle the jelly into hot, clean, dry jam jars, leaving 25mm (1in) head-space. Cover, label and store in a cool, dark, dry place. Yield is about 2.75kg (5-6lb).

Note: This jelly is a delicious accompaniment to cold roast veal or pork.

Crab Apple Jelly

2kg (4lb) crab apples
1-1.50 litres (2-3 pints) cold water
Rind of 2 lemons
Sugar

Wash the apples and cut out any bad portions. Quarter the apples and place them, complete with peel and core, in

Crab Apple Jelly is a traditional British preserve. Serve it with pork, or use it as a filling in puff pastry envelopes.

a large saucepan. Pour enough cold water into the pan to cover the apples, then add the lemon rind. Place the pan over high heat and bring the water to the boil. Reduce the heat to moderately low and simmer for 1 hour or until the apples are tender and mushy.

Pour the apples and liquid into a jelly bag and leave overnight for the juice to strain into a pan.

Measure the final amount of juice and pour it back into the pan. Add 450g (1lb) of sugar for every 600ml (1 pint) of juice.

Place the pan over low heat and stir the juice to dissolve the sugar. Increase the heat to high and bring the juice to the boil. With a metal spoon skim off any scum from the surface. Boil briskly for about 10 minutes or until setting point is reached. Remove the pan from the heat and let the jelly cool. Pour it into hot, dry jam jars and cover, label and store in a cool dark place. Yield will be about 1.35kg (3lb).

Rosemary Jelly

2.25kg (5lb) cooking apples, sliced
600ml (1 pint) water
4 tablespoons fresh rosemary leaves
250ml (8fl oz) malt vinegar
Granulated or preserving sugar
6 drops green food colouring

Place the apples and water in a preserving pan or large saucepan. Stir in half of the rosemary. Bring the water to the boil over high heat. Reduce the heat to low and simmer the fruit for 40 to 50 minutes or until it is soft and pulpy. Add the vinegar and boil for 5 minutes.

Pour the apple pulp into a jelly bag or cloth and allow the juice to drain through for at least 12 hours. When the juice has completely drained through, discard the remaining pulp.

Measure the juice before returning

Rosemary Jelly is a very good alternative to mint jelly to serve with cuts of lamb. Rosemary is a sturdy shrub and will respond to quite extensive cutting.

it to the rinsed preserving pan or saucepan. Add 450g (1lb) of sugar to every 600ml (1 pint) of juice. Place the pan over low heat and stir until the sugar has dissolved. Increase the heat to high and bring the mixture to the boil. Boil briskly, without stirring, for about 10 minutes or until the jelly has reached setting point.

Skim the foam off the surface of the jelly with a metal spoon. Sprinkle the remaining rosemary and the green food colouring over the jelly and stir well.

Ladle the jelly into hot, clean, dry jam jars, leaving 10mm ($\frac{1}{2}$in) space at the top of each jar. Label and store in a cool, dark, dry place. Yield will be approximately 3kg (7lb).

Note: Mint jelly can be made in the same way, substituting 5 tablespoons of fresh chopped mint leaves for the rosemary leaves. Green food colouring may be added according to taste.

Redcurrant Jelly

1.75kg (4lb) redcurrants
600ml (1 pint) water
Sugar

Wash the redcurrants and place in a preserving pan with the water. Bring to the boil then reduce the heat and simmer for 45 minutes to an hour until the fruit is very soft.

Mash well and strain through a jelly bag. Measure the juice, return to a clean pan and bring to the boil. Reduce the heat and add 450g (1lb) sugar to each 600ml (1 pint) juice. When the sugar has dissolved boil rapidly for 10 minutes until setting point is reached.

Bottle, cover and seal. Yield will be about 1.75kg (4lb).

Note: For a thicker jelly to be used as a condiment, the fruit may be cooked with no water. After straining add 550g (1$\frac{1}{4}$lb) sugar to 600ml (1 pint) hot juice. The yield will be slightly less.

Redcurrant Jelly is another standard accompaniment to roast lamb, but is equally good with turkey or venison.

87

Left: Adding the sugar to marmalade – in this case Five Fruit Marmalade (recipe overleaf). The pan should be returned to the stove and the sugar dissolved slowly over low heat, stirring all the time. For dark marmalade, such as Dark Seville (this page) or Dundee (overleaf) use brown sugar – light or dark depending on taste. A further refinement is to add brandy or whisky for a really luscious breakfast spread. Brandy Marmalade can be made by adding 150ml (5fl oz) of brandy to Orange Seville Marmalade, after the sugar has been dissolved and before the pulp is finally boiled up to reach setting point. Whisky Marmalade can be made in the same way by adding 150ml (5fl oz) whisky to Dark Seville or Dundee Marmalade.

Seville Orange Marmalade

1.35kg (3lb) Seville oranges
Juice of 2 lemons
3 litres (6 pints) water
2.75kg (6lb) sugar

Use either method 1, 2 or 3 for preparation and cooking. The above quantities will yield approximately 4.50kg (10lb).

Dark Seville Marmalade

1.35kg (3lb) Seville oranges
2 lemons (prepared as for oranges)
2.75kg (6lb) soft dark brown sugar
2 tablespoons black treacle
3 litres (6 pints) water

Use either method 1, 2 or 3 for preparation and cooking. The approximate yield will be 4.50kg (10lb).

Orange Jelly Marmalade

1.75kg (4lb) Seville oranges
4 litres (8 pints) water
Juice of 2 lemons
Sugar

Prepare fruit, then cook and finish as given under Jelly Marmalade (page 69).

Grapefruit Jelly Marmalade

1kg (2lb 2oz) grapefruit
1 orange and 1 lemon : total weight 450g (1lb)
3 litres (6 pints) water
Sugar

Prepare fruit, then cook and finish as given under Jelly Marmalade.

Lime Marmalade

1.35kg (3lb) limes, washed
2 litres (3½ pints) water
2.75kg (6lb) sugar

With a sharp knife, cut the fruit in half and squeeze the juice into a medium-sized mixing bowl. Reserve the pips.

Chop the pulp and peel coarsely and place in a very large saucepan or preserving pan. Add enough water to cover the fruit. Soak overnight. Drain the pulp and peel well.

Add the fruit juice and the water to

the peel. Tie the pips in a piece of cheesecloth and place it in the pan. Bring the mixture to the boil over high heat. Reduce the heat to low, half cover the pan and simmer for 2 hours or until the peel is soft. Remove the cheesecloth bag, pressing it against the side of the pan with the back of a wooden spoon to squeeze out as much juice as possible. Discard the bag.

Add the sugar, stirring with a wooden spoon until it has dissolved. Increase the heat to high and bring the marmalade to the boil. Continue to boil rapidly for about 20 minutes, or until setting point has been reached. Skim the scum off the surface of the marmalade with a slotted spoon. Remove the pan from the heat. Let the marmalade stand for 10 minutes before

Marmalades are generally served at breakfast, to spread on bread or toast. Shown here (top to bottom) are Dark Seville Marmalade, Seville Orange Marmalade and Lime Marmalade.
Breakfast is a meal in which many preserved foods come into their own: jams, such as Cherry Jam (page 78), can be served as an alternative to marmalade, and dried fruits (in the form of stewed apricots or raisins and sultanas in muesli) make a change from the usual corn flakes or porridge!

filling the jars. Cover, label, and store in a cool dry place. Yield will be about 4.50kg (10lb).

Dundee Marmalade

1.35kg (3lb) bitter Seville oranges, washed
2 lemons, washed
1.75 litres (3 pints) cold water
2.75kg (6lb) preserving sugar

Prepare by method 3.
    When setting point has been reached, let the marmalade stand for 10 minutes – this is to prevent the peel from rising.
    Pour the marmalade into dry, warmed jars, cover and store in a cool place. Yield will be about 4kg (9lb).

Grapefruit Marmalade

1.35kg (3lb) grapefruit
2 teaspoons citric acid
2.75kg (6lb) sugar
3 litres (6 pints) water

Use either method 1, 2 or 3 for preparation and cooking. The approximate yield will be 4.50kg (10lb).

Five Fruit Marmalade

1 orange
1 grapefruit
1 lemon
1.25 litres (2½ pints) water
1 large cooking apple
1 pear
1.35kg (3lb) sugar

Prepare the fruit and use either method 1, 2 or 3 for cooking. Peel and dice the apple and pear before adding them to the mixture. The approximate yield will be 2.25kg (5lb).

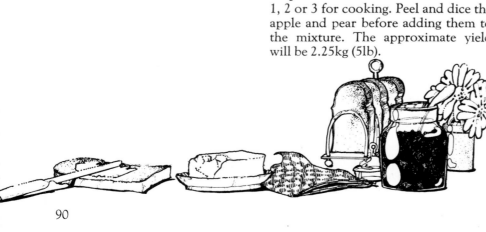

The fruit of the lemon tree may be impossible to eat raw, but it has hundreds of culinary uses. Lemon Curd is an underrated preserve which has an undeserved reputation for being difficult to make. However, if care is taken not to hurry the process and keep the heat low there is no reason why any curd should not be successful. Use Lemon Curd for tarts and flans or as a filling for a lemon sandwich cake, but of course it is equally delicious simply spread on fresh bread and butter.

Lemon Curd

350g (12oz) butter, cut into small pieces
900g (2lb) castor sugar
Thinly pared rind and juice of 6 large lemons
8 eggs, beaten

Place all the ingredients in a heatproof bowl placed over a saucepan of boiling water or in the top of a double boiler. Cook, whisking gently until the butter has melted and the sugar has dissolved. Pour the mixture through a strainer placed over a bowl. Discard the lemon rind. Return the mixture to a clean heatproof bowl or top of the double boiler. Cook, stirring frequently, until the mixture thickens (about 40 minutes).

Pour into clean, dry, warm bottles up to the rim. The yield will be about 1.35kg (3lb). Cover and label, store in a cool place.

Note: Lemon curd does not keep for as long as jams and jellies and should be used within 3 to 4 months.

Gooseberry Curd

1kg (2lb 2oz) gooseberries, trimmed and washed
50ml (2fl oz) water
50g (2oz) butter
3 eggs, lightly beaten
450g (1lb) sugar

In a large saucepan, bring the goose-berries and the water to the boil over high heat. Reduce the heat to low, cover the pan and simmer for 20 to 25 minutes, or until the gooseberries are soft and mushy.

Remove the pan from the heat and push the fruit through a strainer into a medium-sized mixing bowl, pressing down on the fruit with a wooden spoon. Discard the skins left in the strainer.

In another bowl set over a pan of simmering water, melt the butter. Stir in the eggs, sugar and the gooseberry purée. Cook the mixture, stirring frequently, for 25 to 30 minutes, or until it thickens.

Remove the bowl from the heat and pour the curd into clean, dry, warmed jam jars. Seal and cover as for jam.

Using tongs, carefully immerse the filled jars to within 25mm (1in) of the top in boiling water for 5 minutes to sterilize them.

Label the jars and keep them in a cool, dry place. Yield will be about 1kg (2lb).

Orange Curd

Thinly pared rind and juice of 5 medium-sized, bright-skinned oranges
1 tablespoon lemon juice
2 teaspoons orange-flower water
350g (12oz) butter, cut into small pieces
900g (2lb) castor sugar
8 large eggs, well beaten

Place the orange rind and juice, lemon juice, orange-flower water, butter and sugar in a large heatproof mixing bowl and place it over a large saucepan half filled with hot water.

Set the pan over moderately low heat and cook the mixture, stirring constantly with a wooden spoon, until the butter has melted and the sugar has dissolved.

Using a wire whisk or rotary beater, beat in the eggs, a little at a time. Cook the mixture, beating constantly, for 40 to 45 minutes, or until the curd thickens.

Remove the pan from the heat. Lift the bowl out of the pan. With a slotted spoon, remove and discard the orange rind.

Ladle the curd into clean, dry jam jars. Cover, label and store in a cool,

dry, dark place. Yield will be approximately 1.35kg (3lb).

Mincemeat

450g (1lb) sultanas
450g (1lb) currants
450g (1lb) raisins
675g (1½lb) hard cooking apples, peeled, cored and finely chopped

450g (1lb) minced or finely chopped beef suet
75g (3oz) chopped mixed peel
450g (1lb) soft, dark brown sugar
Grated rind and juice of 1 orange
Grated rind and juice of 2 lemons
1 tablespoon mixed spice
50g (2oz) blanched, shredded almonds
150ml (5fl oz) dry sherry
100ml (4fl oz) brandy

Place all the ingredients except the brandy in a large mixing bowl and stir well to mix. Cover with a clean cloth and set aside for 3 days. Stir the mixture several times each day. If at the end of this time the mixture looks too dry, before bottling add a little extra sherry or rum.

Spoon the mixture into jars to within 25mm (1in) of the top and pour a tablespoon of brandy on top of each jar. Cover and label. The yield will be about 3kg (7lb).

Allow to mature for at least 4 weeks before using in pies, tarts or crumbles.

Mincemeat is very easy to make and children especially enjoy helping in the preparation as a prelude to Christmas. You might be able to use your own dried fruit (page 183) and candied peel (page 105). Although mincemeat is usually made into pies or tarts, it can be used as the basis for a fruit crumble. Served with custard, cream or brandy butter (page 243), it is a wholesome and filling winter pudding to eat hot or cold.

Fruit butters & cheeses

The spicy taste of fruit butters and cheeses make a refreshing change from jams and jellies. Butters made from apples, cranberries and damsons are given in the recipes overleaf, but many other fruits could be used. The essential piece of equipment is a sieve; these preserves are based on pulped fruit and have a much thicker consistency than ordinary jams. The spices – cloves, cinnamon and mace – are among those used in the recipes. They are shown in their natural form, though it is advisable to use ground spices so that you can control the flavouring according to your personal taste.

Fruit butters and fruit cheeses are both old fashioned names for preserves made with fruit purée and sugar. They have been used as a form of preserve in Britain for several centuries, and are also particularly associated with the early American settlers. Fruit butters are nowadays a speciality of the Pennsylvania Dutch, but they are also popular all over the United States.

Fruit butters are so called because of their buttery consistency. They were originally made when there was a glut of wild fruits, and can still be used to use up windfall apples or other fruit. Less sugar is required for this sort of preserve so it was particularly economical at a time when sugar was an expensive and rare luxury. Spices were also added to help preserve the fruit. However it does not keep quite as long as fruit cheese.

Fruit cheeses are made from a stiff fruit purée. This is a good way of preserving fruit which has a lot of pips or stones. They use a larger proportion of sugar to purée than fruit butters.

To make fruit cheese, simmer the fruit in a little water until soft then press it through a nylon strainer. Measure the purée and place it in a preserving pan. Add sugar in the proportion of 450g (1lb) to 450g (1lb) of pulp. Simmer gently, stirring frequently, until the sugar is dissolved. Increase the heat slightly and, stirring occasionally, simmer the mixture for one to one and a half hours. Spoon the mixture into small wide-necked jars which have been greased with glycerine, and cover as for jam. Store in a cool, dry place for two to three months before using. Fruit butters are made in a similar way to fruit cheese, except they contain less sugar and have a softer consistency (see recipes overleaf).

Fruit cheese may be turned out in one piece and cut with a knife. Serve it as a condiment to cold meat or poultry or spread it on bread and butter. As an added bonus, it is delicious served as a cold dessert with cream.

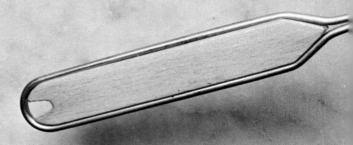

Recipes for fruit butters and cheeses

Three traditional recipes for using up surplus fruit like the tart wild crab apple or the rich old-fashioned damson.

Apple Butter

2.75kg (6lb) crab apples
1 litre (2 pints) water
1 litre (2 pints) dry cider
Sugar
1 teaspoon ground cinnamon
1 teaspoon ground cloves
½ teaspoon ground allspice
Finely grated rind ½ lemon

Wash the apples, remove any bruised parts and cut into pieces. Place the fruit in a preserving pan with the water and cider. Bring to the boil then simmer until the apples are very soft.

Push the fruit and cooking liquid through a sieve. Measure the pulp and allow 350g (¾lb) sugar to each 450g (1lb) of pulp. Return the pulp to the pan and simmer until it is thick. Add the sugar, cinnamon, cloves, allspice and lemon rind. Boil, stirring frequently, until no liquid remains.

Spoon into clean, dry, warm jars. Cover and label. Yield will be about 2.75kg (6lb).

Cranberry Cheese

2.75kg (6lb) cranberries
1 litre (1¾ pints) water
2.75kg (6lb) sugar
Juice and finely grated rind of 1 orange
1 tablespoon lemon juice
1 teaspoon ground cinnamon
½ teaspoon ground mace

Trim and wash the cranberries, and place them in a preserving pan or large saucepan. Pour over enough water almost to cover them. Bring to the boil, reduce the heat and simmer until the cranberries are very soft. Mash them occasionally with the back of a wooden spoon to release the juice.

Pour the mixture into a sieve placed over a large bowl, and press through using the back of a wooden spoon. Return the purée to a clean pan. If it is very liquid boil it for a few minutes to reduce slightly.

Add the sugar and cook gently until it has dissolved. Add the orange rind and juice, the lemon juice, and cinnamon. Bring to the boil, then simmer until the cheese is fairly stiff. Pour into small, clean, dry, warm jars, cover, seal and label. Yield will be about 2.75kg (6lb).

Note: Cranberry Cheese is delicious served with roast turkey or goose.

Damson Cheese

2.75kg (6lb) damsons
300ml (10fl oz) water
2 teaspoons ground allspice
Sugar

Wash the damsons and place them in a preserving pan with the water. Cover the pan and simmer gently until the fruit is tender. Sieve the fruit to form a purée then measure it. Allow 450g (1lb) sugar to each 450g (1lb) pulp. Return the pulp and the sugar to the pan and cook, stirring all the time until it is very thick.

Bottle, cover and label. Yield will be about 2.75kg (6lb).

Note: Other suitable fruits are blackcurrants, gooseberries and quinces.

Fruits for the recipes given here. Below: Cranberries; Right: Damsons; Far right: Crab apples.

Left: The Pennsylvania Dutch settlers imported the tradition of fruit butters and cheeses to America's East Coast. Every year in the Autumn a whole day would be given aside to making Apple Butter in huge vats usually placed in outdoor cookhouses, and large quantities of the apple mixture were made and carefully tended by the women of the settlements.

Candying & crystallizing

Although candied and crystallized fruits can be bought ready prepared, they are generally very expensive. It is well worth making your own, particularly when home-grown fruits are in season. They are easy and economical to prepare, although the actual processing takes several days. The fruit makes an attractive decoration for desserts or served on its own after dinner with coffee, and can also be packed in pretty boxes or jars to become most acceptable gifts.

The basic process of candying fruit consists of covering it with a light, hot sugar syrup and continuing from day to day with increased amounts of sugar until the water in the fruit is diffused slowly and the fruit is impregnated with sugar. Candied fruit is often finished by crystallizing, which gives it a sugary appearance or glazed in a syrup solution, which gives it a glacé finish.

Fruit for candying

Firm fruits such as apricots, cherries, grapes, peaches, pineapples and plums give better results than the soft fruits – raspberries, strawberries and blackberries – as these break up during the processing and turn mushy. Canned fruits may be used for candying but satisfactory results are not always obtained, owing to the different quality of the fruit and the density of the syrup.

Angelica, orange, lemon and grapefruit peel may also be candied and are ideal for use as decoration or as ingredients in cakes, buns and breads. Flower petals and mint leaves can also be crystallized but they require a different method which is dealt with at the end of this section.

Preparing fruit for candying

Fruit used for candying should be fresh and firm. Small fruits such as cherries should be stoned, and fruit that is candied whole, such as crab apples or apricots, need to be pricked with a silver fork so that the syrup can soak into the fruit. Larger fruits should be peeled, halved and, if necessary, quartered. It is better to candy each type of fruit separately, otherwise the individual flavour of the fruit will be lost.

After preparing the fruit weigh it and place it in a large saucepan. Cover with hot water, bring to the boil then simmer the fruit until it is just soft but not overcooked. Drain the fruit into a heatproof bowl. Make sure the bowl is large enough to keep the fruit covered when topped up with the syrup, and reserve the cooking liquid.

Making the syrup

For every 450g (1lb) of fruit, make a syrup with the reserved cooking liquid, making it up to 300ml ($\frac{1}{2}$ pint) with water if neces-

Above: Candied fruits are often used as decoration for cakes or pastries. Opposite: Fresh flowers make an attractive decoration for springtime cakes, but for year-round colour it is worth crystallizing your own. Small blooms such as violets, mimosa and primroses are particularly suitable.

sary. Add 175g (6oz) sugar, or 50g (2oz) sugar and 125g (4oz) of glucose – the latter formula is preferable particularly when candying citrus peel, as it gives a clearer appearance. Bring the sugar and water slowly to the boil and cook until a thin syrup forms. If by any chance there is not enough syrup to cover all the fruit make up another batch – it can always be re-heated for future use.

Candying the fruit
Candying is a lengthy business; note that this method may take up to two weeks or even longer for large pieces of fruit.

1. Pour the hot syrup over the fruit, making sure it is well covered, and set aside for 24 hours.

2. The next day, drain off the syrup into a saucepan and add 50g (2oz) of sugar. Bring to the boil and pour the syrup over the fruit. Repeat this process for two more days, making sure you add the 50g of sugar to the syrup *each* time.

3. On the *fifth* day of processing drain off the syrup again into a saucepan and add 75g (3oz) sugar to the syrup. Add the fruit and boil for three minutes. Return fruit and syrup to the bowl and set aside for 48 hours.

4. Repeat process number 3, leaving the fruit to soak in the syrup for four more days. At the end of this time the syrup should be thick and have a consistency like honey. If for some reason it is not very thick then repeat number 3 again.

Drying the fruit

Lift the fruit out of the syrup with a slotted spoon. Spread it out on a cake rack placed over a baking sheet. Dry the fruit out in a warm place (an airing-cupboard if space is available) at a temperature not higher than 50°C (120°F). If the heat is continuous the fruit will dry in a few hours. On the other hand it could be left in the oven, using residual heat from previous cooking, and will take two to three days, (assuming the oven is used during this time). Remove the fruit from the oven when it is actually in use. As with ordinary drying, you could also use the top of a central heating boiler for this purpose

Candied fruits piled up on a pretty dish or cake stand make a very attractive centrepiece for the tea or dinner table. Choose firm fruits like apples, pears, apricots, grapes and cherries. Large, firm strawberries can be used if they are not hulled, thus lessening the chance of disintegration during the processing. However, smaller soft fruits such as raspberries, loganberries, blackberries or currants are not recommended for candying.

(see page 179).

Turn the fruit occasionally so that it dries on all sides. When it is dry and not sticky the fruit is ready for use.

Crystallizing candied fruit
Dip the dried candied fruit in boiling water, drain well and roll each piece of fruit in granulated sugar.

Glacé fruit
This method gives the fruit a shiny finish and is particularly suitable for chestnuts, the basis of *Marrons Glacés*, a classic French sweetmeat (see page 106), and for whole candied cherries.

Prepare a thick syrup by dissolving 450g (1lb) sugar in 150ml ($\frac{1}{4}$ pint) water and bring it to the boil. Pour a little into a small bowl. (Cover the remaining syrup to keep it hot and prevent it from evaporating.) Dip the candied fruit in boiling water for about 15 to 20 seconds and drain it well. Using a fine skewer, dip each piece of fruit one by one into the syrup. Remove at once and place on a baking sheet. If the syrup begins to go cloudy before all the fruit has been glazed, replace it with the remaining hot syrup. Place the baking sheet in a warm, dry place with a temperature not higher than 50°C (120°F). and turn it occasionally When the fruit is shiny but not sticky it is ready.

Packing the fruit
Candied, crystallized or glacé fruits should be packed in wooden or cardboard boxes lined with waxed paper. The layers of fruit should also be interleaved with waxed paper to prevent them sticking together. Cover the boxes with a lid or waxed paper secured with string. The fruit may also be packed into glass jars but must not have an airtight cover otherwise the fruit will go mouldy.

Candied angelica
Angelica is a showy herb, which grows wild in the mountains and northern parts of Europe, but it is usually cultivated in the garden. Ideally the stalks should be picked in spring when they are young and tender and their colour is at its best.

Remove and discard the root ends and leaves and place the stalks into a saucepan. Pour over a brine, made from 4 teaspoons salt to 1 litre ($1\frac{3}{4}$ pints) of water, and bring to the boil. Boil the stalks for about ten minutes until they have softened slightly. Drain them and rinse well under cold running water. With a sharp knife scrape off the outside fibrous layer and cut the stalks into lengths of about 10cm (4 inches).

To process one pound of angelica, make a syrup with 450g (1lb) sugar – or half sugar and half glucose – and 600ml (1 pint) water. When the sugar has dissolved bring it to the boil and boil for ten minutes. You could add a few drops of green food colouring to the syrup to give the angelica a really bright green colour. Add the angelica to the syrup and boil for 20 minutes.

Remove the angelica from the syrup, using a slotted spoon, and place it on a wire rack. Cover the syrup and set aside. Leave the angelica to dry in a warm place for three days. At the end of this time, bring the syrup to the boil, add the angelica and boil for 20 minutes or until the angelica has absorbed most of the syrup.

Angelica is a member of the parsley family. Its crisp, firm stem is ideal for the crystallizing process, as it does not lose its shape.

Remove the angelica and place on a clean, dry, wire rack. Dry it in a very cool oven – 110°C (225°F, Gas Mark $\frac{1}{4}$) – or in a warm, dry, place like an airing cupboard. When it is dry sprinkle it with sugar and store in an air-tight jar in a cool, dark place.

Candied peel

Choose bright coloured and firm citrus fruits (oranges, lemons, limes or grapefruit) and wash them thoroughly. Divide each fruit into quarters, remove the peel and discard most of the white pith. Weigh the peel and make a note of the amount.

Place the peel in a large saucepan and cover with cold water. Bring to the boil and then reduce the heat and simmer until the peel is tender. If using grapefruit change the water two or three times as this will improve the flavour. Drain the peel into a heat-proof mixing bowl and reserve the cooking liquid.

For every 450g (1lb) of peel make a syrup with 300ml ($\frac{1}{2}$ pint) of the cooking liquid and 225g (8oz) of sugar, or for a better appearance use half sugar and half glucose. Bring to the boil and cook until a thin syrup forms or until the temperature reaches 104°C (220°F) on a sugar thermometer. Pour the syrup over the peel and set aside for 24 hours. Strain the syrup into a saucepan and add 100g (4oz) sugar. Bring the syrup to the boil and cook for one minute. Pour the syrup over the peel and set aside for another 24 hours.

Next day place the syrup and peel into a saucepan, bring to the boil then simmer for 30 minutes or until the peel is almost transparent. Allow the peel to cool in the syrup. You can either dry it at once, or, if you prefer, the peel may be left in the syrup for two to three weeks before drying without any ill effects.

Old-fashioned roly-poly pudding is one of the many recipes which make use of candied orange or lemon peel. Many cakes, fruit breads, pastries and puddings call for a few grams, usually chopped, especially to complement dried fruits such as sultanas and raisins. Spiced Apple Cake (page 197), Christmas Cake (page 236) and Mincemeat (page 94) all include candied peel in their ingredients.

Remove the peel from the syrup with a slotted spoon and place it on a wire rack over a baking tray. Cover the peel with a clean, dry cloth or greaseproof paper and dry it out in a warm place or in a very cool oven – 120°C (250°F, Gas Mark ½).

When the peel is dry, give it a glacé finish (see page 104). Store it in screw-top jars with a piece of waxed paper between each layer to prevent the pieces from sticking to each other.

Marrons Glacés

These glazed chestnuts are not the same as the commercially prepared ones that come from France, which are not possible to produce under home conditions, but they are delicious to eat and well worth while making when chestnuts are in season. Sometimes it is difficult to keep the chestnuts whole during processing but if some disintegrate the pieces can be formed into balls or kept separately to sprinkle over ice-cream or other cold desserts. (This method is for 1kg (2lb 2oz) of whole chestnuts.)

To remove the shells from the chestnuts, make a slit in the hard skin at the pointed end of each nut with a sharp knife. Place them in a saucepan and cover with cold water. Bring to the boil and cook for two minutes. Remove the nuts a few at a time with a slotted spoon and peel off the outer shell and inner skin. When they are all shelled and skinned, place them in a large saucepan and cover with cold water. Bring the water slowly to simmering point and cook until the chestnuts are tender.

Meanwhile make a syrup with 450g (1lb) sugar, 450g (1lb) glucose and a generous 300ml (just over ½ pint) water in a saucepan large enough to contain the chestnuts as well. Bring the syrup to the boil, add the drained chestnuts and bring back to the boil. Remove the pan from the heat, cover and leave overnight in a warm place.

Remove the cover and bring the syrup and chestnuts to the boil and leave again overnight. The next day add about eight drops of vanilla essence and bring to the boil. Allow the syrup to cool slightly then lift the chestnuts out of the syrup and drain on a wire rack. To give them a glacé finish, follow the method on page 104.

Surplus syrup

If there is any syrup left over after any of the above processes it can be kept and used to sweeten fruit salads or stewed fruit. If it is to be kept for any length of time the syrup should be poured into heat-proof bottles and sterilized (see page 51) at a temperature of 88°C (190°F) for 15 minutes.

Crystallized flowers

Crystallized flower petals are fun to make at home and look far more attractive than the commercial ones. They make pretty decorations for cakes and cold desserts like trifles and mousse.

Use any flower *except* those grown from bulbs, as they will be poisonous. The most attractive and suitable ones are violets, primroses, roses, flowering cherry or apple blossom. Select whole flowers or petals which are fresh and undamaged and pick them on a dry day when there is no rain or dew on them.

There are two methods of crystallizing flowers – one uses gum arabic and rose water (these are available from most chemists), and the other uses syrup. Both methods are excellent but the first one

Below: Fresh sweet or Spanish chestnuts can be collected in many gardens, parks and woods where the tall chestnut trees grow, their single large pointed leaves distinguishing them from the five leafed 'hand' of the horse chestnut. Chestnuts are encased in a very distinctive spiny outer covering, and the nuts themselves need to have the hard brown skin removed by blanching in boiling water.
Right: Once processed, your own Marrons Glacé can be packed in individual sweet cases or wrapped in foil inside pretty boxes to give as presents. Most candied fruits make very acceptable gifts; interleave them with greaseproof paper so that they can be removed easily from their containers.

Crystallized flowers can be used to decorate many different types of cake. Here little buns encased in glacé icing are given a finishing touch with a single crystallized violet.

takes a longer time and is slightly more complicated.

Method 1 Place 15g (½oz) gum arabic in a screw-top jar with 2 table-spoons of rose water. Screw the top on and shake for two to three minutes. Set the jar aside for between one and three hours shaking occasionally until the gum arabic is completely dissolved.

Pour the mixture into a small bowl, and then line a baking sheet with grease-proof or waxed paper.

Cut the stalks from the flowers; if you are using small bunches leave 5mm (¼in) of stalk near the flower or remove the petals from the heads.

Using a small, soft, fine paint brush, brush the flower petals on both sides with the gum arabic mixture. Dip the flowers into castor sugar and place them on the baking sheet. (Use only small amounts of sugar at a time and replace it as soon as it becomes damp).

Leave the flowers in a warm place for 24 hours or longer until they are dry and hard. Store them in a glass jar with a tight-fitting lid.

Method 2 Make a syrup with 450g (1lb) sugar and 225ml (6fl oz) water and boil it for five minutes. Drop the flower heads or petals into the syrup and boil for one minute. Using a slotted spoon remove the flowers from the syrup and place them on a baking sheet, lined with greaseproof or waxed paper. If necessary separate the flower heads or petals to arrange them in their original shapes. (A pair of clean tweezers is useful for this.) Leave the flowers in a warm dry place for 24 hours or longer until they are dry and hard, and store them in a glass jar with a tight-fitting lid.

Many fruits and flowers can be crystallized and though it is a lengthy process, it is very rewarding. Above: Flowering cherry blossom crystallizes well, as does apple blossom. Left: Candied fruits look so attractive it is a good idea to store them in glass jars, but take care these are not airtight as the fruit will go mouldy.

Chutneys

Chutney is a condiment made with a mixture of fruits and/or vegetables which are preserved by the addition of vinegar, salt and spices. Although they are now a popular and accepted preserve all over the world they actually originated in India – the name being derived from the Hindu word *chatni*.

One of the great advantages of making chutney is that many types can be made at any time of the year without being confined to seasonal produce. For example, many chutneys are made with dried fruits, others use fresh fruits and vegetables that are available in greengrocers and markets throughout the year. Then there are those which are made with fruits and vegetables at the height of their season. This is the time for those with kitchen gardens to use up surplus produce and, as chutneys are so easy to make, it is certainly worthwhile. Unlike many other ways of preserving fruit and vegetables – many of which require perfect, unblemished produce – chutney can be made with misshapen or bruised ingredients (but with the bruised or damaged parts removed and discarded) which also makes it an economical method of preserving.

The scope of chutney is endless and the combinations and permutations can be varied according to personal taste and the ingredients available – they can be sweet, sour, hot or mild but if you are experimenting with different mixtures then it is better to make a small quantity just to be sure it is what you like!

The success of a good chutney is that it should be relatively smooth in texture and have a rich mellow flavour. To achieve this it requires long, slow cooking and then, ideally, it should be left to mature for at least three months.

Chutneys are very versatile: almost any combination of fruit or vegetable can be made into this delicious condiment. Long slow cooking, plenty of vinegar, sugar and spices, are all that is needed for one of the easiest ways of preserving fruit and vegetables.

Equipment

Pans should be large enough to contain all the ingredients and if you are a keen jam-maker as well it is well worth investing in a special preserving pan. Brass, copper or iron pans should *not* be used as they react with the vinegar and give a metallic flavour to the chutney.

A long-handled wooden spoon is required which should be reserved for chutney-making only. The wood becomes impregnated with the spiciness of the chutney and will taint other recipes.

Heat-proof jars of any type can be used to contain the chutney. These should be clean, dry and warm before pouring in the chutney.

A large ladle or heat-proof jug is useful, especially when making a large quantity of chutney, to make it easier to fill the jars.

The covers are most important. Paper or jam covers should not be used as these allow the vinegar to evaporate and after a month or so the chutney will shrink and become very dry. Special vinegar-proof paper is available, usually in rolls, and this is secured to the jars by tying with a piece of string. Special preserving or bottling jars are suitable, either with screw-on or clip-on lids. Jars with tight-fitting corks may also be used, providing the corks are new. They should be boiled before using, then covered with a piece of grease-proof paper and tied into the tops of the jars with string. Make sure that any metal cover is well lacquered and not scratched. To be on the safe side it is advisable to place a disc of vinegar-proof paper on top of the chutney before screwing on metal lids.

All chutneys should be labelled with the name and date then stored in a cool, dry, dark place. Providing they have been correctly covered and stored most chutneys will keep for one to two years.

Vinegar, sugar and spices

Vinegar is one of the most important ingredients in successful chutney-making, so it should be of good quality and have an acetic acid content of at least five per cent. Bottled vinegar is better than that sold from barrels. Any well-known brand of malt vinegar is suitable, or use wine vinegar for a special flavour.

As vinegar has a slightly hardening effect on some produce, particularly onions, carrots and other firm vegetables, it is advisable to cook them in water for a few minutes, then drain them, before adding to the other ingredients.

Sugar used may be granulated or brown; the latter is often used in dark-coloured chutneys. Prolonged cooking of any sugar has a darkening effect on chutney which is usually desirable. If a lighter colour is preferred then the sugar should only be added when the fruit and/or vegetables are already soft and mushy.

Ground spices are preferable to whole ones in chutney making as they give a better flavour. If whole spices are used, double the amount given in the recipe, bruise them and tie them in a muslin bag before adding to the pan. The bag is then removed before the chutney is poured into the jars.

Equipment for making chutneys and pickles is very straightforward: a large pan, jars, measuring jug, and a wooden spoon which should be used only for this purpose. Any type of jar can be used but it is important to use a vinegar-proof covering otherwise the vinegar may evaporate and the chutney dry up and shrink.

Vinegar is an essential
ingredient of chutney.
Specially flavoured vinegar
can be made by infusing fresh
herbs in the bottle for a week
or two before use. Right:
Thyme vinegar. Below:
Tarragon vinegar. Other
herbs to use could be marjoram
or rosemary.

113

Above: Home-grown tomatoes are most economical for chutney making.

Recipes for chutney

Time-honoured accompaniments to cold meats, curries and savoury cheese dishes, chutneys are easy to make and almost infinitely variable. Here are some well-known recipes plus some which may be less familiar, using all sorts of fruits, vegetables and spices.

Red Tomato Chutney

1.75kg (4lb) ripe tomatoes, peeled and chopped
450g (1lb) dessert apples, peeled, cored and chopped
450g (1lb) onions, peeled and very finely chopped
350g (12oz) sultanas
350g (12oz) raisins
1 teaspoon dry mustard
2 teaspoons ground allspice
1 tablespoon salt
1 teaspoon cayenne pepper
675g (1½lb) soft brown sugar
900ml (1½ pints) vinegar

Place all the ingredients into a preserving pan and bring to the boil. Reduce the heat and simmer, stirring frequently, until the chutney is thick.

Bottle, seal and label. The yield is approximately 3.4kg (7½lb).

Green Tomato Chutney

450g (1lb) onions, peeled and chopped
2.25kg (5lb) green tomatoes, peeled and sliced
2 teaspoons salt
50g (2oz) mixed pickling spice, tied in a piece of muslin
600ml (1 pint) vinegar
450g (1lb) sugar

Boil the onions in a little water until they are soft. Drain and place in a preserving pan with the tomatoes, salt and pickling spice. Bring the mixture to the boil, then reduce the heat and simmer for 1 hour. Add a little of the vinegar when the mixture thickens.

Stir in the remaining vinegar and the sugar, and cook, stirring frequently, until the chutney is thick. Remove and discard the bag of pickling spice.

Bottle, seal and label. The yield is approximately 2.25kg (5lb).

Left: Green Tomato Chutney is an interesting variation, which could make use of late tomatoes which are often slow to ripen fully. Although a spice bag is recommended for this particular recipe, you can use ground spices – in this case mustard, allspice and cayenne. As a further variation, try Green Tomato and Cucumber Relish (recipe on page 120).

115

Apple Chutney is a great favourite of those who make chutney regularly. The recipe for Apple and Raisin Chutney is an interesting variation.

Apple and Raisin Chutney

1.75kg (4lb) cooking apples, peeled cored and chopped
4 medium-sized onions, peeled and finely chopped
2 cloves of garlic, crushed
Juice of 1 lemon
1 tablespoon mustard seeds
900ml (1½ pints) vinegar
450g (1lb) raisins
1 tablespoon ground ginger
2 teaspoons salt
1kg (2lb 2oz) soft brown sugar

Place the apples, onions, garlic, lemon juice, mustard seeds and 600ml (1 pint) of the vinegar in a preserving pan. Bring to the boil then reduce the heat and simmer for 1 hour until the mixture is soft. Add the raisins, ground ginger, salt, sugar and remaining vinegar and simmer, stirring frequently, until the chutney is thick.

Bottle, seal and label. The yield is approximately 3.20kg (7lb).

Mango Chutney

1.35kg (3lb) green mangoes, peeled, halved and stoned
75g (3oz) salt
2 litres (3½ pints) water
450g (1lb) sugar
600ml (1 pint) vinegar
75g (3oz) fresh root ginger, peeled and finely chopped
6 cloves of garlic, crushed
2 teaspoons hot chilli powder
1 50mm (2in) piece cinnamon stick
125g (4oz) raisins
125g (4oz) dried dates, chopped

Cut the mangoes into small pieces and place in a mixing bowl, sprinkle the salt over the top and pour in the water. Cover and set aside for 24 hours.

Drain the mango pieces and set aside. Place the sugar and vinegar in a preserving pan and bring to the boil. When the sugar is dissolved add the remaining ingredients and bring the mixture back to the boil, stirring occasionally.

Reduce the heat and simmer the chutney, stirring frequently, until it is thick; then discard the cinnamon stick.

Bottle, seal and label. The yield will be about 1.75kg (4lb).

Lemon and Mustard Seed Chutney

3 lemons, washed, chopped and seeds removed
1 tablespoon salt
3 small onions, diced
300ml (10fl oz) cider vinegar
1 teaspoon ground mixed spice or allspice
2 tablespoons mustard seed
225g (8oz) sugar
50g (2oz) raisins

Norfolk Fruit Chutney is a succulent, spicy chutney which is delicious in Cheddar cheese and tomato sandwiches, or with cold roast turkey or other cold meats.

Place the chopped lemons in a bowl and sprinkle with the salt. Cover the bowl with a clean cloth or kitchen paper towels and set aside for about 10 hours.

In a large saucepan, combine the salted lemons with the onions, vinegar, mixed spice or allspice, mustard seed, sugar and raisins.

Place the pan over high heat and bring to the boil. Reduce the heat to low, cover and simmer for 50 minutes, or until the lemons are soft.

Remove the pan from the heat. Ladle the chutney into clean, warm jam jars. Seal and label the jars and store them in a cool, dry place until ready to use. It is particularly good with grilled fish, or kebabs. Yield is about 1kg (2lb).

Norfolk Fruit Chutney

1kg (2lb 2oz) apricots, halved, stoned and chopped
1kg (2lb 2oz) tart cooking apples, peeled, cored and chopped
4 medium-sized peaches, peeled, halved, stoned and chopped
2 medium-sized onions, finely chopped
225g (8oz) raisins
50mm (2in) piece fresh root ginger, peeled and finely chopped
$\frac{3}{4}$ teaspoon grated nutmeg
$\frac{3}{4}$ teaspoon ground allspice
$\frac{3}{4}$ teaspoon dry mustard
Finely grated rind of 1 large lemon
Juice and finely grated rind of 2 oranges
750ml ($1\frac{1}{4}$ pints) white wine vinegar
450g (1lb) sugar
450g (1lb) soft brown sugar

In a very large saucepan, or preserving pan, combine the apricots, apples, peaches, onions, raisins, ginger, nutmeg, allspice, mustard, lemon rind, orange juice and rind and 600ml (1 pint) of the vinegar.

Place the pan over moderately high heat and bring the mixture to the boil,

117

stirring constantly. Reduce the heat to low and simmer, stirring occasionally, for 1 to 1½ hours or until the fruit mixture is very soft and pulpy.

Stir in the sugars and the remaining vinegar and simmer, stirring occasionally, for 40 to 50 minutes, or until the chutney is very thick.

Remove the pan from the heat. Ladle the chutney into clean, warm dry jars. Seal, label and store in a cool, dry, dark place for 6 weeks before serving. Yield is about 3.35kg (8lb).

Gooseberry Chutney

225g (8oz) onions, peeled and chopped
1.75kg (4lb) gooseberries, trimmed and washed
350g (12oz) raisins
675g (1½lb) sugar
1 tablespoon salt
2 teaspoons ground ginger
1 teaspoon cayenne pepper
600ml (1 pint) vinegar

Boil the onions in a little water until they are soft then drain off the water. Place the onions with the other ingredients into a preserving pan. Bring to the boil then reduce the heat and simmer, stirring frequently, until the chutney is thick.

Bottle, seal and label. The yield will be about 2.25kg (5lb).

Oriental Relish

3 lemons
2.25kg (5lb) canned, peeled tomatoes
10 medium-sized apples, peeled, cored and coarsely chopped
4 × 50mm (2in) pieces fresh root ginger, peeled and finely chopped
2 tablespoons mixed spice or ground allspice
1kg (2lb) sugar
450g (1lb) soft brown sugar

Cut the lemons into quarters and remove any pips. Place the lemon quarters in a blender and blend for 30 seconds. Alternatively, grate the lemon rind and chop the remaining pith and flesh very finely.

Place the blended lemons and tomatoes with the can juice, apples, ginger and mixed spice or allspice in a

Oriental Relish is a fairly sharp chutney which, like Mango Chutney (previous page), goes well with curry. If a hotter relish is preferred add about three-quarters of a teaspoon of chilli powder or two whole chillis, finely chopped.

very large saucepan. Set the pan over high heat and bring the mixture to the boil, stirring constantly. Boil for 3 minutes. Reduce the heat to low and stir in both sugars. Simmer the mixture, stirring occasionally, for 2 to 2½ hours or until it is thick.

Remove the pan from the heat. Ladle the relish into clean, warmed jars. Cover and store in a cool dry place until ready to use. Yield will be about 2.75kg (6lbs).

Note: As this recipe does not include vinegar it may not keep quite as long as other chutneys or relishes.

Mixed Fruit Chutney

450g (1lb) onions, peeled and chopped
1.35kg (3lb) mixed fruits – apples, pears, plums, tomatoes etc
100g (4oz) dried dates, chopped
2 cloves of garlic, crushed
1 teaspoon salt
1 teaspoon mixed spice
1 teaspoon dried mustard
450g (1lb) soft brown sugar
600ml (1 pint) vinegar

Boil the onions in a little water until they are soft then drain off the water.

Wash, peel and core the fruits and chop into pieces.

Place all the ingredients into a preserving pan, bring to the boil then reduce the heat and simmer, stirring

The recipe for Mixed Fruit Chutney allows you to use any produce, fresh or dried, that you have available, so you can experiment with different tastes. Bananas make a welcome addition to any fruit chutney, their soft consistency and slightly sweet taste blending well with the vinegar and sugar and with other fruit.

frequently until the chutney is thick.

Bottle, seal and label. Yield is about 1.35kg (3lb).

Old Fashioned Date Chutney

450g (1lb) canned peeled tomatoes
225g (8oz) stoned dates
125g (4oz) raisins
125g (4oz) currants
125ml (4fl oz) vinegar
1 teaspoon salt

$\frac{1}{2}$ to 1 teaspoon cayenne pepper

Combine all the ingredients in a large saucepan. Place the pan over moderate heat and bring the mixture to the boil, stirring frequently.

Reduce the heat to low and simmer the chutney, stirring occasionally, for 1 to 1$\frac{1}{2}$ hours or until it is thick. Taste the chutney and add more seasoning if necessary.

Remove the pan from the heat. Spoon the chutney into jars. Cover, seal and label. This chutney will not keep for more than a month. Yield is about 1kg (2lb).

Rhubarb Chutney

2.75kg (6lb) rhubarb, sliced
450g (1lb) onions, peeled and finely chopped
1 clove of garlic, crushed
2 tablespoons mixed spice
1 tablespoon salt
1 litre (1¾ pints) vinegar
1kg (2lb 2oz) sugar

Place the rhubarb, onions, garlic, spice, salt and half the vinegar into a preserving pan. Bring to the boil then reduce the heat and simmer until the rhubarb is very soft. Add sugar and remaining vinegar, simmer, stirring frequently, until the chutney is thick.

Bottle, seal and label. The approximate yield is 2.75kg (6lb).

Cucumber and Green Tomato Relish

1kg (2lb 2oz) green tomatoes, peeled
1kg (2lb 2oz) pickled cucumbers
1 large onion
1 large green pepper
2 tablespoons salt
½ teaspoon ground allspice
1 tablespoon pickling spice
1 teaspoon dry mustard

Surplus kitchen garden produce can be used for many chutneys and relishes. Rhubarb grows prolifically on the 'cut and come again' principle. Right: A well-established pear tree usually yields enough fruit for many types of preserve.

150g (5oz) soft brown sugar
375ml (15fl oz) cider vinegar

Chop all the vegetables very finely. Put in layers in a large saucepan, sprinkling each layer with salt. Leave to stand overnight.

Drain off the excess moisture. Add the spice, mustard, vinegar and sugar. Boil the mixture uncovered for about half an hour, stirring frequently, until it is fairly stiff but still moist. Pack the relish into sterilized jars, filling right to the top. Cover, seal and label. Yield will be about 1.35kg (3lb).

ready. Yield is about 1.75kg (3lb).

Pear Chutney

1.35kg (3lb) pears, peeled, cored and chopped
2 tart apples, peeled, cored and chopped
2 medium-sized onions, sliced
450g (1lb) raisins
1 teaspoon hot chilli powder
50mm (2in) piece fresh root ginger, peeled and finely chopped
1 garlic clove, crushed
1 teaspoon salt
½ teaspoon grated nutmeg
12 cloves
Juice and grated rind of 2 oranges
450g (1lb) soft brown sugar
600ml (1 pint) white vinegar

Place all the ingredients in a very large saucepan and stir well with a wooden spoon. Set the pan over high heat and bring the mixture to the boil, stirring occasionally.

Reduce the heat to low and, stirring occasionally, simmer the chutney for 3 hours or until it is thick. Remove the pan from the heat. Ladle the chutney into clean, warmed jam jars. Cover, label and store in a cool, dry place until

Corn Relish

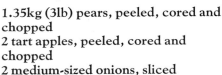

1 litre (1¾ pints) cider vinegar
225g (8oz) sugar
1 teaspoon salt
½ teaspoon ground cloves
1½ tablespoons dry mustard
1 teaspoon turmeric
450g (1lb) white cabbage
2 medium-sized onions
2 red peppers
2 green peppers
1kg (2lb 2oz) corn kernels
2 tablespoons flour

Place the vinegar, sugar, salt, ground cloves, mustard and turmeric in a large saucepan and bring to the boil. Finely chop the cabbage, onions and peppers. Add them with the corn to the vinegar mixture. Bring to the boil and stir in the flour. Then simmer for 45 minutes stirring frequently, until the mixture is fairly stiff but still moist. Pour into sterile jars, cover, seal and label. Yield will be about 2kg (4lb).

Left: Green tomatoes and cucumbers combine to make a sharp green relish that goes very well with real American hamburgers. Below: Peppers are an essential ingredient of Corn Relish, another American favourite. Overleaf: Chutneys, pickles and relishes are ideal for cold buffet lunches. They can be served simply as condiments as in the case of Red Tomato Chutney, Oriental Relish, Mango Chutney or Pickled Oranges, or as part of the meal, such as Spiced Eggs, Pickled Cucumbers, Corn Relish (which is delicious with salad) and many of the other whole pickled vegetables.

Oriental Relish

Pickles

Pickles and chutneys are often thought of as similar. However, while both are preserved with vinegar and spices, there the similarity ends. Pickles require a different processing method – they do not need to be cooked for such a length of time – the exception being fruit pickles, when the fruit is heated gently to allow the vinegar and spices to penetrate. Chutneys are generally made with a mixture of ingredients but most pickles are made from individual fruits or vegetables.

Vegetables used for pickling are first soaked in brine (salt and water solution), or dry salt, for up to two days. This preliminary process removes excess moisture in the vegetables, helping them to remain crisp and preventing the development of bacteria. Brine is

used for most vegetables but dry salt is better for those with a high water content such as courgettes, marrows and cucumbers.

After salting the vegetables must be rinsed in clean, cold water and well drained before being packed into jars and bottles and covered with spiced vinegar.

Equipment
Pickling uses the same types of pans, jars, bottles and covers as Chutneys. (See page 111). A large bowl or bucket (not metal) is needed as well for the preliminary soaking of vegetables.

Types of pickle
Pickles may be made from a wide variety of fruit and vegetables. As with all methods of food preservation, the produce must be of good quality, fresh, firm and clean. Large vegetables – cauliflowers, cucumbers, cabbage and marrows – are best if they are separated or cut into pieces. Small vegetables such as onions (the small pickling variety), mushrooms and tomatoes can be left whole and only require to be peeled, halved or quartered and the pips removed. Fruits that are usually pickled whole, such as damsons, plums and cherries, should be pricked before the preliminary cooking otherwise they will shrivel and dry up. Generally fruits that are most suitable for

Pickling in vinegar is one of the simplest, and therefore one of the most popular, methods of preserving, especially for vegetables. However, though pickling is particularly suited to vegetables as it keeps them crisp, it is not confined to them: fruit, nuts and even eggs can all be pickled successfully. A selection of whole pickles are shown here: methods for all are given from page 130 . Left to right: Apple Pickle, Pickled Onions, Pickled Beetroots, and Pickled Cucumbers (or gherkins).

125

pickling are larger ones like apples, pears and peaches – berry fruits go mushy and are not pleasant to eat.

As well as fruit and vegetables, boiled eggs may be pickled, and also some nuts, particularly walnuts.

Salt, vinegar and spices

Salt. Block, coarse or sea salt gives better results than refined table salt; the latter may give a cloudy effect to the finished product. If brine is used to soak the vegetables an average solution is 450g (1lb) salt to 4l (1 gallon) of water. The salt must be dissolved in boiling water, left to cool and then strained before using. It is essential that the vegetables are completely covered with the brine. A large plate with a small weight placed on top of them will ensure that the vegetables do not rise and float above the liquid. If dry salt is used the vegetables should be placed in layers with a generous sprinkling

of salt over each layer. Use about 1 tablespoon of salt to each 450g (1lb) of vegetables.

Vinegar must be good quality, and have an acetic acid content of at least five per cent. Brown malt vinegar is suitable for all pickles but if a light colour is required, particularly for light-coloured fruit and vegetables, then white malt, wine or cider vinegar may be used.

Spices are added to vinegar to give it a good flavour and they also help as a preservative. Whole spices should be used for spiced vinegar as ground ones will make the vinegar cloudy. The spices used may be varied depending on the type of pickle and personal taste.

In the following recipes there are some variations; however where only spiced vinegar is mentioned this basic recipe may be used: 50mm (2in) piece cinnamon; 1 teaspoon cloves; 2 teaspoons allspice; 1 teaspoon black peppercorns; 1 teaspoon mustard seed; 2-3 bay leaves; 1 litre (2 pints) vinegar. Place the spices and vinegar in

You can vary the flavour of the vinegar depending on the type of produce. For instance, a mild, sweet vinegar would be best for Peach Pickle (page 134), whereas a dark vinegar flavoured with mustard seed and chillis would be suitable for Marrow Pickle (page 138).

Above: Black peppercorns are used whole for spicing vinegar. Right: For a different flavour, use a herb vinegar such as marjoram vinegar as the basis of spiced pickling vinegar.

a saucepan, cover and bring just to the boil (do not allow the liquid to bubble). Remove the pan from the heat and set aside for two and a half to three hours. Strain the vinegar and if it is not going to be used immediately pour it into clean, dry bottles.

Spiced vinegar is used either hot or cold. Usually cold vinegar is best for the vegetables that should be kept crisp – onions, cauliflower and cabbage – while hot vinegar gives a better result to the softer fruit pickles.

Although it takes a considerably longer time, an alternative method of making spiced vinegar is to steep the spices in the unheated vinegar, in a bottle, for two to three months. The bottle should be shaken occasionally. The advantage of this method is that the full flavour of the spices really penetrates the vinegar.

Mixed pickling spice can be bought ready prepared and gives a fairly good result but preparing your own means a wider variety of flavours to the many different types of pickle.

Above: Bay leaves are always included in the pickling spices needed for spiced vinegar. If you are able to infuse the spices in cold vinegar over a period of time, use whole fresh leaves. Otherwise crush dried bay leaves and mix with the other spices. Other herbs and spices can be used, such as chervil (far left) and allspice (left).

Recipes for pickles

Eighteen pickles, sharp and crunchy, to use on their own as vegetables in winter salads, or as accompaniments to savoury dishes, or – like gherkins or pickled walnuts – to serve on their own with drinks.

Mixed Pickle

675g (1½lb) onions, peeled and chopped
1 medium-sized cauliflower, trimmed and separated into flowerets
1 cucumber, cut into cubes
450g (1lb) French beans, trimmed and sliced
Fresh red or green chillis
1 litre (1¾ pints) spiced vinegar

Place the vegetables in a large mixing bowl and cover with brine. Soak for 24 hours. Drain and lightly pack into jars, adding a chilli to each one.

Fill each jar with cold spiced vinegar, making sure there is enough vinegar to surround each piece of vegetable.

Cover, seal and label. Yield will be about 1.35kg (3lb).

Piccalilli

2.75kg (6lb) prepared vegetables – cucumber, cauliflower, pickling onions, tomatoes etc
450g (1lb) coarse salt
1 litre (1¾ pints) vinegar
1 tablespoon turmeric
1 tablespoon dry mustard
1 tablespoon ground ginger
2 cloves of garlic, crushed
175g (6oz) sugar
3 tablespoons cornflour

Spread the vegetables on a large dish and sprinkle with the salt. Set aside for 24 hours. Drain and rinse in cold water.

Place most of the vinegar into a preserving pan and add the spices, garlic and sugar. Bring to the boil and add the vegetables. Simmer the mixture until the vegetables are still just crisp.

Blend the cornflour with the remaining vinegar and stir into the vegetable mixture. Boil for 2-3 minutes,

stirring gently.

Spoon into jars and cover, seal and label. Yield will be about 2.75kg (6lb).

Orange Pickle

6 oranges
1 teaspoon salt
450g (1lb) sugar
2 tablespoons golden syrup
175ml (6fl oz) malt vinegar
125ml (4fl oz) water
Seeds of 6 cardamoms
6 black peppercorns, crushed
½ teaspoon ground cinnamon
¼ teaspoon mixed spice or ground allspice
12 cloves

Put the oranges and salt into a large saucepan. Pour over enough hot water just to cover them and place the pan over moderate heat. Bring the water to the boil, reduce the heat to low and simmer the oranges for 50 minutes or until they are tender.

Remove the pan from the heat. Drain the oranges and place them on a board to cool. In a medium-sized saucepan, bring the sugar, golden syrup, vinegar, water, cardamom seeds, peppercorns, cinnamon, mixed spice or allspice and cloves to the boil over moderate heat, stirring constantly. Reduce the heat to low and simmer the mixture for about 10 minutes. Remove the pan from the heat and set aside to cool.

Using a sharp knife, cut the oranges into thin slices. Pour the sugar and vinegar mixture through a strainer into a large saucepan. Discard the flavourings. Add the orange slices. Place the pan over moderate heat and bring the mixture to the boil, stirring frequently. Reduce the heat to low and simmer for 20 minutes.

Remove the pan from the heat and allow the mixture to cool for 5 minutes. Ladle the pickle into clean, warm, dry

Piccalilli is a well-known mustard pickle with crisp shallots and cauliflower flowerets, which goes splendidly with most cold cuts of meat, especially ham and pork.

Chow-Chow is another of the many pickles and preserves associated with the Pennsylvania Dutch. This delicious mix of fresh vegetables, spices and vinegar could be used as part of a winter salad.

jars. Cover and label the jars and store them in a cool, dry place for at least three weeks before use. This pickle is delicious with roast goose, duck or pork. Yield is about 1.75kg (4lb).

Chow-Chow

350g (12oz) kidney beans, soaked overnight in cold water and drained
4 red or green peppers, white pith removed, seeded and sliced
1 medium-sized cauliflower, trimmed and separated into flowerets
450g (1lb) French beans, trimmed and sliced
225g (8oz) sweetcorn
1 litre (1¾ pints) vinegar
175g (6oz) soft brown sugar
25g (1oz) dry mustard
3 tablespoons mustard seed
2 teaspoons turmeric

Cook the vegetables separately in boiling salted water until they are only just tender. Drain them and place in a large mixing bowl.

Place the vinegar, sugar, mustard, mustard seed and turmeric in a saucepan. Cook gently until the sugar has dissolved, then bring the mixture to the boil. Add the vegetables and heat through for a few minutes.

Spoon the pickle into jars. Cover, seal and label. Yield will be about 1.75kg (4lb).

Maine Cauliflower and Tomato Pickle

2 medium-sized firm cauliflowers, separated into flowerets
675g (1½lb) firm tomatoes, quartered
4 medium-sized onions, coarsely chopped
1 medium-sized cucumber, coarsely chopped
175g (6oz) salt
1 teaspoon dry mustard
1 teaspoon ground ginger

1 teaspoon black pepper
225g (8oz) soft brown sugar
1 teaspoon pickling spice
600ml (1 pint) white wine vinegar

Arrange the vegetables in layers in a large deep dish, sprinkling equal amounts of the salt on each layer. Pour over enough cold water to cover the vegetables. Cover the dish with aluminium foil and set it aside in a cool place for 24 hours.

Next day, place the vegetables in a large collander and rinse them thoroughly under cold running water to remove the excess salt. Drain off the water, shaking the collander, and place the vegetables in a large saucepan.

Sprinkle over the mustard, ginger, pepper, sugar and pickling spices. Pour over the vinegar. Set the pan over moderate heat and bring the liquid to the boil, stirring frequently.

Reduce the heat to low and simmer, stirring occasionally, for 15 to 20 minutes, or until the vegetables are tender but still firm when pierced with the point of a sharp knife.

Remove the pan from the heat. Pack the vegetables into pickling jars. Pour in enough of the cooking liquid to fill each jar. Label, cover and store them in a cool, dry, dark place. Yield will be about 2.75kg (6lb).

Maine Cauliflower and Tomato Pickle is another American mixed vegetable recipe. Use a strong spiced vinegar, using black peppercorns and a small dried chilli to heighten the flavour.

133

Beetroot is particularly good when pickled – many people prefer it served with a little vinegar anyway. It is best to use raw beets. However, if you buy cooked beets, place them in a saucepan of water and bring to the boil for no more than a minute or two. Then use the liquid as suggested in the recipe.

Beetroot Pickle

6 medium-sized beetroots, preferably uncooked
Cold water
350ml (12fl oz) wine vinegar
1½ tablespoons dry mustard
½ teaspoon salt
275g (9oz) sugar
2 onions, sliced
2 teaspoons dill seeds

Boil the beetroots until they are tender. Drain and set aside, reserving 300ml (10fl oz) of the liquid. When the beetroots are cool, slice off the tops and bottoms. Then, using your fingers, slip off the skins. Slice the beetroots and set aside.

In a medium-sized saucepan bring the vinegar and reserved cooking liquid to the boil over moderate heat. Add the mustard, salt and sugar. Stir to mix, and bring to the boil again. Remove the saucepan from the heat and set aside.

Arrange the beetroot slices and onions in layers in clean, screw-top jars. Add the dill seeds. Cover with the hot vinegar mixture. Tightly screw on the tops of the jars. Cool and place in the refrigerator. Allow the beetroot to stand for a few days before using.

Serve very cold. Yield will be about 1.25 litres (3 pints).
Note: Small, whole beetroots could be pickled in the same way.

Peach Pickle

1 tablespoon whole cloves
1 tablespoon allspice berries
75mm (3in) piece cinnamon stick
50mm (2in) piece root ginger, crushed
Rind of half a lemon
1kg (2lb 2oz) sugar
600ml (1 pint) white wine vinegar
2.25kg (5lb) peaches, peeled, stoned and halved or quartered, depending on size

Tie the cloves, allspice, cinnamon, ginger and lemon rind in a double piece of muslin. Place the sugar and vinegar in a preserving pan and heat until the sugar has dissolved. Bring the syrup to the boil and add the peaches and bag of spices. Simmer the peaches for about 5 minutes or until they are just soft.

With a slotted spoon remove the peaches and pack them into jars.

Boil the syrup until it has reduced by one-third. Discard the bag of

spices. Pour the syrup over the peaches, allowing the syrup to penetrate through. If necessary add more until the jars are full.

Cover, seal and label. Yield will be about 2.25kg (5lb).

Note : If there is any syrup left over bottle it, as the peaches may need topping up during storage.

Pears and damsons may also be preserved in the same way.

Apple Pickle

1kg (2lb 2oz) sugar
600ml (1 pint) spiced vinegar
1kg (2lb 2oz) cooking apples,
quartered and cored

Place the sugar and vinegar in a preserving pan and heat until the sugar has dissolved. Reduce the heat and add the apples, cook until they are just tender and not broken. With a slotted spoon remove the apples and carefully pack them into jars. Boil the syrup until it reduces to 300ml (½ pint) then pour over the fruit. Cover and

label. Yield will be about 1kg (2lb).

Note : This is an excellent way of preserving crab apples. Leave them whole, wash them and prick them – this allows the syrup to penetrate the fruit more quickly.

Pickled Red Cabbage

1 head red cabbage
Salt – 3 teaspoons to 450g (1lb)
cabbage
600ml (1 pint) white wine vinegar
1 tablespoon soft brown sugar
1 tablespoon pickling spice

Shred the cabbage finely. Put it in a large bowl and sprinkle each layer with salt. Leave for 24 hours. Drain off any liquid and rinse off any surplus salt.

Put the vinegar, sugar and pickling spice into a pan and bring to the boil. Simmer for 5 minutes and allow to cool for at least 2 hours. Strain.

Pack the cabbage loosely into jars and cover with the spiced vinegar. Cover with plastic lids, label and store in a cool, dark place. This cabbage can

Top : Red cabbage should be salted for 24 hours before pickling. Above : To core apples evenly it is usually best to use a proper apple corer.

135

Above: Small onions, usually grown especially for the purpose, are best for pickling. Right: Spiced Cleos look very attractive packed in special glass jars. Make sure the skins are pricked so that the vinegar can penetrate to the centre of the fruit.

be used after a week but will begin to lose its crispness within 2 to 3 months.

As a variation a hard, round white cabbage can be pickled in the same way.

Pickled Onions

Small pickling onions
600ml (1 pint) brine for each 450g (1lb) onions
Cold spiced vinegar

Place the onions, unpeeled, in a mixing bowl and cover with brine. Set aside for 12 hours. Then drain and peel the onions. With fresh brine, cover and set aside for 2 days. Drain the onions thoroughly and pack into jars. Cover with cold spiced vinegar. Cover, seal and label.

Spiced Cleos

16 small cleos or clementines, or any fruit of the tangerine family
½ teaspoon bicarbonate of soda
12 allspice berries
1 cinnamon stick
10mm (½in) fresh ginger root
12 cloves
300ml (10fl oz) white wine vinegar
450g (1lb) light brown sugar

Wash the cleos and pierce a few holes in their skins with a fork. Put them in a large heavy-bottomed pan, cover with water, add the bicarbonate of soda and boil for 12 minutes.

Place the spices in a piece of muslin and tie with string to make a small bag. Add the spice bag and the vinegar to the pan, cover with a lid and simmer for 20 minutes.

Remove the spice bag and turn the heat down low. Pour in the sugar, stir until it has dissolved, then bring to the boil and simmer for a further 20 minutes, again covering the pan with a lid.

Lift the fruit from the cooking liquid with a slotted spoon and pack into a sterilized jar or jars. Continue to simmer the liquid in the covered pan for 10 minutes more, cool slightly, then pour over the cleos and seal the jars. Store in a cool place.

Spiced Cleos look pretty and remain in good condition for several months providing the fruit is fully immersed in the liquid. They make an excellent and decorative accompaniment to game or pork.

Spiced Eggs

2 teaspoons roughly crushed black peppercorns
2 teaspoons roughly crushed allspice berries
2 teaspoons ground ginger
1 teaspoon salt
1 litre (1¾ pints) wine or herb vinegar
16 small fresh eggs

Place all the seasonings in a piece of muslin and tie into a little bag with string.

Pour the vinegar into a saucepan and add the spice bag. Bring to the boil then simmer for 20 minutes in a covered pan. Allow the liquid to cool in the pan and stand for 2 hours before removing the spice bag.

Meanwhile boil the eggs for at least 10 minutes. Place the cooked eggs in cold water to cool, then carefully remove the shells.

Divide the eggs between sterilized jars, pour on the cold spiced liquid, making sure the eggs are completely immersed in the liquid, and seal with airtight lids.

Leave for 1 month before opening.

Pickled French Beans

1½ teaspoons salt
1 litre (1¾ pints) white wine vinegar
125g (4oz) sugar
4 garlic cloves, peeled
2 bay leaves
2 onions, thinly sliced
6 black peppercorns
2 teaspoons dill seed
1kg (2lb 2oz) fresh French Beans

In a medium-sized saucepan, combine 1 teaspoon of the salt, vinegar, sugar, garlic, bay leaves, onions, peppercorns and dill seed.

Place the pan over moderate heat and bring the liquid to the boil. Reduce the heat to low, cover the pan and simmer for 30 minutes.

Meanwhile, half fill another medium-sized saucepan with water and bring it to the boil over moderate heat. Add

Pickling small boiled eggs is a well-tried method of preserving them over a period of time.

the remaining salt and the beans and cook for 3 to 5 minutes. Remove the pan from the heat and drain the beans. Place them upright in dry, clean, preserving jars. Set aside.

Remove the vinegar mixture from the heat. Strain the mixture over the beans up to the tops of the jars. Seal the jars and store in a cool, dark place until they are required. Yield will be about 1.75kg (4lb).

Pickled Cucumbers

1kg (2lb 2oz) pickling cucumbers
Brine
1.75 litres (3 pints) spiced vinegar
Dill seeds

Pickling cucumbers can vary greatly in size: if they are very large they should be sliced lengthways into convenient pieces to fit available pickling jars. Prick the skins all over so that the vinegar thoroughly penetrates them.

Place the cucumbers in a mixing bowl and cover with brine (page 126). Set aside for 3 days, drain well and pack into jars. Pour hot spiced vinegar into the jars, cover tightly and leave for 24 hours. Strain off the vinegar, bring it to the boil and then pour it over the cucumbers again. Repeat this process until the cucumbers have a good green colour. They should be completely covered with vinegar so it may be necessary to add more. Add dill seeds to the vinegar before sealing to add a piquant flavour. Cover, seal and label. Yield will be about 1kg (2lb 2oz) pickled cucumbers.

Pickled Walnuts

450g (1lb) young green walnuts
Brine
Spiced vinegar

Walnuts used for pickling must be young and green, and used before the hard outer skin has begun to form on them. Test by pricking with a needle and if any thin shell is felt this can be removed.

Place the walnuts in a mixing bowl and cover with brine (page 126). Set aside to soak for up to a week. Drain the nuts and soak in fresh brine for another week. Drain well and spread

out on shallow dishes. Keep in a dry airy place for 1-2 days until the nuts turn black. Pack the walnuts into jars and cover with spiced vinegar. Cover, seal and label. Yield will be about 450g (1lb) pickled walnuts.

Pickled Peppers

6 large red peppers, white pith removed, seeded and halved lengthways
1 litre (1¾ pints) white wine vinegar
½ teaspoon salt
6 black peppercorns
Bouquet garni, consisting of 4 parsley sprigs, 1 thyme spray and 1 bay leaf tied together
4 tablespoons olive oil

Preheat the grill to high. Place the peppers, skin sides up, on the grill rack and grill for 5 to 8 minutes or until the skin of the peppers is black and charred. Remove the peppers from the grill and, with your fingertips, rub off the charred skin.

Cut the peppers into 50mm (2in) slices and pack them in sterilized preserving jars. Set aside.

In a medium-sized saucepan, combine the vinegar, salt, peppercorns and bouquet garni. Place the pan over moderate heat and bring the vinegar to the boil. Boil for 5 minutes, then remove the pan from the heat. Strain equal amounts of the vinegar into each jar and set aside, uncovered, at room temperature until it has cooled. When the vinegar is cool, pour 1 tablespoon of the olive oil on top of each jar. Cover tightly and store in a cool, dark place.

Marrow Pickle

Walnuts for pickling should be young and green, and are pickled whole without removing the shell.

1 large vegetable marrow, peeled, seeded and diced
450g (1lb) onions, chopped
2 tablespoons salt
2 tablespoons ground ginger
2 tablespoons turmeric
1 teaspoon cloves
4 green chillis, slit lengthways and seeds removed
12 peppercorns
350g (12oz) soft brown sugar
2 litres (4 pints) malt vinegar

In a large bowl, make layers of marrow and onions, sprinkling each layer generously with salt. Cover the bowl with a cloth and set aside for 9 hours or overnight. Drain off all excess liquid and set aside.

In a large saucepan or preserving pan, combine the ginger, turmeric, cloves, chillis, peppercorns, sugar and vinegar. Bring the mixture to the boil over high heat, stirring occasionally. Reduce the heat to low and simmer for 30 minutes.

Add the marrow and onion and stir well. Increase the heat to high and bring the mixture to the boil. Then simmer, stirring occasionally, for 1½ hours, until it is thick.

Spoon the pickle into warm jars, cover, label and store. Yield is about 2kg (4lb).

Indian Lime Pickle

20 whole limes
20 green chillis
6 tablespoons coarse rock salt
4 bay leaves, crumbled
175g (6oz) fresh root ginger, peeled and cut into thin matchstick shapes
300ml (10fl oz) lime juice

Wash the limes in cold water and dry them with kitchen paper towels. Using a silver or stainless steel knife, make four cuts through the limes to quarter them to within 5mm (¼in) of the bottom of the fruit. Remove the pips.

Slit the green chillis lengthways and scrape out the seeds, leaving the chillis whole with their stalks.

Arrange a layer of limes on the bottom of a large pickling jar. Sprinkle with salt and crumbled bay leaves. Add 2 or 3 chillis and about 2 tablespoons

of the ginger. Repeat the layering process until all the ingredients, except half of the salt, are used up. Pour in the lime juice and give the jar a good shake to settle the contents.

Cover the mouth of the jar with a clean cloth and tie it in place with string. Place the jar in a sunny place for at least 6 days, adding half a tablespoon of the remaining salt each day. Shake the jar at least twice a day. Each night, place the jar in a dry place in the kitchen. Be sure to turn the jar each day so that all sides are exposed to the sun's rays.

After the 6 days, keep the pickle on a kitchen shelf for 10 days. Cover the jar with a lid and shake the jar every day. After 10 days the pickle will be ready to eat. Yield will be about 1.35kg (3lb). This is a very hot pickle, best eaten with curry.

Pickled Red Peppers can be used in salads and when chopped combine well with cold sweetcorn kernels.

Sauces & ketchups

Sauces and ketchups are very similar although the name 'ketchup' is actually derived from the Malaysian *kepchop* meaning the brine from pickled fish. However, nowadays ketchup is a name applied to some sauces, particularly in America. Ketchups usually have a slightly thinner consistency than sauces, and both sauces and ketchups are made from similar ingredients to those used for chutneys. The preparation and method are also generally the same, the main difference being that sauces are sieved to produce a smooth purée before bottling.

Equipment
The equipment for sauce-making is the same as for chutneys; however a nylon or hair sieve is essential, if a food mill or electric blender are not available. Ideally it is more practical to fill small bottles or jars as sauces and ketchups are generally used in small quantities. If large bottles are used the contents will evaporate unless it is used within one or two months. Another advantage of small containers is that several may be opened giving a wider selection at mealtimes. Almost any type of bottle or jar may be used – commercial sauce bottles, tonic water bottles, small wine bottles, baby food jars etc. Whichever you choose, they should be washed thoroughly and dried before use. If the tops are metal they must have a plastic coated lining and if not, a small circle of vinegar-proof paper can be placed over the bottle before the top is screwed on. If bottles without tops are used, such as uncorked wine bottles, then they require clean corks covered with a piece of vinegar-proof paper. If the bottles are to be processed the covers should be lightly screwed on or the corks secured with fine wire on string (this ensures they are kept in place during the heating process). When the bottles are cool, the covers should be screwed on tightly or the wire or string removed and the corks pushed firmly into the bottles. (Corks should be dry before this is done.) The necks of the bottles should then be dipped into melted paraffin wax up to 10mm ($\frac{1}{2}$in) to make a complete air-tight seal.

Label the bottles with the name of the sauce and date, and store in a cool, dry place.

It is worth making many different sauces so that you have them to hand for every occasion. Mushroom Ketchup, Tomato Sauce, Mustard Sauce, Horseradish, Mint, Worcestershire – all these and more are covered in the next few pages of recipes. A sieve or good food mill are useful for sauces, but a blender is the ideal implement to give them the smooth consistency they need.

An adaptation of a traditional recipe, Mushroom Ketchup is an unusual and tasty accompaniment to many informal savoury dishes such as flans, pies and cold meats.

Recipes for sauces

Sauces serve a rather different purpose from chutneys and pickles. Here are some useful recipes for every cook.

Tomato Sauce

12 pickling onions or shallots, peeled and chopped
50ml (2fl oz) olive oil
1.35kg (3lb) fresh tomatoes, skinned and chopped
150ml (5fl oz) wine or cider vinegar
2 tablespoons soft brown sugar
2 teaspoons salt
1 teaspoon black pepper

Soften the onions in the olive oil in a large saucepan. Add the tomatoes and all the other ingredients. Bring to the boil and simmer for 15 minutes, stirring occasionally.

Turn into a blender, food mill or sieve and purée the mixture. Check for seasoning and adjust to taste. Return the sauce to the saucepan and bring to the boil. Pour into prepared bottles leaving 25mm (1in) headspace, seal and sterilize as for Fruit Syrups (page 51). Label and store. Yield will be about 1 litre (1¾ pints).

Mushroom Ketchup

1.35kg (3lb) mushrooms, trimmed
100g (4oz) salt
1 small onion, peeled and chopped

Tomato Sauce has to be poured liberally over a real hamburger – along with mustard, relish and melted cheese!

1 clove of garlic, crushed
1 tablespoon pickling spice, crushed
600ml (1 pint) vinegar

Chop the mushrooms and place in a mixing bowl. Sprinkle with the salt and set aside for 24 hours, stirring occasionally. Drain the mushrooms and rinse in cold water.

Place the mushrooms in a saucepan with the onion and garlic. Add the pickling spice and vinegar. Bring the mixture to the boil then reduce the heat, cover the pan and simmer for 30 to 45 minutes until the mushrooms are soft. With the back of a wooden spoon push the mixture through a nylon sieve placed over a mixing bowl. Return the purée to a clean saucepan and bring to the boil.

Pour into the prepared bottles, leaving 25mm (1in) headspace, seal at once and sterilize as for Tomato Sauce.

Seal and label. Yield will be about 1 litre (1¾ pints).

Mustard Sauce

2 green peppers
1 red pepper
100g (4oz) green tomatoes
2 onions
Half a cucumber
200g (8oz) gherkins or pickled cucumbers
1.2 litres (2 pints) water
1 tablespoon salt
600ml (1 pint) white wine vinegar
200g (8oz) soft brown sugar
1 tablespoon mustard seed
1 tablespoon flour
$\frac{1}{4}$ teaspoon turmeric

Remove the pith and pips from the red and green peppers, and skin the tomatoes. Roughly chop these and all the other vegetables. Place them in a large bowl, add the water and salt, and leave overnight in a cool, dry place. Next day, strain the vegetables, discarding the salt water, and place them in a large heavy-bottomed pan. Add the vinegar, sugar and mustard seed and bring to the boil.

Place the flour and turmeric in a saucer, add a drop of water and mix into a paste. Gradually stir the paste into the vegetable mixture.

Simmer the contents of the pan, uncovered, for $1\frac{1}{4}$ hours, or until the sauce has thickened, stirring occasionally. Turn the mixture into a blender or put it through a food mill, then pour the sauce into sterilized bottles or jars, seal and label. The yield will be about 900ml ($1\frac{1}{2}$ pints).

Cranberry and Orange Sauce

4 tablespoons water
4 tablespoons fresh orange juice
125g (4oz) sugar
225g (8oz) fresh cranberries, washed and picked over
1 tablespoon finely grated orange rind

Pour the water and orange juice into a medium-sized saucepan and add the sugar. Place the pan over low heat and stir with a metal spoon to dissolve the sugar. Increase the heat to moderately high and add the cranberries. Bring the liquid to the boil and cook for 5 minutes, stirring occasionally, until the cranberries are just tender and their skins begin to burst.

Remove the pan from the heat and mix in the grated orange rind. Leave the sauce to cool to room temperature. It may then be poured into glass jars, covered and stored in the refrigerator for future use. Serve with turkey or other roast meat. Yield is about 600ml (1 pint).

Horseradish Sauce

Horseradish roots
Distilled malt vinegar

Use fresh horseradishes and remove all the leaves. Scrape or peel the white roots, wash and dry with kitchen paper towels or a clean cloth.

Grate or shred the horseradishes into a mixing bowl. Spoon into clean, dry

Leaves of the horseradish plant.

144

preserving jars or bottles, packing it down tightly. Cover with distilled malt vinegar which has been boiled for 1 minute and left until cold. Leave 10mm (½in) headspace. Seal with air-tight covers and store in a cool, dry place.

To serve: Mix a little of the horse-radish with salt, pepper and mustard to taste and add sufficient double cream to give a smooth consistency.

Worcestershire Sauce

1 litre (1¾ pints) malt vinegar
4 shallots, or 1 small onion, peeled and very finely chopped or minced
1 clove of garlic, crushed
6 tablespoons walnut ketchup
4 tablespoons anchovy essence
4 tablespoons soy sauce
½ teaspoon cayenne pepper
½ teaspoon black pepper
1 teaspoon salt

Place all the ingredients in a large bottle or jar and cover tightly. Shake the bottle or jar a few times a day for 2 weeks.

Strain the mixture into a large mixing bowl. Pour the sauce into clean, dry bottles and seal them tightly. Store in a cool, dry place. Yield will be about 1 litre (1¾ pints).

Mint Sauce

Mint leaves
Malt vinegar

Use only young, fresh mint leaves, discarding the stalks. Wash and dry the leaves with kitchen paper towels or a clean cloth. Chop the mint leaves and pack into clean, dry preserving jars.

Pour in enough malt vinegar to cover the mint, making sure the vinegar penetrates it. Leave 10mm (½in) head-space and cover with air-tight covers. Store in a cool, dry place.

To serve: Remove some mint (about 1 tablespoon per person) and add extra vinegar, water, sugar, salt and pepper to taste.

Note: An unusual and even more delicious way of serving mint sauce is to add chopped lettuce leaves and a little chopped onion to the mint sauce as well as the extra vinegar, water, sugar, salt and pepper. (Use about 3 lettuce leaves and 1 small onion to 4 tablespoons of the basic mint sauce.) This version is a speciality of the Tyne and Wear areas in the North East of England and is especially good served with roast lamb or lamb chops.

Top: Using mint from your own garden or window box is the cheapest way of making Mint Sauce. Below: Mustard seed can be dark or light, depending on the variety. Use whichever you prefer for hot Mustard Sauce.

Home freezing

Freezing as a form of long term food preservation is a relatively new technique. However, home freezing has become very widespread recently and is recognized as one of the most versatile methods of food preservation. The chilling of food to retard spoilage has been known for a long time; even in the days of the Roman Emperor Nero, snow and ice from mountain slopes were packed around freshly killed meat and fish in cone-shaped pits, lined with straw. The same idea was used in the 17th and 18th centuries in England when natural ice collected from nearby lakes and streams was packed into large, brick-lined, egg-shaped holes in the grounds of country houses. The tops of these ice houses which protruded above ground level were usually kept shaded from the sun by planting trees on the south side. Ice became a much sought-after commodity and was imported from Norway or America in fast clippers. Although blocks of ice were still used in kitchen ice-safes and ice-chests for cooling food and drinks right up until the 1920s, in 1834 Jacob Perkins, an American engineer living in London, invented the first machine for the mechanical production of cold. It was first used in the 1880s to bring chilled meat to this country in refrigerated cargo ships. The invention of mechanical refrigeration led to the introduction of household refrigerators in the early 1920s and to the first household food freezers in the 1950s.

It was Clarence Birdseye, an American explorer, who noted when trapping furs in Labrador in the winter of 1924 that the flavour and quality of fish caught by cutting holes in the ice was preserved naturally if left to freeze by the side of the hole in the very low temperature ice. Even months later, on the return journey, the fish was virtually indistinguishable from freshly caught fish when cooked.

The fish had retained its natural flavour and texture because it was really fresh at the time of freezing, had been frozen very quickly in the low temperature ice, covered in a glaze of ice to prevent drying and was then held at a steady low temperature. These are the principal requirements for successful food freezing at home.

Food freezers

The requirements for an efficient food freezer are that it should be capable of freezing a specified weight of food from 25°C (77°F) to −18°C (0°F) while at the same time maintaining the temperature of any frozen food already being stored in the freezer at about −18°C (0°F). Most freezers are now marked with the food freezer symbol (figure 1) and this distinguishes them for conservators or frozen food storage compartments which may be marked with star markings (figure 2) indicating that they are intended only for the storage of already-frozen food. These are often part of the average domestic

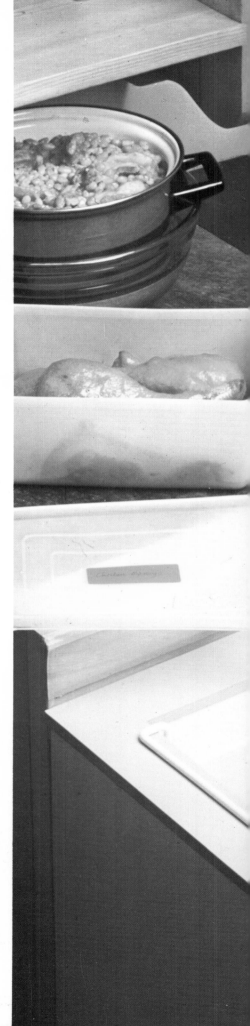

The NEW DUPLEX REFRIGERATOR, Registered. For Wenham Lake or Rough Ice. PRIZE MEDAL REFRIGERATORS. Fitted with Water Tanks and Filters. The New American DOUBLE-WALL ICE WATER PITCHER. Suitable for Wine Cup, &c. The American BUTTER DISH, with revolving lid, for use with ice. WENHAM LAKE ICE delivered in town for less than 1d. per lb., or forwarded into the country, in packages of 2s. 6d., 4s., 8s., and upwards, by "Goods Train," without perceptible waste. Illustrated Price Lists free on application.

WENHAM LAKE ICE COMPANY

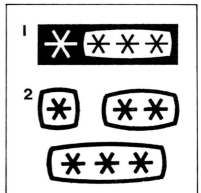

Refrigerators and freezers have come a long way since the early days. Top: This ice house in the grounds of Hatchlands, near East Clandon in Surrey, is typical of many built in the late eighteenth century.
Centre: An early refrigerator – really an ice-box, as it was not mechanically operated.
Above: Food Freezer symbols.

refrigerator. Make sure that the freezer you choose complies with the standard specifications of a reputable national or local consumer protection group, and, in Britain, carries the 'kitemark' of the British Electrotechnical Approvals Board or an equivalent national symbol.

Freezers are available in a wide range of sizes, ranging from about 55 litres (2cu ft) to about 800 litres (28cu ft). Each 28 litres (about 1cu ft) of space will hold about 9kg (20lbs) of frozen food. At least 55 litres (2cu ft) is the minimum requirement for each person in the family, though you should bear in mind the usual number of people to be catered for: families that do a lot of home entertaining will probably require a much larger freezer.

Food freezers and refrigerators should be located in a dry, well ventilated place, on a level floor, so that the lid or door will close correctly. All freezers, except those with fully automatic defrosting,

Equipment needed for successful freezing includes many types of container (polythene, waxed or aluminium foil), tough polythene bags, freezer paper, cling film, tubs, a blanching basket and ice cube trays.

need to be defrosted occasionally; follow the manufacturers' instructions on how and when to defrost.

Foods for freezing

With a few exceptions which are listed below almost all fresh and cooked food can be preserved by freezing and there are only a few simple rules to follow to ensure complete success.

1. Choose only really fresh food of prime quality – this especially applies to fish and sea foods. (You can always find other uses for over-mature or bruised fruit and vegetables – particularly for chutneys and sauces!)

2. Cooked foods must be freshly prepared and allowed to cool, before packing and freezing.

3. Food for freezing must be sealed in a container or wrapped to exclude air – this is to avoid dehydration, loss of colour, texture and flavour, and cross-flavouring, during storage.

4. Pack foods in probable mealtime proportions, interleaving chops, beefburgers, fish fillets, etc, with polythene, aluminium foil or freezer paper for easy separation.

5. Follow the freezer manufacturer's instructions when loading fresh food and *avoid placing fresh food in direct contact with food already frozen.* It is good practice to depress the fast freeze switch, if one is fitted, a few hours before loading the freezer with fresh food. Return the fast freeze switch to its normal position after about 24 hours. The thermostat setting for normal storage should keep frozen food at a temperature not warmer than –18°C (0°F).

6. The usual rules of hygiene in the preparation of food must be followed. In particular make sure that all packaging, kitchen tools and utensils, cutting boards – and hands – are thoroughly washed between handling fresh and cooked foods.

7. A few foods are not recommended for freezing. These include hard-boiled eggs, mayonnaise, baked egg custard pies and tarts, royal icings and frostings, single cream, soft meringues, boiled potatoes (except if new), stuffed poultry, bananas and vegetables intended for use in salads. Foods which contain a high proportion of gelatine do not freeze satisfactorily.

Packaging food for freezing

The low temperature air in a food freezer is very dry, and any food not properly sealed will lose its natural moisture and may develop freezer burn. Inadequately packaged food is not unsafe, but will be unpleasant to eat after storage at low temperatures.

The packaging materials must be free from taint and odours, and moisture and vapour proof to prevent loss of natural moisture and juices in the food. They should be resistant to cracking and breaking at freezer temperatures, a suitable shape to ensure fast freezing by keeping the packages as thin as possible or flexible, so that dry foods can be wrapped snugly excluding as much air as possible. (Square shaped rigid containers make better use of storage space and stack more easily than round ones.)

Packaging materials which fill these requirements include:

Polythene bags. These are available in many sizes, for fruits, vegetables, fish, meat, poultry, loaves of bread and baked foods.

Polythene sheeting, freezer paper and heavy duty aluminium foil. These are especially useful for wrapping irregular shaped food and

Freezers come in two main types: the chest (see page 152) and the upright (below). Upright freezers are often more convenient as they do not take up much floor space. However, chest freezers generally have a larger capacity so are suitable for large families or those who entertain often.

It is a good idea to wrap meat in cling film or freezer paper before wrapping it firmly in aluminium foil or in polythene bags sealed with freezer tape.

interleaving individual portions of meat, fish, poultry, hamburgers, yeast or pastry dough etc.

Polythene tubs and cartons with tightly fitting lids for soft fruit, sauces, stews, casseroles and all liquids.

Aluminium and waxed paper dishes, trays, basins, etc, using aluminium foil or polythene sheet to cover.

Plastic covered wire and freezer tape for sealing.

Ideally, each package should be labelled and marked with details of contents and the date of freezing. Different colours for labels and marking are helpful for later identification – such as green for vegetables, red for meat, blue for fish, etc.

The charts on pages 158-161 give an immediate reference for most types of produce. General remarks on the preparation of different types of food are given on the following pages.

Meat

With all kinds of meat, prepare for freezing by trimming off all excess fat and remove bones as far as is practicable to save space and packaging material. Bones which have been removed can be used to make stock, which can then be frozen in convenient sized containers after skimming off all fat. The airtight wrapping of meat is especially important to prevent dehydration. Protect outer packaging by first covering any sharp projecting bones with greaseproof paper or clean muslin. Exclude as much air as possible before sealing in aluminium foil or polythene bags. Interleave steaks, chops and small cuts with aluminium foil or polythene sheet. Larger joints of meat should be cut into meal time or family size portions before freezing and it must be remembered that joints of 1kg (2lb 2oz) and larger will probably require at least 48 hours to freeze through to the centre of the joint.

Hamburgers can be frozen in ready-to-cook portions, and stored in sealed polythene bags, with each hamburger interleaved with freezer paper. You can also freeze the buns.

151

Using your freezer economically means keeping it well stocked with the sorts of food which you know you will be using on a regular basis, as well as dishes which you can use for special occasions. It is a good idea to spend a day a month 'stock-taking': check the dates on the food already frozen and their storage life, and re-stock with a new batch of fresh produce and cooked food. (Remember to keep already-frozen and fresh foods completely separated.) Shown here are many of the different ways foods can be frozen: in the foreground strawberries are being prepared for single freezing, so that they can then be transferred to a freeflow pack. Cooked dishes are being frozen in aluminium foil containers so they can simply be removed from the freezer and cooked in the same dish. Soup has been frozen in a large, sealed polythene bag, while other items are stored in rigid containers. Bread can be frozen quite satisfactorily, whether shop-bought or home-made, and of course fruit and vegetables can be frozen ready for use at any time.

Vegetables need to be blanched before freezing by plunging them in boiling water for the times given on the chart (see page 159). It is best to freeze a vegetable such as cauliflower ready-prepared for cooking by separating the flowerets and discarding the leaves and stalks before blanching. The flowerets can be frozen separately to produce a free flow pack. There is no need to thaw vegetables before cooking.

Freezing cooked meat

As is the case with fish, fruit and vegetables, and poultry, meat which has been home or commercially frozen can be used as an ingredient for a recipe, such as a stew or casseroles and then refrozen providing it is well cooked before freezing. It is especially important for hygiene and cross-contamination reasons to avoid handling fresh and cooked meat and poultry at the same time when preparing for freezing. Providing fat has been skimmed, the storage life of cooked stews and casseroles prepared in this way is up to two months.

Fish

Fresh fish deteriorates very quickly after being caught even if well chilled, so fish purchased from an inland fishmonger is unlikely to be fresh enough for home freezing. All fresh fish suitable for freezing should be washed, cleaned, gutted, and head, tail and fins removed then washed again. Prepare the fish as for cooking, either whole, filleted or in steaks. To increase storage life, whole round and flat fish, after freezing and temporary packing can be glazed by dipping in an ice cold solution of salt and water (50g (2oz) salt to 600ml (1 pint) of water).

Game birds

Game birds should be prepared for home freezing in the same way as for poultry (see chart, page 159), but the birds should be hung for a time according to the taste and flavour preferred. In any case, the hanging time should be a little less than that for immediate cooking. After preparation, pack in polythene bags or aluminium foil and seal.

Vegetables

As a general guide, all vegetables which are normally cooked before eating will freeze and store satisfactorily. Some, like tomatoes and onions, will lose their original crispness and texture after freezing, but are very useful for stews, casseroles and sauces. After washing and trimming most vegetables must be blanched in boiling water for a short time before packaging and freezing. This retards the action of enzymes and prevents 'off' flavours. The few exceptions are given in the chart. Blanching is most easily done by putting small quantities of vegetables in a wire basket and immersing this in a pan of boiling water, normally at a ratio of not more than 450g (1lb) of vegetables to $3\frac{1}{2}$ litres (6 pints) of water. Blanching time begins as the water returns to the boil and ends by plunging the vegetables into ice cold water. Most vegetables can be packed into conveniently sized polythene bags or rigid cartons and many can be frozen individually to produce a free flow pack (see below).

Fruit

Fruit can be frozen whole, in halves or in slices and in a dry pack in dry sugar, in a sugar syrup or as a fruit puree. The addition of sugar or sugar syrup helps to protect colour and flavour. Light coloured fruits like apples, pears and peaches will darken after peeling and slicing. This discoloration can almost be eliminated by working quickly and placing the fruit in a solution of ascorbic acid and water, using 500mg ascorbic acid to 600ml (1 pint) of water. Do not use iron or copper pans for this solution.

Freezing separately. After cleaning the fruit, using as little water as

possible, dry it and lay it out in a single layer in a polythene bag, laid on a flat aluminium baking tray. Freeze the fruit in this position. Small fruit will freeze in a few hours and can then be shaken gently down into the bag. Fill the bag using fruit from other trays. Although time-consuming, this method is best for small fruit like raspberries, strawberries and blackberries, producing a free flow pack. (The

method applies to other kinds of food as well – diced vegetables and peas for example.)

Dry pack. This is suitable for fruits with a relatively tough skin – gooseberries and currants for example need only be washed and dried before freezing in closed bags, especially if they are to be used only as recipe ingredients or for jam-making.

Dry sugar pack. After cleaning and drying, sprinkle the fruit with sugar using 100g (4oz) sugar to each 450g (1lb) of fruit, shaking or stirring the fruit gently to ensure an even coating.

Sugar syrup. Prepare sugar syrup and allow to cool before adding to fruit. Add sugar to boiling water and simmer only long enough for all sugar to be dissolved. Sugar syrup can be used in one of three strengths:–

1. Light sugar syrup: 225g (8oz) sugar to 600ml (1 pint) water.
2. Medium sugar syrup: 330g (12oz) sugar to 500ml (17fl oz) water.
3. Heavy sugar syrup: 500g (1lb) sugar to 500ml (17fl oz) water.

If recommended add 500mg ascorbic acid to the solution when cold.

Purées and juices. Fruit which has been discarded because of over-ripeness, blemishes or bruises could be frozen in purée form

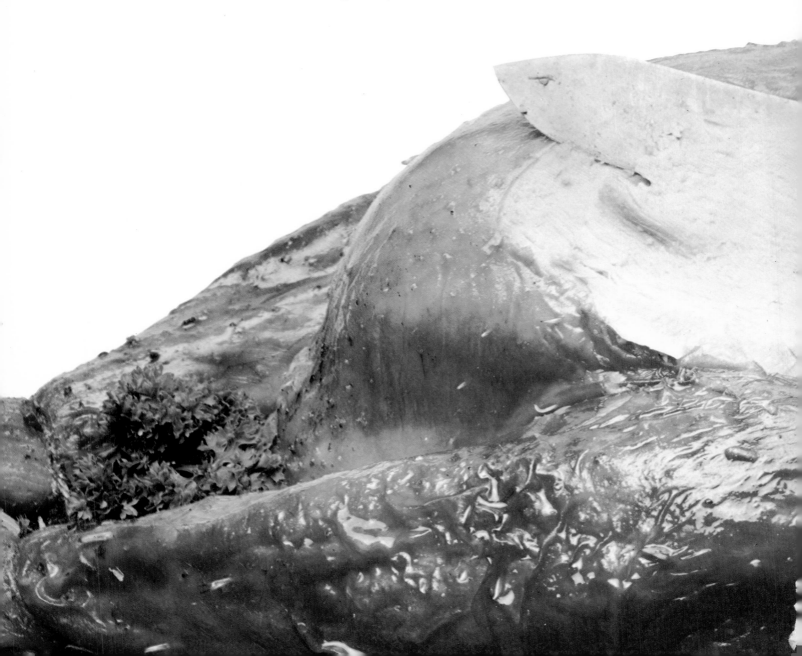

after blemished or bruised parts have been removed. Pass the fruit through a nylon sieve or food mill and add sugar at the ratio of about 100g (4oz) of sugar to 450g (1lb) fruit according to taste. Apples and tomatoes should be cooked before sieving.

Storage life. With a few exceptions, most fruit will freeze and store satisfactorily at –18°C (0°F) for up to nine months when packed in dry sugar or in sugar syrup. The storage life is normally reduced to about six months if fruit is packed dry.

Cooking home frozen foods

Small portion sizes of fish, meat, poultry and all vegetables can be cooked straight from the freezer without thawing. Ensure that fish, meat and poultry portions are cooked through to the centre of the food. Vegetables which have been blanched should be cooked in the minimum quantity of boiling, salted water. They normally need less cooking time than fresh vegetables.

It is important that large joints of meat, whole fish and all whole birds should be thawed before cooking. This is especially important with chickens, ducks, geese and turkeys, bearing in mind that a frozen bird of above 10kg (22lb) will require about three days in a cool, clean place to thaw through to the centre.

It is very important to thaw poultry thoroughly before cooking. This should be done in a cool place, keeping the bird covered lightly on a tray or dish. Remove the polythene covering as soon as it is possible to do so. Bear in mind that a large frozen bird such as a turkey or goose may need as much as three days to thaw, so it should be removed in good time from the freezer to avoid disappointment at a special occasion such as Thanksgiving or Christmas.

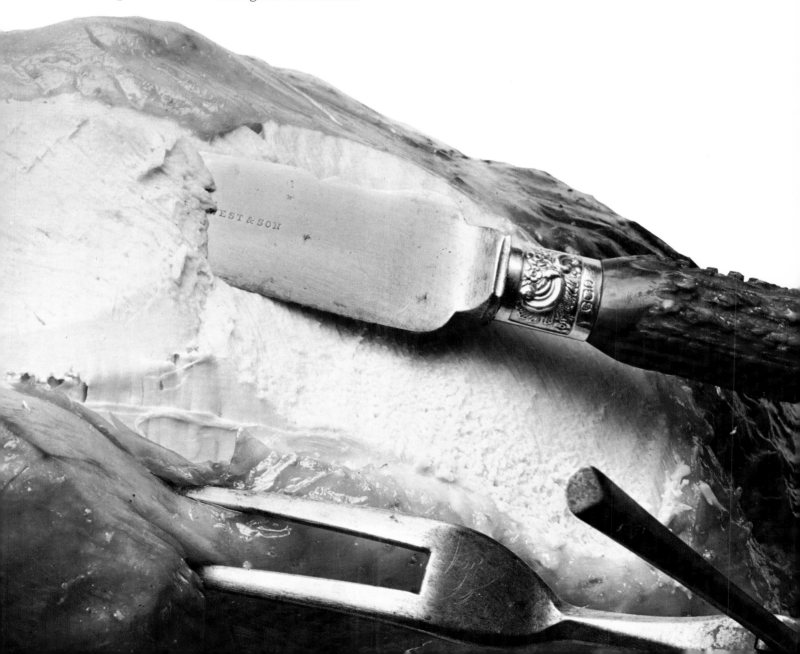

Freezing Chart

Preparation and storage life

Food	Preparation	Storage life up to
Bread and cakes		
Bread, rolls, croissants, Danish pastries	Bake and cool before wrapping in polythene bags, seal and freeze. If sliced, individual slices can be toasted without thawing. Freeze bread crumbs in convenient sized polythene bags.	1 month
Cakes, scones, biscuits	Bake and cool before wrapping in polythene bags or sheet. Preferably fill and decorate cakes during thawing. In recipes use egg yolks rather than whole eggs, high quality margarine instead of butter. Interleave layers of sandwich cakes with freezer paper or polythene sheet.	6 months
Unbaked yeast dough	Yeast does not remain stable very long when frozen. Pack the unrisen dough in greased polythene bags. Leave headspace and seal. Rising time may need to be increased: compensate by adding more yeast in doughs to be frozen.	2 months
Unbaked pastries and pies	Pastry is better frozen unbaked. Prepare in conveniently sized thin slabs. Wrap in foil or polythene sheet, roll out after thawing. Pies with a pastry base and/or covering should be prepared as for cooking. Cook and cool savoury fillings before covering with pastry. Fruit does not require cooking. Foil dishes are ideal for packing: over-wrap with foil before freezing.	6 months
Dairy Foods		
Whole eggs	Lightly beat yolks and whites together either with 1 tablespoon sugar or 1 teaspoon salt to every 6 eggs. Pack in waxed carton or tub leaving headspace. Seal well. Alternatively freeze in ice cube tray and store frozen blocks in polythene bag. Seal well.	6 months

	Preparation	Freezer storage life up to
Egg yolks	Store better than whole egg. Gently mix yolks. Add a little sugar or salt. Freeze and pack as for whole eggs.	9 months
Egg whites	Pass through sieve, mix gently, add a little sugar or salt. Freeze and pack as for whole eggs.	9 months
Milk	Freeze only homogenized milk in waxed carton leaving head space.	3 months
Cream	Freeze only double cream (not less than 40 per cent butter fat) and whipping cream. Preferably add sugar – one tablespoon to each 500ml (1 pint) cream. Pack in waxed cartons leaving head space.	3 months
Ice-cream	Store bought ice-cream in original container. Home-made in wax cartons, leaving headspace.	3 months
Butter	Overwrap commercial packaging or tubs with polythene sheet or aluminium foil. Seal well.	salted up to 3 months; unsalted up to 6 months
Cheese	Hard cheese may become crumbly after freezing. Cream and cottage cheeses mixed with whipped cream make good sandwich fillings. Grated cheese freezes and stores well for use in recipes or for garnishing. Pack in tubs or cartons and grated cheese in polythene bags.	soft cheese up to 3 months; grated hard cheese up to 6 months
Fish		
White fish – cod, haddock, plaice, sole, whiting etc	Small fish can be frozen whole after preparation. Glaze if preferred and pack in polythene bags or aluminium foil. Larger fish should be filleted or cut into steaks. Interleave individual fillets and steaks with aluminium foil, polythene sheet or freezer paper. Pack in flat wax or foil containers. Wrap in polythene or foil.	6 months
Oily fish – halibut, herring, mackerel, mullet, salmon, turbot, trout, etc	Prepare and freeze as for white fish. Storage life for oily fish is shorter than white fish.	3 months
Shellfish – crab, lobster	Only freeze shellfish if it is less than 24 hours since it was taken from the water. Cook crab and lobster, remove meat from shells and claws and pack in tubs, cartons or aluminium foil containers leaving head space.	3 months

		Storage life up to
Oysters, scallops	Best frozen uncooked, remove from shells, retain natural juices. Wash fish in salt and water then pack in polythene tubs, cartons or aluminium foil containers with natural juices. Leave head space before sealing.	3 months
Prawns and shrimps	Best frozen uncooked after washing in salt and water. Remove the heads and tails and pack in tubs, cartons or aluminium foil containers. The shells and veins should be removed during thawing.	3 months

Beef and lamb	Preparation	Storage life up to
Large cuts	Remove bones and excess fat. Pad any projecting bones and seal as snugly as possible in aluminium foil or polythene bags. Seal well. Make stock from bones, freeze in ice-cube trays and pack in polythene bags.	9 months
Small cuts	Remove excess fat, wrap in aluminium foil or in polythene bag. Interleave chops, steaks etc with aluminium foil, freezer paper or polythene sheet, draw out as much air as possible before sealing well in aluminium foil or polythene bags.	6 months
Pork and Veal	Prepare and pack as above.	
Large cuts		4 months
Small cuts		3 months
Offal	Prepare and pack as for small cuts. Maintain strict hygiene standards.	2 months
Minced meat and sausages	Prepare and pack as for small cuts. Freeze only freshly minced meat and bought sausages. Avoid salt in sausages as this reduces storage life.	1 month
Poultry and game	Remove head, tail and feathers. Clean and truss as for cooking, pad any projecting bones. Do not stuff poultry before freezing. Pack in polythene bags, excluding as much air as possible, and seal well. Make stock from giblets, skim all excess fat after cooling and freeze in tubs or cartons leaving head space.	Chickens up to 9 months. Ducks, geese, turkeys and game up to 6 months
Poultry joints and quarters	Freeze and wrap individually in polythene bags or aluminium foil. Several portions can be frozen in one package providing pieces of poultry are interleaved with aluminium foil or polythene sheet.	Chicken up to 9 months. Duck, goose, turkey portions up to 6 months

Vegetables	Preparation	Blanching time in minutes	Storage life up to
Artichokes (globe)	Trim off coarse outer leaves, stalks, tops and stems. Add lemon juice to blanching water.	7	12 months
Asparagus	Wash, scrape stalks, trim to approx equal lengths. Divide up into thick, medium and thin stalks. Pack in rigid containers.	thin – 2 thick – 4	12 months
Aubergines	Wash well and cut into about 10mm (½in) slices with stainless steel knife. Pack in rigid containers.	4	12 months
Beans (broad)	Pick young tender beans. Shell and discard any blemished beans.	3	12 months
Beans (French and runner)	Wash and trim ends, leave whole or slice thickly or cut into pieces about 25mm (1in) long	whole – 4 sliced – 3	12 months
Beetroot	Select young and small beets. Cook whole beets until tender, rub off skins and pack in rigid containers. Large beets should be sliced or diced after cooking.	none	6 months
Broccoli	Wash, and trim stalks cutting away any woody stalks. Divide up into thick, medium and thin stems. Pack in rigid containers, sprig to stalk. Separate layers with polythene film or freezer paper.	thick – 5 thin – 3	12 months
Brussels sprouts	Trim and remove discoloured leaves. Cross-cut the stalks and wash in salted water. Can be frozen individually. Pack in rigid containers or polythene bags.	small – 3 large – 5	12 months
Cabbage	Trim outer coarse leaves. Wash in salted water. Cut or tear into shreds. Drain well and dry. Pack in rigid containers or polythene bags.	2	6 months
Carrots	Remove tops and tails. Scrape and wash. Leave small new carrots whole, but slice or dice larger carrots. Small	whole – 5 sliced – 3	8 months

159

	Preparation	Blanching time (minutes)	Storage life
	whole carrots can be frozen individually.		
Cauliflower	Select firm white heads. Remove most of outer coarse leaves. Separate into equal sized sprigs. Wash in salted water, drain and pack in rigid containers. Add lemon juice to blanching water to retain colour.	3	8 months
Celeriac	Wash, trim, scrape and slice, dry and pack into rigid containers or polythene bags.	6	9 months
Celery	Best suited after freezing for use as ingredient in recipes. Remove outer coarse stalks and strings. Cut into 50 to 75mm (2-3in) lengths. Freeze hearts whole. Pack in containers or polythene bags.	hearts – 8 stalks – 4	12 months
Corn on the cob	Remove outer husks, trim ends and wash. Freeze separately and pack in polythene bags.	5 to 8 depending on size	12 months
Corn kernels	Remove outer husks, and scrape kernels off the cob. Wash, drain and pack in rigid containers or polythene bags. Can be added to other vegetables before freezing, eg peas.	5	12 months
Courgettes	Wash and cut into 25mm (1in) slices. Drain and pack into rigid containers interleaving layers with freezer paper or aluminium foil.	3	12 months
Leeks	Remove coarse outer leaves and trim root end. Wash well, leave whole or slice and pack into rigid containers or polythene bags. They freeze well in white sauce. Seal well to prevent cross-flavour in storage	whole – 4 sliced – 2	6 months
Mushrooms	Wash and peel field mushrooms. Trim stalks. Leave whole or slice. Add lemon juice to blanching water – or sauté in margarine – dry well and pack in rigid containers without blanching.	whole – 4 sliced – 2	12 months
Onions	Use only for cooking after freezing. Peel, slice into rings. Pack in small rigid containers and seal well to prevent cross-flavour in storage. They freeze well in white sauce.	2	3 months
Parsnips	Choose young and small parsnips, scrape and wash. Cut into quarters or slices. Drain and pack into rigid containers or polythene bags.	3	12 months
Peas	Choose young sweet peas, pod and discard any blemished peas. Blanch in small quantities. Drain well and pack in containers or polythene bags.	1½	12 months
Peppers (red and green)	Wash, halve and remove seeds and stalk. Can then be sliced if preferred. Remove only tops and seeds if later to be stuffed. Freeze individually, whole or sliced. Drain and pack in polythene bags.	2	12 months
Spinach	Choose young tender leaves. Wash well in running water, drain and press out as much water as possible. Pack in rigid containers or polythene bags in portions or family mealtime quantities.	2	12 months
Turnips and swedes	Remove thick peel and cut into 25mm (1in) cubes. Pack in rigid containers or polythene bags.	3	12 months
Herbs – mint, parsley, sage, thyme etc.	Wash, drain and dry. Chop finely and freeze in ice cube tray. Wrap cubes in aluminium foil or polythene bags. After freezing and storage, colour and flavour may be reduced.	1	3-6 months

Fruit	Preparation		Storage life up to
Apples	Peel, core and slice. Use ascorbic acid to prevent browning. Blanch (see vegetables) for two or three minutes for dry pack. Alternatively pack in dry sugar or medium sugar syrup with ascorbic acid.		9 months

160

Fruit	Preparation	Storage
	Pack in bags or tubs. Leave headspace in syrup pack.	
Apple purée	Peel, core and slice, cook until tender and sieve. Add sugar and pack in tubs leaving headspace.	6 months
Apricots	Peel, remove stones and freeze in halves or slices in medium sugar syrup with ascorbic acid. Pack in tubs leaving headspace.	9 months
Avocados	Peel, remove stone and convert flesh to purée, adding 10ml (1 teaspoon) of lemon juice to each 500ml (1 pint) of purée. Season with salt and pepper and pack in tubs leaving headspace.	2 months
Bilberries and blackberries	Pick firm berries, remove stalks, wash and dry. Freeze as dry pack, individually, or as dry sugar pack or in heavy syrup. Pack in tubs leaving headspace.	9 months
Blackcurrants	Strip firm currants off stem, wash and dry. Freeze as dry pack individually for jam making, or in dry sugar pack or in heavy sugar syrup. Pack in tubs leaving headspace.	9 months
Cherries	Pick fully ripe, firm fruit, wash and dry. Remove stones and freeze as dry pack for jam making or in light sugar syrup. Pack in tubs leaving headspace.	9 months
Citrus fruits: lemons, oranges, grapefruit	Peel and remove pith and pips. Separate into segments and pack in tubs with medium sugar syrup leaving headspace. Alternatively wash, dry and freeze whole, especially Seville oranges for marmalade making.	9 months
Cranberries	Remove stalks, wash and dry. Freeze whole in dry sugar for sauce or sieve for purée, then pack in tubs leaving headspace.	6-9 months
Damsons	Wash, halve and remove stones. Pack dry for jam making in dry sugar pack for cooking and dessert varieties in heavy sugar syrup. Pack in tubs leaving headspace.	9 months
Grapes	Seedless varieties of grapes can be frozen whole; otherwise halve, remove seeds and pack in a light sugar syrup leaving headspace.	9 months
Loganberries	Select firm berries, remove stalks, wash and dry and pack dry, individually or in dry sugar; pack in tubs leaving headspace.	9 months
Melon	Peel and halve the fruit to remove the seeds. Cut into slices, cubes or balls and immerse immediately into light sugar syrup. Alternatively sprinkle prepared melon pieces with lemon juice and pack in dry sugar. Leave headspace in cartons or tubs.	9 months
Peaches	Peel, remove stones and cut into slices. Immediately immerse in medium sugar syrup with ascorbic acid. If dry sugar pack is preferred, dip slices into ascorbic acid solution before sprinkling with sugar.	9 months
Pears	Peel, core and cut into quarters or slices. Immediately sprinkle with lemon juice to avoid discolouration. Then cook for about five minutes in light sugar syrup. Drain the fruit, cool and pack in tubs in medium sugar syrup with ascorbic acid leaving headspace. Freeze and store best as a purée.	6-9 months
Pineapple	Peel and core, then cut into slices, rings or cubes. Pack into light sugar syrup using any juice from the fruit. Leave headspace in tubs and cartons.	3 months
Plums	Wash, halve and remove stones. Pack dry or in dry sugar pack for jam making. For dessert use pack in heavy sugar syrup with ascorbic acid, leaving headspace in tubs.	9 months
Raspberries	Select firm berries and wash only if necessary. Freeze individually or in dry sugar pack.	9 months
Redcurrants	Strip currants off stems, wash and dry. Freeze individually or dry pack for jam making. Alternatively pack in tubs leaving headspace with heavy sugar syrup for desserts.	9 months
Rhubarb	Select only young and tender stalks. Cut into 25mm (1in) pieces and lightly cook. Drain and cool and pack in dry sugar for pie fillings and jam making, or in heavy sugar syrup for dessert use, leaving headspace in tubs.	9 months
Strawberries	Remove hulls and wash only if necessary. Freeze individually or in dry sugar pack.	9 months
Tomatoes	Best frozen as a purée, otherwise wash, dry and freeze individually whole if to be used for cooking.	6-9 months

Recipes for freezing

Preservation of fresh food when it is at its best is the primary function of a freezer, but of course there is the secondary, labour-saving function of pre-cooked meals which can be served effortlessly and weeks later. The recipes given here will show the potential of a properly-utilized freezer. Game has the shortest season of any meat, so we have included a pâté, pie and casserole which make use of it when available, and can be served as marvellous dinner party dishes. In addition there are interesting soups which can be made in bulk and then frozen, some irresistible desserts including a spectacular cheese-cake, and of course, lots of versions of that wonderful standby, home-made ice-cream.

Game Pâté
8-10 servings

25g (1oz) plus 1 teaspoon butter
2 tablespoons vegetable oil
150g (6oz) pig's liver, washed and chopped
100g (4oz) lean bacon, finely chopped
1 small onion, finely chopped
1 clove of garlic, crushed
2 tablespoons flour
$\frac{1}{2}$ teaspoon salt
$\frac{1}{4}$ teaspoon black pepper
2 pheasants, jointed, the flesh removed from the bone and cut into strips, or
1 medium-sized duck or rabbit, jointed, the flesh removed from the bone and cut into strips
1 tablespoon chopped fresh parsley
1 tablespoon chopped fresh chives
$\frac{1}{2}$ teaspoon dried tarragon

In a medium-sized frying-pan, heat 25g (1oz) of the butter with the oil over moderate heat. When the foam subsides, add the liver and bacon pieces and cook them, stirring and turning occasionally, until the liver is cooked through. Add the onion and garlic to the pan and cook, stirring occasionally, until the onion is soft and translucent. Remove the pan from the heat, then remove the meat and onion and mince very finely. Set aside.

On a large plate, combine the flour, salt and pepper. Dip the pheasant, duck or rabbit strips in the flour, shaking off any excess.

Preheat the oven to moderate 180°C (350°F, Gas Mark 4).

Return the frying-pan to moderate heat and when the oil is hot again, add the meat strips to the pan. Cook them, stirring and turning occasionally, for five minutes, or until they are lightly browned. Remove the pan from the heat and set aside.

Lightly grease a deep aluminium foil dish or terrine with the teaspoon of butter. Spread about half the liver and onion mixture on the bottom of the dish. Top with a layer of about half of the meat strips, sprinkled with half of the parsley, half of the chives and half of the tarragon. Cover with the remaining meat strips and herbs and finish off with a layer of the liver and onion mixture. Cover the top of the pâté with aluminium foil.

Place the dish or terrine in a large, deep baking tin half-filled with boiling water and place the tin in the oven. Bake the pâté for $1\frac{1}{2}$ hours, or until it is well browned and has shrunk slightly from the sides of the container. When cooked, set it aside to cool to room temperature.

To freeze: If the pâté has been made in an aluminium foil dish, cover it securely with foil, and label. If it has been made in a terrine, place the terrine inside a sealed polythene bag or wrap securely in foil. Label and store.

Freezer storage life: Up to 4 months.

To serve: Remove from the freezer and allow to thaw for at least four hours at room temperature. Serve accompanied by fresh or Melba toast and butter.

Avocado Mousse
4-6 servings

3 avocado pears
Juice of 1 lemon
4 tablespoons olive oil
175ml (7fl oz) double cream
2 teaspoons sugar
Salt and pepper, to taste

Halve the avocado pears, remove the stones and scoop the flesh out into a mixing bowl. Mash the flesh with a fork and beat in the lemon juice; then gradually add the oil, beating all the time. Stir in the cream, sugar and season to taste. (This can be done in an electric blender.)

To freeze: Spoon the mousse into a large container or individual small ones, leave 10mm ($\frac{1}{2}$in) headspace. Cover, seal and label.

Freezer storage life: Up to 2 months.

To serve: Leave to thaw out for 4-6

Left: Game pâté is a rich, textured pâté which could be served with toast as a dinner party first course, or eaten with French bread as part of an informal lunch. Below: An avocado pear.

163

hours. If necessary give it a gentle stir. Spoon into individual serving dishes and garnish with a sprinkling of cayenne pepper and a few prawns if liked.

Chilled Summer Soup
4-6 servings

35g (1½oz) butter
½ lettuce, chopped
1 bunch watercress, chopped
1 bunch spring onions, chopped
400ml (¾ pint) homogenized milk
400ml (¾ pint) water
1 chicken stock cube
Salt and pepper
150ml (5fl oz) yogurt

Heat the butter in a large pan. Add the lettuce, watercress and spring onions, and cook, covered, over a gentle heat for 10 minutes. Add the milk, water, stock cube and seasoning, bring to the boil and simmer for 20 minutes or until the vegetables are tender. Remove from the heat, and either sieve or purée in a blender.

To freeze: Remove any fat from the surface, pour into rigid containers leaving 10mm (½in) headspace. Cover, seal and label.

Freezer storage life: Up to 4 months.

Many types of cream soup can be made which freeze well and can be cooked straight from the freezer. Using the basic recipes given here and overleaf you can vary the ingredients, using almost any combination of vegetables. Chicken, tomato, cucumber or carrot could all be used as well as mushrooms and clams. The important point to remember is that these soups freeze better if the cream is omitted initially, and only added immediately before serving.

To serve: Thaw in the refrigerator overnight, or 3 hours at room temperature. Stir in the yogurt.

Cream of Mushroom Soup
4 servings

50g (2oz) butter
225g (8oz) mushrooms, wiped and sliced
2 shallots or spring onions, finely chopped
350ml (12fl oz) chicken stock
150ml (5fl oz) milk
2 tablespoons flour
150ml (5fl oz) single cream
½ teaspoon salt
½ teaspoon white pepper

In a medium-sized saucepan, melt three-quarters of the butter over moderate heat. Add the mushrooms and shallots or spring onions and sauté them for 3 minutes. Add the chicken stock and milk to the pan and bring to the boil.

Reduce the heat to low, cover the pan and simmer for 20 minutes.

Put the liquid and vegetables in a blender or through a food mill to make a smooth purée.

In a large saucepan, melt the remaining butter over moderate heat. Remove the pan from the heat and stir in the flour, mixing to a smooth paste. Return the pan to the heat and gradually add the blended soup, stirring continuously until it comes to the boil. Lower the heat and stir in the salt and pepper. Allow to cool.

To freeze: Remove any fat from the surface, pour into rigid containers and cover leaving 10mm (½in) headspace. Seal and label.

Freezer storage life: Up to 3 months.

To serve: Bring the soup to the boil. Cool slightly and add the cream and

seasoning, a little at a time. Do not let the soup boil once the cream has been added.

Cream of Clam Soup
4 servings

2 tablespoons butter
1 medium-sized onion, minced
1 clove of garlic, crushed
1 tablespoon flour
250ml (8fl oz) fish stock, strained
125ml (4fl oz) white wine
Bouquet garni, consisting of 4 parsley sprigs, 1 thyme spray and 1 bay leaf tied together
½ teaspoon salt
½ teaspoon white pepper
450g (1lb) canned minced clams with their juice
175ml (6fl oz) single cream
1 tablespoon chopped fresh parsley

In a large saucepan melt the butter over moderate heat. Add the onion and garlic and cook until they are soft but not brown. Remove the pan from the heat and stir in the flour, mixing to a smooth paste. Gradually add the fish stock, white wine, bouquet garni, salt and pepper to the pan and return it to the heat. Bring the liquid to the boil, stirring constantly. Reduce the heat and simmer, covered, for 15 minutes.

Add the clams and their juice to the pan. Raise the heat to high and bring the mixture to the boil. Reduce the heat to low and simmer for 5 minutes. Remove and discard the bouquet garni. Allow to cool.
To freeze: Skin off any fat, pour into rigid containers leaving 10mm (½in) headspace. Cover, seal and label.
Freezer storage life: Up to 3 months.
To serve: Bring the soup to the boil, then cool slightly. Add the cream to the soup, a little at a time, stirring constantly. Heat the soup gently until it is hot but not boiling.

Pour the soup into a warmed tureen and sprinkle it with parsley. Serve at once.

Jerusalem Artichoke Soup
4 servings

450g (1lb) Jerusalem artichokes
25g (1oz) butter or margarine
1 onion, chopped

4 sticks celery, chopped
600ml (1 pint) stock, or water and a chicken stock cube
300ml (½ pint) homogenized milk
1 tablespoon cornflour
Salt and pepper
1 tablespoon chopped fresh parsley

Peel the artichokes under cold running water to prevent discoloration. Chop roughly. Melt the butter in a pan and sauté the artichokes, onion and celery gently, covered, for about 10 minutes. Add the stock, cover, and simmer gently for about 35 minutes or until the vegetables are very soft. Either rub the soup through a sieve or purée in a blender. Gradually blend the milk into the cornflour. Heat the soup to boiling point, then add the milk and seasoning

Left: Pea and Celery Soup can be garnished with chopped parsley.
Above: Celery stalks are 'earthed up' during cultivation to blanch the stems and improve the flavour.

and continue to cook, stirring all the time until the soup has thickened. Taste, and adjust the seasoning. Remove from the heat and allow to cool.
To freeze: Place the cooled soup in a rigid tub leaving 10mm ($\frac{1}{2}$in) headspace, cover, seal and label.
Freezer storage life: Up to 3 months.
To serve: Reheat the soup gently until piping hot. Sprinkle with parsley and serve with croûtons.

Celery and Pea Soup
4 servings

50g (2oz) butter
1 head celery, washed and sliced
1 onion, peeled and chopped
1 litre (1$\frac{3}{4}$ pints) chicken stock
225g (8oz) peas
Salt and pepper to taste

Melt the butter in a large saucepan and fry the celery and onion for 2 minutes, stirring occasionally. Add the stock and simmer for 15 minutes or until the celery is soft. Add the peas and simmer for a further 15-20 minutes. Season to taste. Sieve or blend the soup and allow to cool.
To freeze: Remove any fat from the surface, pour into containers leaving 10mm ($\frac{1}{2}$in) headspace. Cover, seal and label.
Freezer storage life: Up to 4 months.
To serve: Bring soup to the boil and serve with croûtons or Melba toast.

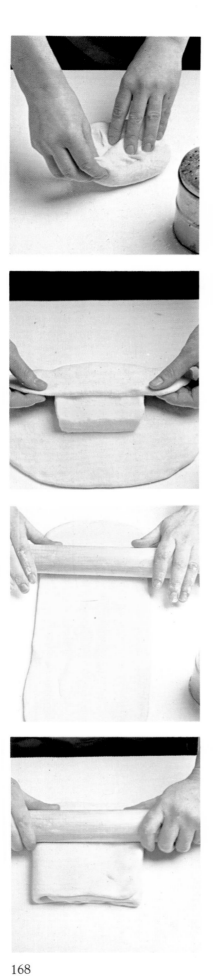

Venison Pie
4-6 servings

**675g (1½lb) boned shoulder of
venison cut into 25mm (1in) cubes**
**225g (8oz) lambs' kidneys, prepared,
cleaned and chopped**
1 teaspoon salt
½ teaspoon black pepper
**¾ teaspoon mixed spice or ground
allspice**
¼ teaspoon ground mace
1 large onion, finely chopped
2 tablespoons chopped fresh parsley
250ml (8fl oz) home-made beef stock
175 (6oz) puff pastry dough
50ml (2fl oz) red wine
1 tablespoon red wine vinegar
2 tablespoons olive oil
1 egg yolk, lightly beaten

Place the venison, kidneys, salt, pepper,
mixed spice or allspice, mace, onion
and parsley in a large saucepan. Pour
over the stock.

Place the pan over high heat and
bring the liquid to the boil. Cover the
pan with a well-fitting lid, reduce the
heat to low and simmer for 2 hours,
until the meat is tender.

Remove the pan from the heat. Set
aside to cool completely. When the
meat mixture is cold, skim off and discard any fat from the surface of the
juices.

On a lightly floured board, roll out
the dough into a 25cm (10in) circle.
Using a sharp knife, cut a strip from
the outside of the circle approximately
25mm (1in) wide. Press the strip on to
the rim of a 23cm (9in) pie dish.

Using a slotted spoon, transfer the
venison and kidneys to the pie dish.
Pour over 75ml (3fl oz) of the cooking
liquid, the wine, vinegar and oil. Discard the remaining cooking liquid.
Place a pie funnel in the middle of the
dish. Moisten the edges of the dough
already in the dish with a little water.
Lift the dough circle on to the pie dish
and press the edges together to seal
them. Trim the edges, and using a
pastry brush, brush the dough with the
beaten egg yolk.

To freeze: Cover the dish with
aluminium foil or polythene sheet.
Seal with freezer tape and label.

Freezer storage life: Up to 3 months.

To serve: The pie may be cooked
while still frozen or left to thaw out
for 6 to 8 hours at room temperature.

Preheat the oven to fairly hot, 200°C
(400°F, Gas Mark 6).

*Left: Venison Pie is a rich and
satisfying dish, covered with a puff
pastry case. Far left: Making puff
pastry. Make a dough from 450g
(1lb) flour, ½ teaspoon salt, 125g
(4oz) butter and 250ml (8fl oz) iced
water. Crumble the butter and
salted flour together and add enough
water to make a firm dough. Knead
it for a few minutes to make it
smooth and pliable. Chill for 15
minutes. Beat 350g (12 oz) butter
into an oblong. Roll out the dough
and place the butter on it. Fold the
four sides of the dough over the
butter to enclose it completely in a
neat parcel. With folds downwards
roll out the pastry away from you.
Fold the rolled dough in three, and
then turn so the open end is away
from you. Roll out again into an
oblong, fold it as before and chill in
the refrigerator, before rolling out
and covering the pie dish.*

Pheasant Casserole is a good dish to serve at a special occasion. Use mature pheasants as plump young pheasants are best roasted whole.

If frozen, cook the pie for 45 to 55 minutes or until the centre is hot. If the pastry starts to brown too quickly cover it with aluminium foil.

If thawed, cook the pie as above but for a shorter time – about 25 to 30 minutes should be sufficient.

Pheasant Casserole
4 servings

2 mature pheasants
25g (1oz) butter
1 tablespoon oil
1 large onion, sliced
50g (2oz) flour
600ml (1 pint) stock, or water and a stock cube
Grated zest and juice of 1 orange
1 tablespoon redcurrant jelly
125ml (5fl oz) port
1 bay leaf
1 sprig of parsley
Salt and pepper

Heat oven to 170°C (325°F, Gas Mark 3). Cut the pheasants into four pieces. Heat the butter and oil in a pan and quickly fry the pheasants on all sides until they are a good golden colour.

Remove from the pan and place in a casserole. Add the onion to the pan and cook until soft. Mix in the flour and cook, stirring for a few minutes until golden brown. Gradually add the stock and bring to the boil, stirring all the time. Allow to thicken and add the remaining ingredients. Pour over the pheasant, cover, and cook for about 3 hours, depending on the age of the bird.

To freeze: Remove any fat from the surface, spoon into rigid containers or

aluminium foil dishes, leaving 25mm (1in) headspace. Cover, seal and label.
Freezer storage life: Up to 3 months.
To serve: Allow to thaw for 3 to 4 hours at room temperature. If packed in rigid container spoon into a heat-proof dish and reheat in the oven at original temperature for 45 minutes.

Russian-Style Beef
4-6 servings

650g (1½lb) rump steak
25g (1oz) butter
1 tablespoon vegetable oil
2 onions, peeled and chopped
2 cloves of garlic, crushed
2 tablespoons flour
2 tablespoons tomato paste
200g (8oz) tomatoes, peeled and chopped
3 teaspoons paprika

Salt and pepper to taste
300ml (10fl oz) red wine
250ml (8fl oz) soured cream

Cut the steak into thin strips and fry in the butter and oil until brown. With a slotted spoon remove the steak and place it in a saucepan. Fry the onions and garlic in the remaining butter and oil for 2 minutes. Stir in the flour, tomato paste and tomatoes and stir to blend. Pour the mixture into the saucepan with the steak, stir in the paprika, salt, pepper and wine. Bring to the boil then reduce the heat and simmer for 30 minutes. Set aside until cool.
To freeze: Remove any fat from the top and pour the mixture into a foil dish. Cover, seal and label.
Freezer storage life: Up to 3 months.
To serve: Allow to soften slightly then place the stroganoff in a saucepan and bring slowly to the boil. Add the soured cream and serve at once.

Russian-Style Beef is an adaptation of the classic Russian dish Beef Stroganoff, specifically designed for home freezing. It is easy to prepare after freezing so is an ideal dish for unexpected but important guests. Add 175g (6oz) whole button mushrooms before the final cooking. Serve with rice and a green vegetable or salad.

Redcurrant Cheesecake is a spectacular dessert which freezes well and would bring a welcome touch of summer to a winter meal.

Redcurrant Cheesecake
6-8 servings

100g (4oz) plus 1 teaspoon butter, melted
200g (8oz) crushed digestive biscuits
1 teaspoon ground cinnamon
450g (1lb) cream cheese
50g (2oz) castor sugar
475ml (19fl oz) double cream
550g (1¼lb) redcurrants, trimmed
10g (½oz) gelatine, dissolved in 2 tablespoons boiling water
1 egg white, stiffly beaten

Lightly grease a 23cm (9in) loose-bottomed cake tin with the teaspoon of butter. Set aside.

Combine the crushed biscuits, the remaining melted butter and the cinnamon together with a wooden spoon. Line the base of the cake tin with the biscuit mixture, pressing it firmly against the bottom of the tin with your fingers or with the back of the wooden spoon. Set aside

Beat the cream cheese and sugar together with the wooden spoon until the mixture is smooth and creamy. Stir in 100ml (4fl oz) of cream and 450g (1lb) of the redcurrants. Beat in the dissolved gelatine mixture and spoon it on to the biscuit base. Place the tin in the refrigerator to chill for 30 minutes or until the mixture has set.

Meanwhile beat the remaining double cream until it forms stiff peaks. With a large metal spoon, fold the egg white into the cream.

Remove the cake tin from the refrigerator. Spoon the cream mixture on to the cheesecake, making swirling patterns with the back of the spoon.

Then sprinkle the remaining redcurrants over the cream.

Note: This cheesecake would be equally spectacular made with blackcurrants, raspberries, blueberries or loganberries.

To freeze: It is probably best to leave the cheesecake in its tin to freeze, wrapping it securely in aluminium foil, sealing and labelling it.

Freezer storage life: Up to 3 months.

To serve: Thaw for 2 to 3 hours at room temperature or, better still, overnight in the refrigerator. Serve with extra whipped cream, if liked.

Frozen Gooseberry Fool
4 servings

450g (1lb) gooseberries
300ml (½ pint) water
Sprig of mint
100g (4oz) sugar
A little green food colouring
300ml (½ pint) double cream, lightly whipped

Top and tail the gooseberries. Put them in a pan with the water and mint, cover, and simmer gently for about 15 minutes until soft. Remove from the heat, stir in the sugar and a little green colouring. Discard the mint sprig. Sieve, or purée in a blender and then sieve to remove all the pips. Allow to cool, and blend the cooled mixture with the lightly whipped cream.

Note: When fresh gooseberries are not obtainable, use 650g (1½lb) canned or bottled gooseberries and omit the sugar and water. Drain off all but 6 tablespoons of the fruit syrup, then sieve or purée in a blender.

To freeze: Place in a covered plastic container and label.

Freezer storage life: Up to 3 months.

To serve: Allow to soften for 1 hour before serving. Turn into 4 ramekin dishes and decorate each with a sprig of mint or a few extra gooseberries.

Gooseberries can be frozen either in a free-flow pack or in light sugar syrup. Frozen Gooseberry Fool freezes them in another form, ready-prepared to serve at very little notice, since it must be served cold.

Ice-cream can either be made 'still-frozen' or with an ice-cream churn or electric ice-cream maker. Still-frozen ice-cream must be beaten during freezing. This should be done 30 minutes after first placing the ice-cream in the storage compartment or freezer, and again when the mixture is almost solid. If you use an electric ice-cream maker (below), you will have much softer, velvety ice-cream, so it is well worth investing in one if you make ice-cream regularly. The apparatus fits into the freezer or storage compartment. The mixture is poured into a container equipped with paddles, which churn it continuously during freezing. This breaks up the ice crystals and aerates the mixture. When the paddles are no longer able to turn, the ice-cream is ready.

Vanilla Ice-Cream
4 servings

300ml (10fl oz) milk
3 egg yolks
50g (2oz) castor sugar
½ teaspoon vanilla essence
300ml (10fl oz) double cream, beaten until thick

Place the milk in a saucepan and bring almost to the boil. Beat in the egg yolks, sugar and vanilla essence. Strain into a clean saucepan and cook over low heat until the mixture thickens and coats the back of a wooden spoon.

Pour into a mixing bowl and place in the freezer for about an hour, until almost hard. Whisk well and add the cream.

Spoon into a waxed or aluminium container, leaving 10mm (½in) head-space. Cover, seal and label. Return to the freezer.

Freezer storage life: Up to 6 months.
To serve: Leave to soften for about 10 minutes, then serve.

For Chocolate Ice-Cream, add 50g (2oz) melted plain chocolate to the hot milk.

For Coffee Ice-Cream, add 1 tablespoon coffee essence to the mixture before adding the cream.

For Raspberry or Strawberry Ice-Cream, add 300ml (10fl oz) of fruit purée instead of the whipped cream.

Minted Lemon Ice
8 servings

175g (6oz) castor sugar

375ml (12fl oz) water
Grated rind and juice of 3 large
lemons
4 tablespoons finely chopped fresh
mint
150ml (5fl oz) double cream
3 tablespoons single cream
(optional)

Place the sugar and water into a saucepan. Stir gently over low heat until the sugar dissolves, then bring to the boil.

Remove the pan from the heat and stir in the grated rind of lemon and strained lemon juice – there should be 125ml (4fl oz) of lemon juice. Stir in the chopped mint and, when cool, pour the mixture into ice trays, cover with aluminium foil and freeze. After 1 hour, when the ice is firm, remove it from the freezer, and break it up with a fork until mushy and smooth.

Lightly whip the creams together in a large mixing bowl. Then gradually fold in the lemon ice.

To freeze : Pour the mixture into rigid containers, leaving 10mm (½in) headspace. Cover, seal and label.

Freezer storage life : Up to 3 months.

To serve : Thaw slightly, then spoon the ice into demi-tasses or small glasses and top each with sprigs of fresh mint.

Lemon Sorbet
6 servings

Grated rind of 1 lemon and juice
of 2 lemons
Cold water
75g (3oz) castor sugar
1 teaspoon gelatine
2 egg whites

Mix lemon rind and juice and add cold water to make 1 litre (1¾ pints). Place in a saucepan with the sugar and bring to the boil. Remove from the heat and whisk in the gelatine. Pour into a mixing bowl and place in the freezer until just beginning to harden.

Meanwhile whisk the egg whites until stiff and beat into the lemon mixture.

Pour into containers, leaving 10mm (½in) headspace, cover, seal and label. Return to the freezer.

Freezer storage life : Up to 6 months.
To serve : Leave to soften for about 30 minutes then spoon into serving dishes. Decorate with a slice of fresh lemon and serve with sponge fingers.

For Orange Sorbet, use the juice of 1 orange and grated rind of 3 oranges or a can of frozen orange juice diluted with 1 tablespoon of grated orange rind. Both orange and lemon sorbet can be frozen, and then served, in their scooped-out skins. Slice the tops off carefully, remove all the flesh and as much of the pith as you can with a sharp fruit knife and chill before packing with the sorbet mixture.

For Strawberry, Raspberry and other soft fruit sorbets, use 300ml (10fl oz) of fruit purée in place of the lemon or orange rind and juice.

Brown Bread Ice-Cream
8 servings

475ml (17fl oz) vanilla ice-cream
4 small slices brown bread
1 teaspoon ground cinnamon
125ml (4fl oz) water
75g (3oz) sugar

Place the ice-cream in a large mixing bowl and allow it to soften a little, breaking it up with a fork if it is very frozen.

Remove the crusts from the bread and discard. Crumble the rest and mix it with the ground cinnamon.

Place the water and sugar in a small pan and stir over medium heat until the sugar dissolves. Then increase the heat and boil until the mixture caramelizes and turns golden. Remove the pan from the heat and stir in the breadcrumbs, then swiftly blend the mixture into the ice-cream before the breadcrumbs form large lumps.

To freeze : Turn the mixture into a rigid container, leaving 10mm (½in) headspace. Cover, seal and label.
Freezer storage life : Up to 3 months.
To serve : Leave to soften for about half an hour before serving.

Right: Lemon or Orange Sorbets are among the lightest and most refreshing desserts and are especially recommended to be served after a fairly rich main course. Far right: So many ice-creams can be made successfully at home: shown here, from top to bottom, are Brown Bread Ice-Cream, Apricot Ice-Cream, Coffee Ice-Cream, Strawberry Ice-Cream and Minted Lemon Ice-Cream.

Drying

Drying is another of the very early methods of preserving food. In prehistoric times cereals, berries, nuts and fruit were left in the sun and then stored for the winter months. The American Indians dried meat in the same way – it was known as *pemmican*. It is interesting to note that samples of dried food found in archaeological digs at Jericho have been estimated to be 4,000 years old!

Even today sun drying is carried out in some parts of the world. In addition air or wind drying, mainly of fish, is carried out in northern areas of Europe. Cod and herring are usually salted before drying, and in Scandinavia they are produced in this way on a commercial scale. It is possible to dry your own fish, although once again this method is not recommended as a long-term method of preserving. It should be done during cold, preferably windy, weather when there is little or no humidity, using freshly caught herring or whiting. Sprinkle the fish generously on both sides with coarse salt and leave them on a flat dish or tray overnight. This will begin the drying process by drawing much of the water out of the fish. Then thread a cane or thin stick through the gills and mouth, or insert 'S' hooks into the jawbones of the fish. Hang them outside in an exposed position for a couple of days. Use them immediately, and, after cleaning, serve fried with plain boiled potatoes and a fresh vegetable. Salt fish is dried in many other parts of the world, especially in African and West Indian communities, and it is stocked by many delicatessens and speciality shops. For further information about salt fish, see page 201.

For all drying, the basic principle is the same: to remove all moisture from the food, usually by heat, thus inhibiting the growth of enzymes which cause rapid deterioration of food.

Some fruits, vegetables and herbs can easily be dried at home, although it may take up to a week to ensure complete evaporation of moisture.

The two main essentials for drying foods at home are correct temperature and plenty of ventilation. The ideal temperature of the circulating air should be between 50°C and 65°C (120°F and 150°F) – if the temperature is too high the food will 'cook' and shrivel up so the end result will be unsatisfactory. The most obvious place for drying food is in the oven; however most ovens do not have a low enough temperature, but you can use the residual heat left after cooking, with the oven turned off. This is quite satisfactory but it does mean the process cannot be continuous and will have to be carried out over several days. Ideal places for continuous drying are an airing cupboard (if there is space) or over a central heating boiler.

Equipment
As previously mentioned, ventilation is important so that the warm

Above: Air-drying fish at Skarsvag in Norway. The cold dry atmosphere of northern Scandinavia is ideal for fish drying. Opposite: Fish drying in Ghana, where the sun's heat is used to evaporate the moisture.

air can circulate freely. Consequently the food should be placed on trays or racks with wooden slats or a cheesecloth base. These may be bought or very easily constructed. An alternative is a fine wire cooling tray covered with a piece of cheesecloth or muslin so that the imprint of the wire does not mark the fruit. If new cheesecloth or muslin is used it should be washed and dried before using, otherwise it could give the food an unpleasant flavour.

Preparation of fruit

The most suitable fruits for domestic drying are apples, apricots, pears and plums. Small fruits and berries are not usually suitable for drying as they discolour and do not retain their original shape when cooked. However some varieties of small grapes, plums, figs and currants can be dried and can be an excellent substitute for commercially dried fruits in fruit cakes, breads and puddings. The fruit should be of the best quality and ripe – under-ripe fruits take much longer to dry and the colour and flavour will be impaired.

Apples and pears require peeling and coring. Apples should be cut

into 5mm (¼in) rings and pears into halves or quarters depending on the size. To prevent discoloration, place the pieces immediately into a bowl of cold, salted water (use about 50g (2oz) salt to 4 litres (1 gallon) water) for a few minutes. Lift out with a slotted spoon and pat dry with kitchen paper towels. Place the pieces of fruit in single layers on the drying tray. Cover the tray with a piece of muslin to keep the fruit clean while it is drying. To test that the apples and pears are completely dry, press two or three pieces together: they should feel rubbery and spring back into shape when the pressure is released. Remove the tray from the heat and leave for 12 hours before packing into airtight jars or containers. Store in a cool, dry place.

Plums and apricots (also figs) may be dried whole but if they are large they are better halved and stoned. Wash the fruit and place it on the tray – if halved they should be placed with the cut sides uppermost so that the juice does not run out. The fruit should be started at the lower temperature of 50°C (120°F) especially if they are whole, otherwise the skins will burst and some of the juice will be lost. When the skins begin to shrivel the temperature may be raised to 65°C (150°F) and the fruit left to dry completely.

Currants and grapes may be dried in the same way, but will probably need less time overall.

To test if whole fruit is dry, squeeze the skin gently. If it does not break or no juice comes out it is ready. Set aside for 12 hours before packing and storing.

Cooking dried fruit

Dried fruit should be soaked in cold water for several hours before use. After this they can be cooked in the soaking water, with sugar added a few minutes before the final cooking time. Alternatively the soaked fruit may be drained and used in pies, fruit crumbles and other hot or cold puddings.

Vegetables for drying

The most suitable vegetables for drying are string beans, haricot, kidney or lima beans, peas, onions and mushrooms, and like all home preserved produce they must be fresh and firm.

Peas and beans. Young tender beans may be dried whole but if they are older and tougher they are better sliced. Beans and peas should be blanched in boiling water for about three minutes, then drained and spread on trays. They should be dried at a temperature starting at 50°C (120°F) and the heat increased slowly until the temperature reaches 65°C (150°F).

The vegetables are dry when they are crisp and hard. They should be packed in jars or bottles with air-tight lids and stored in a dry, dark place. Beans and peas require soaking in cold water before use for about 12 hours or until they are soft, then they should be boiled before serving.

Onions that are to be dried should be medium to large in size, peeled and cut into 5mm (¼in) slices. Separate the slices into rings – use the very small centres for cooking fresh as they are difficult to dry satisfactorily.

Dip the onion rings into boiling water for about 30 seconds, drain and pat dry with kitchen paper towels. Spread the onion rings on to trays and dry at a temperature not higher than 65°C (150°F). When

Left: Dried fruit such as apples, apricots and raisins can be added to a sweet yeast dough to make delicious fruit breads, such as this one, Hutzelbrot from Germany, which is also flavoured with whole hazelnuts, fennel seeds and coriander. Above: Sweet black grapes can be seeded and dried to resemble commercially produced raisins.

183

they are crisp allow them to cool, then pack in bottles or jars with air-tight lids. Store in a dry, dark place.

Before using the onion rings first soak them in warm water for about 30 minutes. If the onions are to be fried or grilled pat them dry with kitchen paper towels.

Mushrooms should be very fresh. Peel if you prefer, or wipe them clean with a damp cloth. Spread the mushrooms on trays or thread them on fine string with a knot between each to prevent them touching each other. Dry at a temperature not higher than 50°C (120°F), until they are dry and shrivelled. Pack in jars or bottles. No lids are required but it is advisable to cover them with clean muslin or other material to prevent dust from entering the jars. Store in a dry place. Alternatively if the mushrooms have been threaded on a string they may be hung up in a dry, cool place.

Dried mushrooms may be used without preparation for casseroles, soups and other dishes with liquid that require long slow cooking. For frying or grilling they should be soaked in cold water for about 30 minutes and well drained before cooking.

Below: Mushrooms can be dried spread out on a tray. A basketwork or bamboo tray such as this would be very effective as the loose weave allows the air to circulate freely. Far right: Dried beans have been in culinary use for centuries as they are particularly suited to the drying process. Shown here, clockwise from the top: Oea, flageolet, black, broad, haricot, pinto, lima, butter, soya and red kidney.

184

*Above: Common marjoram,
Oreganum vulgare, is a
useful herb to store dried.
Right: Bouquets garnis made
from dried chopped herbs can
be stored in the kitchen for use
at a moment's notice in
casseroles, stews and many
other dishes. Tie the herbs in
circles of muslin or cheesecloth.*

Drying your own herbs is satisfying as well as useful. It is easier to store them crushed or chopped in airtight containers, as these do not take up too much valuable space in the kitchen.

Dried herbs

It is most useful to have a selection of herbs in the store cupboard. Of course, commercially dried herbs are freely available, but if you grow your own herbs in a garden or window box or can obtain them fresh from a nursery or market then it is well worth drying some, particularly for use in winter.

The herbs should be picked when the plants are just about to flower, but not immediately after it has rained. After washing and shaking dry, small leaved herbs such as thyme, parsley, rosemary and savory can be loosely tied in a piece of muslin and hung up to dry out in a warm place.

Larger leaved herbs such as bay leaf, mint, sage or basil dry better if the leaves are stripped off the stems and tied in muslin. After drying the leaves may be left whole, or crushed with a rolling pin. Pack the herbs in small bottles with air-tight lids to prevent loss of flavour and store them in a dry, dark place.

As dried herbs have a more concentrated flavour than fresh ones use only half the quantity if fresh herbs are mentioned in recipes.

'Bouquets garnis'

A term frequently referred to in cooking is *bouquet garni* – this is a bunch of herbs – usually consisting of a bay leaf, sprig of parsley and thyme – which are tied together and used in soups and casseroles. It is useful to prepare some of these and dry them so they are ready for instant use. The *bouquet garni* should be removed from the cooked dish before serving.

Recipes for using dried foods

Dried vegetables and fruits can add variety and nourishment to your meals in a number of ways, and the recipes here include many dishes which are particularly satisfying during the lean, cold months of winter.

Boston Baked Beans
6-8 servings

225g (8oz) fat salt pork
1kg (2lb 2oz) dried haricot, pea or kidney beans, washed and drained
2 teaspoons salt
1 large onion
75g (3oz) soft brown sugar
6 tablespoons molasses or black treacle
3 teaspoons dry mustard
1 teaspoon black pepper

Put the salt pork in a large bowl. Add cold water to cover. Soak for 3 hours and drain well.

Place the beans in a large saucepan and add enough cold water to cover. Add 1 teaspoon of salt. Bring the water to the boil over high heat and boil the beans for 2 minutes. Remove the pan from the heat and let the beans soak in the water for an hour.

Return the pan to the heat and bring the beans to the boil again. Reduce the heat to very low, partially cover the pan and slowly simmer the beans for 30 minutes. Drain and discard the liquid.

Preheat the oven to 130°C (250°F, Gas Mark ½).

Place the whole onion in the bottom of a large flameproof casserole. Add a layer of the cooked, drained beans to the casserole.

Thickly slice the drained salt pork and cut each slice into small chunks. Arrange a layer of salt pork over the beans in the casserole. Add another layer of beans and finish with pork.

Mix together the brown sugar, molasses (or treacle), mustard, black pepper and the remaining 1 teaspoon of salt. Spoon the mixture over the beans and pork. Add enough boiling water to cover the beans.

Cover the casserole and place it in the oven. Bake for 5 hours, adding boiling water from time to time so that the beans are always just covered.

Remove the lid of the casserole and bake uncovered for the last 45 minutes. Serve straight from the casserole.

Dried white haricot beans (far right) are the best to use for Boston Baked Beans. This warming dish is perfect for parties or late suppers as you can bake it for almost as long as you like, just checking from time to time that it is not drying out too much. Use your own salt pork, as well as dried beans, for this recipe (see page 212).

Salt Cod with Wine Sauce

4-6 servings

275g (10oz) long grain rice
600ml (1 pint) water
1½ teaspoons salt
1kg (2lb 2oz) salt cod, soaked in cold water for 24 hours
3 tablespoons olive oil
1 large onion, finely chopped
1 garlic clove, crushed
150g (5oz) canned tomato purée
½ teaspoon freshly ground black pepper
250ml (8fl oz) dry white wine
50ml (2fl oz) brandy
25g (1oz) butter

Put the rice in a medium-sized saucepan. Pour over the water and add 1 teaspoon of the salt. Place the pan over moderate heat and bring the water to the boil. Cover the pan, reduce the heat to very low and simmer the rice for 15 minutes, or until all the liquid has been absorbed and the rice is tender. Remove the pan from the heat and set aside in a warm place.

Drain the salt cod and dry it on kitchen paper towels. Skin the cod and chop into 35mm (1½in) pieces. Set aside.

In a large frying-pan, heat the oil over moderate heat. When the oil is hot, add the onion and garlic and cook, stirring occasionally, for 5 to 7 minutes, or until the onion is soft and translucent but not brown. Stir in the tomato purée, the remaining salt and the pepper and cook, stirring occasionally, for 3 minutes. Stir in the wine and bring the mixture to the boil, stirring frequently.

Add the salt cod and brandy to the pan, stirring well to combine all the ingredients. Reduce the heat to low, cover the pan and cook, stirring and turning the salt cod from time to time, for 20 to 25 minutes, or until the fish flakes easily when tested with a fork.

Meanwhile, in a large saucepan, melt the butter over moderate heat. When the foam subsides, add the rice to the pan. Cook, stirring frequently, for 3 to 5 minutes, or until the rice is heated through and is well coated with the butter.

Remove the pan from the heat.

Salt Cod in Wine Sauce is an unusual and exotic Mediterranean dish which turns the unpromising raw material of dried salt cod into a succulent dish fit for a dinner party.

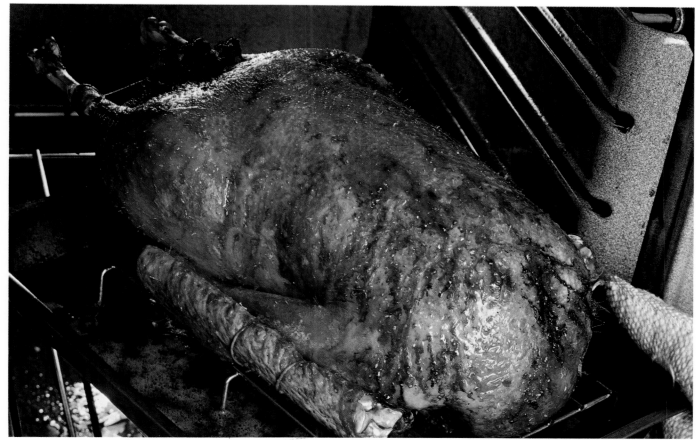

Arrange the rice in a ring on a warmed serving platter. Remove the frying-pan from the heat and spoon the fish and sauce into the centre of the rice ring. Serve at once.

Goose Stuffed with Apple and Prunes

6 servings

1 × 4kg (8lb) young goose
1 tablespoon salt
2 teaspoons ground black pepper
Half a lemon
450g (1lb) prunes, soaked overnight in 250ml (8fl oz) red wine or, better still, port
450g (1lb) dried apples, soaked overnight and drained, then diced

Heat the oven to 220°C (425°F, Gas Mark 7).

Make sure the goose is clean, dry and well trussed with string. Then rub it inside and out with salt, pepper and lemon. Prick the skin lightly all over with a fork to allow the surplus fat to run out while cooking.

Drain the prunes, remove the stones and chop them up. Mix them with the diced apple and stuff the goose with

Roast goose makes a welcome change from the other large birds, and the fruity flavour of dried apple and prune stuffing perfectly complements the taste of the meat.

the mixture.

Place the goose breast upwards in a roasting pan and cook for 15 minutes. Remove it from the oven, turn it on to one side and cover the pan with aluminium foil. Return to the oven and reduce the heat to 180°C (350°F, Gas Mark 4).

After 30 minutes, again remove the goose from the oven. Turn it on to the other side. Spoon 2 tablespoons of boiling water over the bird to help the fat run out, and tip the fat from the roasting pan.

Cook the bird for a further 1¾ to 2 hours, regularly pouring off surplus fat and turning the goose to ensure even cooking. Remove the foil for the final 15 minutes to brown the skin.

Fabada : Spanish Bean and Sausage Soup
6 servings

2 litres (3 pints) water
225g (8oz) dried white haricot beans, soaked overnight and drained
225g (8oz) dried broad beans, soaked overnight and drained
1 large onion, chopped
2 cloves of garlic, crushed
2 morcillas or 100g (4oz) similar blood sausages, sliced
1 teaspoon dried oregano
2 small chorizo or similar sausages, sliced
4 bacon slices, chopped
50g (2oz) smoked ham, chopped
½ teaspoon ground saffron
1½ teaspoons salt
1 teaspoon black pepper

In a large saucepan, bring the water to the boil over high heat. Add the white and broad beans, onion and garlic.

Bring the water back to the boil. Reduce the heat to low, cover the pan and simmer for 45 minutes to an hour, or until the beans are tender.

Add the morcillas or blood sausages, oregano, chorizo sausages, bacon, ham, saffron, salt and pepper and stir to mix. Continue simmering for 30 minutes. Pour into a warmed soup tureen and serve at once.

Centre: Fabada is a warming soup which, with its mixture of Spanish sausage and dried beans, is a meal in itself. Below: Either dried green or, more correctly, yellow split peas can be used to make wholesome Pease Pudding, a well-known British recipe.

Pease Pudding
4-6 servings

450g (1lb) dried peas, soaked overnight in cold water and drained
1 onion, peeled and chopped
2 teaspoons of salt
25g (1oz) butter
1 egg, beaten
Pepper, to taste

Place the peas, onion and salt in a saucepan and cover with cold water. Bring to the boil then reduce heat and simmer for 2-3 hours until the peas are soft.

Drain the peas and onion and push them through a sieve or purée in an electric blender.

Return the purée to a clean saucepan and place over a very low heat. Add the butter, egg and pepper and stir all the time until the mixture is hot. Serve with boiled ham or roast pork.

Black peppercorns are an essential seasoning for both Fabada and Pease Pudding.

193

Above: Mixed Fruit Compôte is a useful and good-looking alternative to fruit salad when fresh fruit is scarce. Right: Zurich Fruit Crumble makes good use of almost any kind of dried fruit.

Mixed Fruit Compôte
4-6 servings

125ml (4fl oz) sweet vermouth
125ml (4fl oz) orange juice
350ml (12fl oz) water
225g (8oz) sugar
1 × 50mm (2in) piece of cinnamon stick
Grated rind of 1 lemon
1kg (approx 2lb) mixed dried fruit – apples, apricots, pears, prunes, raisins etc – soaked overnight in cold water and drained

Place the vermouth, orange juice, water, sugar, cinnamon and lemon rind in a large saucepan. Bring to the boil, reduce the heat and add the fruit. Simmer very gently for 15 to 20 minutes until the fruit is soft.

Remove the fruit with a slotted spoon and place it in a heatproof serving dish.

Strain the cooking syrup into a clean saucepan and boil it for about 15 minutes until it reduces slightly. Pour the syrup over the fruit and serve hot or cold with cream.

Zurich Fruit Crumble
6 servings

300ml (10fl oz) water
250ml (8fl oz) white wine
150g (5oz) sugar
100g (4oz) dried apricots, soaked overnight and drained
100g (4oz) dried figs, soaked

Above: Desiccated coconut is added to the crumble topping of Zurich Fruit Crumble. Above right: Pears, peaches and plums can all be dried for use in desserts.

overnight and drained
**100g (4oz) dried peaches, soaked
overnight and drained
100g (4oz) dried prunes, soaked
overnight and drained
100g (4oz) dried pears, soaked
overnight and drained
100g (4oz) dried apples, soaked
overnight and drained
50g (2oz) shelled pistachio nuts
50g (2oz) shelled Brazil nuts
75g (3oz) desiccated coconut
75g (3oz) flour
75g (3oz) butter, softened**

Pour the water and wine into a large saucepan and set the pan over moderate heat. Add 50g (2oz) of the sugar and stir until it has dissolved. When the sugar has completely dissolved, add the dried fruits and nuts. Increase the heat to high and bring the mixture to the boil, stirring constantly. Reduce the heat to low and simmer for 20 minutes. Taste the syrup and add more sugar if desired.

Preheat the oven to moderate 180°C (350°F, Gas Mark 4).

Remove the pan from the heat and, using a slotted spoon, transfer the fruits and nuts to a large ovenproof dish. Set aside.

In a medium-sized mixing bowl, combine the coconut, flour, butter and the remaining sugar. Using your fingertips, rub the ingredients together until the mixture resembles fine bread-crumbs.

Cover the fruit mixture with the crumble mixture and place the dish in the centre of the oven. Bake for 20 to 30 minutes or until the crumble is cooked and golden brown.

Remove the dish from the oven and serve immediately with cream or custard.

Pear and Ginger Sponge
4 servings

**450g (1lb) dried pears, soaked
overnight in cold water and drained
50g (2oz) crystallized ginger, chopped
50g (2oz) soft brown sugar
50g (2oz) butter or margarine
50g (2oz) castor sugar
1 egg
75g (3oz) self-raising flour**

Preheat the oven to 180°C (350°F, Gas Mark 4).

Slice the pears and place them in an ovenproof dish with the ginger and soft brown sugar.

Cream the butter or margarine with

the castor sugar. Beat in the egg and stir in the flour. If necessary add a little warm water to give a smooth cake-like consistency.

Spread the cake mixture over the pears and bake for 30 minutes until the sponge is risen and golden brown.

Plum Cobbler
4-6 servings

650g (1½lb) dried plums or prunes, soaked overnight in cold water and drained
300ml (10fl oz) water
100g (4oz) sugar
25g (1oz) chopped almonds
75g (3oz) butter or margarine
175g (6oz) self-raising flour
25g (1oz) castor sugar
Milk to mix

Preheat the oven to 200°C (400°F, Gas Mark 6).

Place the plums and water in a saucepan and simmer for 10 minutes. Remove the plums and place them in a greased baking dish with half of the cooking liquid, the sugar and almonds.

Rub the butter or margarine into the flour, add the sugar and enough milk to make a soft textured dough. Roll the dough out to about 10mm (½in) thick and cut into rounds. Place rounds on top of the fruit. Brush the dough with a little milk and sprinkle with castor sugar. Bake for 15-20 minutes or until the topping is cooked and golden brown. Serve hot with custard or cream.

Spiced Apple Cake
6 servings

225g (8oz) dried apples, soaked overnight in cold water and drained
100g (4oz) butter or margarine
100g (4oz) soft brown sugar
2 eggs
225g (8oz) self-raising flour
1 teaspoon mixed spice
1 teaspoon baking powder
Candied orange peel (optional)

Grease an 18cm (7in) cake tin with butter and line with greaseproof paper. Preheat the oven to 180°C (350°F, Gas Mark 4).

Place the drained apples on kitchen paper towels and pat dry. Chop the apples into pieces and set aside.

Cream the butter or margarine and

Spiced Apple Cake can be decorated with slices of candied orange peel (see page 105). Alternatively omit the peel and sprinkle the cake with castor sugar or coat it with glacé icing.

197

Caramel peaches is a sumptuous eye-catching dish which is in fact very easy to make, with dried or bottled peaches. If you like you can spice up the recipe by adding a little chopped preserved ginger with the peaches.

sugar. Beat in the eggs, one at a time. Sieve the flour, mixed spice and baking powder and stir into the butter and sugar mixture. Stir in the apples and, if necessary, add a little milk to make a fairly stiff dropping consistency. Spoon the mixture into the prepared tin and arrange the pieces of orange peel on top, if liked. Bake for about 45 minutes to an hour or until the cake is firm and a skewer inserted into the centre of the cake

comes out dry.

Turn the cake out on to a wire rack and leave to cool.

Caramel Peaches
4 servings

450g (1lb) dried peach halves, soaked overnight in cold water and drained

50g (2oz) blanched, toasted almonds
350ml (12fl oz) double cream
100g (4oz) soft brown sugar

Simmer the peaches in a little water and sugar until they are soft. Drain and place them in a shallow heatproof dish. Sprinkle the almonds over the peaches and set aside to cool.

Whip the cream until it is thick and spread it evenly over the top of the peaches.

Sprinkle the sugar over the cream and place under a hot grill until the sugar caramelizes. Serve at once.

Oriental Fruit Salad
6 servings

125ml (4fl oz) clear honey
75ml (3fl oz) kirsch
10 dried figs, stalks removed and coarsely chopped
20 dried dates, halved and stoned
60g (2½oz) whole unblanched hazelnuts
60g (2½oz) whole unblanched almonds
1 medium-sized melon (honeydew, cantaloup, ogen, etc)

In a medium-sized shallow dish, combine the honey and kirsch. Add the figs, dates, hazelnuts and almonds. Stir well to coat the fruit and nuts with the liquid. Cover the dish and set aside to soak for 4 hours, stirring occasionally.

Using a sharp knife, cut the melon in half. With a sharp-edged metal spoon, scoop out and discard the seeds. Peel the melon and discard the skin. Chop the flesh into cubes.

Stir the melon cubes into the fruit and nut mixture. Place the dish in the refrigerator and chill the fruit salad for at least 1 hour. Divide the fruit, nuts and liquid equally among 6 individual serving glasses and serve immediately.

Curing, smoking & salting

Curing is the method used to extend the edible life of food by salting and smoking. Both fish and meat can be preserved in this way: a well-known example of cured fish is smoked salmon, which may be first salted then smoked. Bacon is an example of cured meat – it may just be salted, or salted and then smoked. In many parts of the country, mainly farming communities, some curing is still done at home but for most city dwellers there is neither the time nor the opportunity to carry out these methods, apart from the fact that the raw material – salmon, or a whole leg of pork – can be very expensive! With the advance of food technology and the wider knowledge of the use of chemical preservatives, commercially cured foods – fish, meat and related products – are more convenient and, in many cases, safer to eat as the preservatives used are controlled by law. Recipes for home curing exclude the use of certain chemical preservatives which might be harmful to health if used indiscriminately. However the process has an interesting background and can be used domestically if great care is taken to follow the instructions and use the *exact* proportions of the ingredients. There are some superb recipes for using many salted or smoked foods. In addition dry salting can be used for some vegetables and nuts.

Salting fish : the background

Salting of fish may be carried out either in dry salt or by pickling in brine – a solution of salt and water. The preservative quality of salt was discovered by primitive man, but the process was originally confined to coastal regions and localities where salt was mined. Both Egypt and Asia Minor were areas rich in salt, and fish such as red mullet, bream, mackerel, eel and sword fish among others were salted and sent by the Romans all over their empire. Some of these fish can still be obtained in salted form in the markets of the Mediterranean. Large fish were usually cut into pieces and, when pickled in brine, spices and herbs were added to give variations of flavour. It is said that 200 recipes for the preparation and salting of fish were listed by the Greek writer Athenaeus in 200 AD.

In Britain salt was an important commodity in the Middle Ages. A connection with salt can be identified in some place names in localities where salt pans were used for the production of salt by evaporation of sea water. Some examples are Saltcoats in Ayrshire, Prestonpans on the Firth of Forth, and a part of the Beccles Fen in East Anglia called Solfon – meaning salt pan!

Although there are still some notable exceptions, especially in Scandinavian countries and the Mediterranean, the commercial salting and pickling of fish has declined in recent times, mainly as a result of considerable improvements in the distribution of fresh fish,

Left: Salmon smoking at the Pinney Smokehouses at Sternfield in Suffolk. The salmon is cured to a special recipe and then smoked over smouldering oak sawdust. Above: A member of the Fulani tribe of Sudanic Africa smokes strips of beef over an open fire.

These pictures were taken at the premises of R. Boston & Sons of Spittal, near Berwick-on-Tweed in Northumberland, on the Scottish Border. This old family firm has been in the fish trade for over a hundred years. The photographs show two crucial stages in the 'Scotch cure' of herrings, a process which remained unchanged in the forty years between which these two photographs were taken, and which was only finally overtaken as a method of fish preservation with the advent of efficient refrigeration. Above: Women sit gutting herrings brought in by the local fishing fleets (This picture dates from the late 1870s.)

a preference for unsalted, natural flavoured fish and more convenient methods of preserving such as canning and freezing. Home preservation methods have followed similar trends and freezing has rapidly become the easiest and most popular method of preserving fish.

Fish may be salted at home but the keeping times are short. However, we have included one method here for interest.

Salting fish at home

The most important factor is that the fish must be really fresh, either just out of the water or bought from a reputable fishmonger. Herring is the fish most commonly salted at home and may be used in a variety of recipes. Other salt fish may be purchased from some delicatessens or fishmongers.

To salt herrings keep them in a brine solution for one to two weeks. Make the brine with 3½ litres (6 pints) hot water, 550g (1¼lb) salt and 125g (4oz) sugar. Place the salt and sugar in a glass or earthenware bowl; pour in the water, stir until the salt is dissolved and set aside to cool. The brine must cover the herrings, so if you need more make it in the same proportions. However, 800ml (1½ pints) of brine are generally required for six to eight herrings. Gut, bone and clean the herrings and place them in the brine. Lightly cover and place in the refrigerator or cold pantry for a week or ten days. Use the fish within two weeks at the most.

Smoking

Drying in the heat of the sun was the earliest method of preserving

but it was more successful for cereals, fruits and vegetables than for fish and meat. Stone Age man discovered that smoke from a fire was more successful for the 'drying' of fish and meat as it kept the insects away, gave the produce a better flavour and helped to keep it edible for a longer time. Even so, the fish and meat were very tough and it was found in later years that preliminary salting improved the texture, flavour and keeping qualities of the food.

The 'Scotch cure' consisted of brining the fish over a period of eight days. Once the barrels were brimful with herrings they were sealed with tight-fitting lids. (This picture was taken in 1910.)

Varieties of smoked fish

Although smoking of fish is carried out in many countries it is a very British speciality, particularly in the North of England and in Scotland. Most fish can be smoked but the most popular are herrings, salmon, cod and cod's roe, haddock, mackerel and trout. Nowadays smoking is not used as a preservative for fish, but rather as a means of giving a subtle and unique flavour. The different flavours are produced by the type of wood used for the smoke and the temperature of the process. 'Hot smoking' uses a high temperature – trout, eels and the small haddocks known as Arbroath smokies are usually smoked in this way which means they are partly cooked as well. The other method is called 'cool smoking' which is done at a lower temperature and is used for salmon and haddock.

Herring is probably the most popular smoked fish and is available in many varieties all with different names. Kippers are fat herrings which are split down the back from head to tail, lightly brined and cool smoked. The word 'kipper' probably derives from the Dutch *kuppen* which means to spawn, and was first applied to out-of-season salmon. As these were thin and lacked fat they were split and smoked to make them more edible. The name goes back as early as the fourteenth century when there were references to the 'kipper time' in connection with salmon fishing on the Thames.

The kippers we know today were claimed to have been first made in the early nineteenth century by a man called John Woodger of Seahouses in Northumberland. The flavour of kippers varies depending on the kind of wood used and undoubtedly today the best kippers come from Loch Fyne in Scotland and the Isle of Man. Thanks to modern refrigerated lorries these may be obtained in most parts of Britain. These kippers are pale gold in colour. Bloaters, a speciality of Great Yarmouth, are whole herrings which are dry salted and very lightly smoked. They have a milder flavour than kippers and because of the light smoking do not keep so well. Bloaters should be split and filleted before cooking Buckling are also whole herrings which are smoked for a longer time and at a higher temperature which gives them a deep gold colour. They require no further cooking and make an excellent hors d'oeuvre.

Haddock is another popular fish that is smoked. It is often known as 'finnan haddie' because the first smoked haddock was said to have been produced in the fishing village of Findon in Scotland. Finnan

haddock is split, gutted and the head removed before being soaked in brine and then smoked. The result is a pale golden coloured fish that should not be confused with the bright yellow boneless fillets, sold in fishmongers and supermarkets, which are usually cod and have colouring added before being smoked.

Smokies, or more correctly Arbroath smokies, are small haddocks which are smoked whole. In the village of Arbroath in Scotland there are family businesses near the quay with their own smoke houses, where people come from far and wide just to buy and eat the local produce. Like buckling, smokies do not need any further cooking but can be heated at home in the oven or under the grill if you prefer them hot.

Trout and salmon are the most expensive smoked fish. Trout have a short storage time even after smoking, but with commercial quick freezing they are available in most parts of the country. Smoked trout do not require any further cooking and are best served cold with horseradish sauce. They also make the basis of a delicious pâté.

Smoked salmon is undoubtedly considered the prize of all smoked fish, not only because of its delicious taste but also because of its comparative scarcity and the skill that is required to smoke it.

Kippers are probably the most familiar of the British varieties of smoked herring. Many commercial brands contain food colouring, but good kippers obtain their warm golden brown colour and fine, moist texture simply from skilled smoking. Kippers have many uses: they are delicious grilled with a little butter, or poached gently in plain water, and eaten with fresh bread and butter. Many people find them particularly good for breakfast. In addition the cold flesh can be mashed to make an unusual pâté (see page 220), which is an economical first course.

Above: An effective smoker can be constructed quite easily from a barrel, as shown here, though an oil drum, packing case or even large cardboard box would do just as well. Stand the barrel on bricks to create an up-draught, and hang the fish from rods fixed across the top. Light a charcoal fire in an old metal bucket or similar container, and sprinkle hardwood sawdust or chips on top. Cover the whole apparatus with an old blanket or tarpaulin.
Right: Arbroath Smokies are small haddocks smoked in a particular way which originated in the fishing community of Arbroath in Scotland. Far right: The zenith of smoked fish, the taste and texture of smoked salmon are actually preferred by some to that of the fresh fish (overleaf). Salmon can be smoked at home if a little care is taken. Soak the fish in brine, with brown sugar or black treacle added, plus crushed garlic or onion, and lemon juice. Do not remove the skin, whatever the size of the piece you are smoking. Brine the fish for about an hour per 450g (1lb). Allow the fish to dry in a cool place for 24 hours, then cool smoke for up to 24 hours for a large piece.

Salmon is caught and smoked in many countries including Japan, Canada, America and Scandinavia but connoisseurs consider the best salmon to come from the Scottish rivers Tay and Dee, as the fish have a more delicate flavour and soft oily texture which make them most suited to smoking.

Home smoking of fish
Fish can be smoked at home although the results will differ from the commercially bought products which have been smoked under controlled conditions. However, providing the important basic rules are followed, it is an interesting and enjoyable process to carry out.

It is important to have the right equipment. Small kilns or smoking boxes can be bought but are relatively expensive and only worthwhile if a considerable amount of smoking is to be done. Otherwise a home smoker can be made from such simple objects as a metal box, metal wheelbarrow or from an old steel or wooden beer barrel.

An adequate supply of heat to produce smoke is also required. This can be a fire made from charcoal or briquets, which are placed in a bucket with holes punched around the sides, then covered with hardwood chips or sawdust to produce the smoke. Alternatively an electric hot plate or butane gas ring could be used, with a pan on top

for the hardwood chips or sawdust. Either way, it should be placed in the bottom of the smoke box.

Racks or hooks are required at the top of the smoker to hang or lay out the fish – these should be arranged so that the smoke reaches all surfaces of the fish.

A good draft is essential to allow the smoke to circulate freely – in a home-made smoker this will occur naturally but if the smoker is a permanent one built into a wall, it requires inlets near the source of heat and at the top. If the smoke is allowed to be too concentrated then the food will have an unpleasant sooty flavour.

It is most unwise to think of smoking food indoors unless you have a large old-fashioned fireplace, since, apart from the lack of draft, the smell will penetrate the whole house. If you have a suitable shed in the garden you could adapt it for use as a smoke house; otherwise situate the smoker in the garden, preferably on flag stones or concrete.

The best type of wood chips or sawdust to use are those from hardwood trees like oak, birch or walnut. Pine should not be used as it gives a resinous and unpleasant flavour to the food. Many sawmills or carpenters will supply wood chips and sawdust, but make sure you ask for the right type.

Methods of smoking

The brining and smoking of fish are based on the same principle whether done domestically or commercially. The strength of the brine can vary from a saturated solution (high salt content) to a weaker one depending on the flavour required. Normally a brine strength of 80° will be found suitable for most purposes. You can measure the strength by adding salt until an egg or peeled fresh potato will float on the surface of the solution. Alternatively, use a 'brineometer'. A brineometer looks rather like a glass thermometer with a large bulb at one end and a scale marked in degrees on the stem. The brineometer floats upright in the solution, and the strength of the brine is measured by reading the degrees on the scale at the surface of the solution.

An 80° strength brine is made with 1.20kg (2½lb) salt to 4 litres (8 pints) of water. (For method see page 202.) Ideally a fresh solution should be used each time but an existing batch of brine may be used again, unless it shows signs of scum, mould or smells 'off'. Extra ingredients can be added to the brine to give different and unusual flavours – for instance sugar, lemon juice, crushed garlic or onion – but they should be added sparingly until you find the exact flavour that is acceptable. Herbs also give a distinct flavour: the most suitable for fish are dill, crushed bay leaves, mace or allspice.

Cool smoking, in which the temperature should not rise above 30°C (70°F), is used for fish that is eaten uncooked like smoked salmon, and for smoked haddock or kippers that are cooked before serving.

The fish should be cleaned, gutted, and filleted if necessary, then soaked in the brine solution, from 30 minutes for small fish or fillets, and up to four or five hours for large whole fish. With home smoking there can be no rigid rules, so if one batch of fish tastes too salty reduce the brining time for the next. Hang up the fish in a clean place to dry slightly before smoking. Again the time for smoking depends on several factors but up to 24 hours is necessary for large fish. The colouring will tell you if the fish is smoked sufficiently, and

the flesh should be dry when pierced with a knife.

Hot smoking, when the fish is smoked and cooked at the same time, is suitable for buckling, mackerel, eel and trout. Soak the fish in brine and leave it to dry as for cool smoking. Start smoking the fish at a lower temperature, about 33°C (75°F) and raise it to 55-65°C (125-150°F).

To test if the fish is sufficiently smoked, pierce it with a knife and if the flesh flakes easily it is ready. If the fish is smoked whole or the pieces are very thick, use a meat thermometer to ensure that the centre is cooked. If it registers 60°C (140°F), the fish is ready.

Remember that smoking is not a true method of preservation. It is advisable to eat the fish within one or two days. For longer storage, the fish may be kept for up to two months in a freezer.

The 'short cut' smoker

For those who like camping or picnicking near rivers or the sea, freshly caught fish can be smoked in minutes in a small portable container which originated in Sweden. It can also be used for cooking outdoors at home, and it is great fun to cook fish this way either for the family or for parties. The fish should be fresh, then cleaned, gutted, and filleted or cut into pieces if large. Rub it with salt and leave for half an hour, then smoke. The smoke box is sold with a bag of sawdust and fuel container for methylated spirits, which is lit to cook and smoke the fish simultaneously.

Curing meat

As with fish, it is not usually advisable to treat home curing as a long term method of meat preservation, unless you are sure you can control the conditions for curing. However, home cured meat, whether salted or smoked, does give many interesting variations of flavour. Meat can be salted and used without being smoked, and beef, tongue and pork are often treated in this way. In addition, meat can be spiced, although spices were originally used to disguise the taste of food which was already stale! The methods given here all use brine made from salt and water. Meat can also be dry salted, but this is a risky process, which is not usually recommended as a method of home curing.

Salting beef

Make a brine solution with 900g (2lb) salt, 1 tablespoon saltpetre, 100g (4oz) sugar and 3 litres (6 pints) water. Bring to the boil and pour into a large mixing bowl or other non-metal container. Allow to cool before soaking the beef.

This quantity of brine is sufficient for a 2.25kg (5lb) piece of beef (the best cuts to use are brisket, silverside or topside). It is important that the brine should completely cover the beef. Cover the container and soak the beef for four to five days. The container must be kept in a cold place, ideally the refrigerator. Before cooking the beef rinse it well in cold running water.

Salting tongue

This method is suitable for the large ox tongues. For a 2kg (4lb) tongue, prepare a brine solution with 3½ litres (6¼ pints) boiling water, 450g (1lb) salt, 75g (3oz) sugar, a level tablespoon of saltpetre, a crushed clove of garlic and about 25g (1oz) pickling spice. Soak the

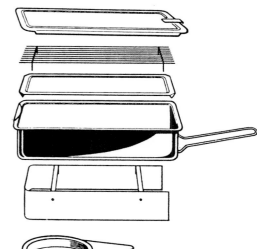

Left: There are several versions of the 'short cut' smoker on the market. Whichever you choose, it will make a welcome change to picnic, camping or fishing party catering. Above: a smoker generally divides into these main components: a small container for methylated spirits sits inside an aluminium guard. The sawdust is sprinkled on the base of the main pan, and is covered with a metal tray. The fish are placed on a rack over this and the smoker is covered with a sliding lid. Heat from the lighted spirit underneath is enough to singe the fine sawdust inside the smoker, thus cooking and smoking the fish simultaneously. Overleaf: Bradenham hams are distinguished by their thick coal black skin, although the flavour is delicate and sweet. The colouring comes from the special cure which is reputed to have originated in Yorkshire in the late eighteenth century, but which is now extensively used elsewhere.

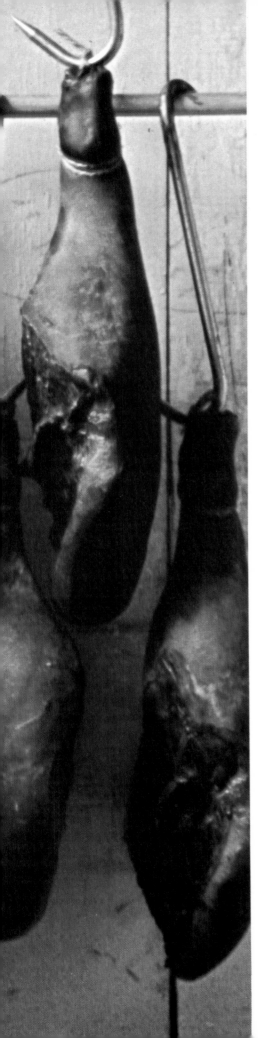

tongue in this brine, after boiling and cooling, for two days per 450g (1lb). Check the brine every two days – if it has become sour, discard it, rinse the tongue, clean and sterilize the bowl or crock as quickly as possible and continue curing in a completely new batch of brine. The tongue should then be boiled for about 4 hours in a large pan of water, with an onion, carrot, bay leaf, half a dozen peppercorns and a few mustard seeds. Allow the tongue to cool, then remove the hard outer skin, the small bones and cartilage from the base of the tongue. It can then be pressed, either in a tongue press or in a cake tin, weighted down with a heavy weight on top of a plate or small board. Turn out when set (this takes about 10 hours, or overnight), and use cold, or as part of a hot dish. Commercially pickled tongues are often very salty, so you may need to soak them for 24 hours in clean, cold water before cooking.

Curing pork
Cured pork is generally referred to as bacon or ham, and is by far the most widely used of the varieties of cured meat. Ham is in fact the hind leg of a pig, cured whole, though the name is used for many forms of cured pork, both smoked and unsmoked. Bacon is the name given to other cuts of cured pork. The flavour of bacon or ham depends on three factors: the food originally fed to the pigs before slaughter, the strength, sweetness or spiciness of the curing brine, and the type of wood used for smoking. When talking about bacon or ham it is difficult to divide the salting and smoking processes, since many well-known cures depend on both for their distinctive flavours.

Curing pork at home
Some of the traditional cures can be carried out at home, though four important safety factors should be borne in mind. Firstly, care should be taken to obtain good fresh meat. It is worth having a word with your butcher so that he can obtain really prime quality meat for you. Secondly, maintain rigid standards of personal hygiene while handling the pork, before and during curing. Scald the equipment before use with boiling water. Thirdly, make sure the meat is completely immersed in the brine or curing liquid: weight it down with a board or plate if necessary. Finally, before you eat the bacon or ham it must be cooked thoroughly to kill off bacteria which could cause food poisoning. The meat should be cooked in high heat, and the interior temperature should reach at least 70°C (140°F). If you are going to embark on home curing it is worth investing in a meat thermometer so that you can be absolutely sure about this.

Simple pickled pork
For pickled pork, or unsmoked 'green' bacon, you simply need to soak the pork in strong brine. It is wise to start with an economical joint such as flank, belly or collar, particularly as the brine penetrates more easily through these relatively thin cuts. The bacon can then be boiled and eaten with pease pudding, or cut finely and used as bacon for frying. Prepare a brine from 2kg (4lb) coarse salt, 60g (1¼oz) saltpetre and 6 litres (1½ gallons) of water. The brine should then be boiled and skimmed until the liquid is clear. When cool, pour the brine over the pork in a glass, earthenware or stoneware container, and steep for 24 hours in a temperature not more than 3-4°C (35-38°F), probably in the refrigerator. (For both pickled and cured bacon, it is

best not to remove the skin until after cooking.) After this time, remove the ham and squeeze it to remove excess liquid and blood. Dry it and store it in the refrigerator. This bacon should be used within a week. For more prolonged preservation, the pork should be cured and smoked.

Smoked meat

The smoking of meat is a centuries-old craft and until recent times in country areas, even the poorest families kept at least one or two pigs which were eventually prepared for smoking to provide ham, bacon and sausages. The oldest method of smoking was done outside over a smouldering fire, but later the process moved into the house and the food was hung over the kitchen fire in the chimney. Some old houses have fire places with a recess on one side of the chimney. These were called 'bacon cupboards', as a side of pork would be left to hang for a month or so until it was well and truly smoked. In some areas a separate smoke-house was built adjacent to the house and some of these are in existence today. Today home smoking of meat is obviously not carried out as extensively as it was before this century. Firstly few modern houses have large enough fireplaces – if at all – and secondly, the wide variety and good quality of commercially smoked meat, and other foods such as poultry and cheese, mean that lengthy home smoking is no longer necessary.

Curing bacon and ham

There are several traditional British cures and many of them are called after the town or area where the particular cure originated. Nowadays the names are used to describe the type of cure and its ingredients.

Many processors or companies have their own 'secret recipe' for the brine, because it is this that gives their bacon the distinctive flavour. Most bacon is cured in a brine solution, although some may be dry cured in salt, which gives it a paler and rougher texture than normal. The bacon is then generally smoked to give it a rich flavour, although unsmoked bacon is also available – it has a milder flavour and a slightly shorter storage life.

Of the well-known British cures, Wiltshire is probably the most widely used by bacon processors. Bradenham is recognized by its black skin and is sweet cured and smoked by a special method. York ham, which is famous throughout the world, has a mild, delicate flavour which is reputed to have originated from use of the sawdust left over from the building of York Minster.

Britain is not the only country to produce smoked pork, in fact most countries have their own specialities – Italy with its famous Parma ham, the Virginia sweet-cure ham of America, the many varieties of smoked sausages from Germany, and the equally numerous varieties of salami, which is said to have originated in Hungary, but which are now made in many European countries.

Smoking pork at home

If you have the facilities to smoke even a small piece of pork, boned loin is probably the best cut for home smoking. It is well worth trying as the flavour will differ from commercially smoked pork. Smoking pork is similar to smoking fish in that it is soaked in a brine solution for a length of time and then smoked for anything from a few hours

Right: This French farmhouse kitchen has the perfect situation for smoking: a solid fuel stove set into a deep chimney breast over which pork belly, garlic sausages and hams can be hung to smoke as long as is needed. Below: Smoked bacon slices are an integral part of many recipes, and are particularly good combined with cheese and cream in egg dishes such as quiche lorraine or omelette.

Above: Clear honey from the comb would be ideal — though expensive — for the sweet cure described on this page.

to several days!

The following method is the one used by the well known gourmet and restaurateur, Paul Leyton who, with his wife, prepare and serve superb meals at The Miners Arms, Priddy in Somerset. The meat is smoked in an old open-hearth fire place and the result is excellent.

Smoked loin of pork

Use a non-metallic container, such as a *white* plastic bucket or bowl of about 20 litres (5 gallons) capacity, to soak the pork in. Prepare a brine with 2kg (4½lb) salt, 20g (¾oz) saltpetre, 125g (4oz) dark brown sugar, 225g (8oz) clear honey, 125ml (4fl oz) lemon juice and 8 litres (14 pints) boiling water. Cover the brine and set aside to cool. Pre-cool the meat to 4°C (40°F) before immersing it in the brine. The amount of brine given here is sufficient for two boned loins of pork. While the pork is being cured it is very important that it is kept at a temperature of 4°C (40°F) or below, and this can normally only be achieved by keeping it in the refrigerator.

Place the pork in the brine for 15 minutes, then remove it and rinse it in cold water. Add 2 litres (3½ pints) of dry cider to the brine. Return the pork to the brine and leave it in the refrigerator for five days. It is important that the pork is completely immersed, so if necessary place a non-metallic weight on top of it. Turn the pork every day.

At the end of this time, remove the pork from the brine, pat it dry with kitchen paper towels and weigh it. This is important since after smoking there should be a 25 per cent loss of weight, which indicates that the smoking process is completed.

Mr Leyton wraps each loin in caul fat and hangs them inside the large chimney where the smoke from a hardwood log fire can billow around them. They are not hung right over the fire as they would become too hot and the smoke would not penetrate through to the centre of the meat.

The temperature will fluctuate between 55°C (130°F) when the fire is burning brightly during the day and 15°C (60°F) when it is damped down at night. The time taken depends on several factors – the weather, the amount of draught in the chimney – so the meat may need to be left to smoke for five to seven days.

After the smoking process if completed, the meat should be cooled quickly and stored in the refrigerator where, uncut, it will keep for several weeks. Providing the meat is correctly wrapped, it will retain its high quality if stored in a home freezer. Wrap the meat in clean muslin, then seal it in heavy polythene, excluding as much air as possible. Storage life is up to six months.

Other cures for pork

Wiltshire. As already mentioned the Wiltshire cure is one of the most popular. This version may not taste exactly like commercially produced Wiltshire ham of course, but you can experiment and may find that your ham tastes even more distinctive. For a 4-5kg (9½-11½lb) boned ham you will need a brine of 650g (1½lb) coarse salt, ¾oz saltpetre, a good litre (2 pints) of beer, 450g (1lb) black treacle or molasses, 10 to 12 juniper berries and 12g (½oz) crushed black peppercorns. Boil all these ingredients together, leave to cool and then pour over a piece of pork which has been pickled for an hour in the brine given on page 212. The pork should be cured in a non-metal container at a temperature of 3°C (35°F), for two days per 450g (1lb) weight. Turn the ham every other day so that all parts are well-covered.

After the curing time, remove the ham and dry it with clean muslin, then place it in a cotton bag. Leave it to dry for 24 hours in a cool place, then hang it near a hardwood fire or in a smoke box, and cool smoke at 25°-30°C (75°-85°F). About 24 hours of smoking is necessary, but if the smoking is intermittent, this could take as long as a week. Weigh the ham before and after smoking to be sure.

Suffolk. This is a light, sweet cure. For the same size piece (4-5kg) prepare in brine as for the Wiltshire cure, then make the cure from a good litre (2 pints) of beer, the same amount of malt vinegar, 650g (1½lb) coarse salt, 12g (½oz) each of peppercorns, cloves and saltpetre, and 450g (1lb) sugar. Boil all these ingredients in a large saucepan. In another saucepan, boil 50g (2oz) hops in a litre (2 pints) of water for half an hour. Then strain this liquid into the rest of the cure. Allow to cool. Place the pork in a non-metal dish and pour over the curing liquid. Leave for two days per 450g (1lb) weight, unless the flesh is very thick, in which case allow three days per 450g (1lb) keeping it at a temperature of no more than 3°-4°C (35°-40°F). Turn and baste every day. Dry the meat for 24 hours in a cool place, then place in a muslin bag and smoke in the same way as for the Wiltshire cure. Remove the bag to look at the bacon at regular intervals, as it should not be allowed to become too dry, Weigh the bacon before and after to make sure you do not smoke it for too long.

When smoking ham or bacon, hang it near enough to the fire to come in contact with the smoke, but not so close that it becomes sooty. Store it in a cool dry larder, hung from the ceiling so there is free circulation of air around it, or store it in the refrigerator. Cook it before use and eat hot or cold. Once cooked it is best stored in the refrigerator and will keep for about a week.

Salted beans

If there is a glut of beans in the garden and no freezer is available a good way to preserve them is by salting. It is however advisable to use them within six months providing they have been correctly prepared – if not they will go slimy and should not be used.

Choose young, fresh runner or French beans. Wash well in cold running water, dry with kitchen paper towels. French beans may be left whole and runner beans are best sliced.

Kitchen salt is the most suitable to use. Table salt contains a preservative and it is difficult to achieve a sufficient density with grated block salt. For every 1.35kg (3lb) beans 450g (1lb) kitchen salt is required.

Place a layer of salt in a glass or earthenware crock or in jars (metal containers must not be used) and cover with a layer of beans. Fill the crock or jars with alternate layers, pressing the beans well down and finishing with a layer of salt. Cover and set aside for two to three days to allow the beans to settle down. Fill the crock or jars with more salt and beans. Cover with a moisture-proof material such as strong polythene, secured with string or with screw-on or clip-on glass covers.

To cook the beans. Rinse thoroughly under cold running water, soak for two hours in warm water and drain. Cook in boiling water for 20 to 30 minutes until they are just tender.

Below: If you grow your own runner beans it is easy to preserve the surplus in dry salt.

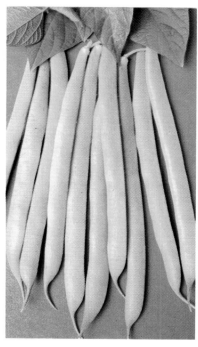

Nuts keep well in a dry place if stored in their shells. Shelled nuts can be roasted and salted, then stored in airtight tins. Most nuts can be treated in this way: try salting an interesting mixture such as pistachios, almonds, Brazils, cashews, peanuts and hazelnuts.

Salted nuts

Almonds, cashews, peanuts and mixed nuts can be brought ready salted, but as they are easy to do at home it is well worthwhile.

Heat 2 tablespoons of oil with 25g (1oz) butter in a frying pan. Add the shelled nuts, about 125g (4oz) at a time, and fry gently, stirring frequently until the nuts are golden brown. Drain the nuts on kitchen paper towels and sprinkle generously with salt. When cold store in an air-tight container. As an alternative to plain salt the nuts may be sprinkled with garlic salt.

Sauerkraut

Sauerkraut is a German term meaning literally 'sour plant'. It is made by placing alternate layers of finely shredded white cabbage and coarse salt (15g ($\frac{1}{2}$oz) per 450g (1lb) cabbage) in a large wooden tub or earthenware crock. It is then covered by a clean cloth and a lid which is weighted down with a heavy weight. The salted cabbage is then

left to ferment and mature for three weeks in a temperature of about 20-25°C (70-80°F). It can be flavoured with caraway seeds or juniper berries if liked. After a few days the brine rises above the level of the lid and a scum forms; remove this every few days. If the brine level falls, top it up with a brine made from 50g (1oz) salt to 1 litre (2 pints) water.

Fresh sauerkraut should be used at once as it does not keep longer than three or four days. Use it on its own with German sausages and mashed potato for a filling meal (the sauerkraut and sausages can be cooked together in the same pot for added flavour), or as part of many other delicious recipes. If you make more sauerkraut than you need for immediate use it can be preserved by bottling. Drain the juice into a saucepan and boil it, add the shredded cabbage and bring back to simmering point. Pack at once into warm sterilized jars, cover and process in boiling water for 25 minutes. Test the seal, cover and store.

Cabbage can be preserved as sauerkraut, a well-known German speciality. It can be served plain or varied with fruit such as apricots or flavouring such as caraway seeds. It is traditionally accompanied by sausages such as saveloys or Frankfurters.

Delicate smoked trout can be eaten whole with horseradish sauce, or pounded with sherry, cream and tabasco to make a fish pâté.

Recipes using cured foods

Salted or smoked foods may seem commonplace – there are so many different types available. Here we give some surprisingly exotic recipes which use both home cured as well as commercial produce, for those who like the special tastes but do not have the facilities to cure their own food.

Kipper Pâté
4 servings

450g (1lb) kipper fillets, cooked, boned, skinned and flaked
50g (2oz) butter, softened
4 tablespoons double cream
1 teaspoon Tabasco sauce
1 tablespoon sweet sherry
Pepper, to taste
50g (2oz) clarified butter, melted

Place all the ingredients, except the pepper and clarified butter, in the jar of an electric blender. Blend, at medium speed, for 1 or 2 minutes until the mixture is smooth. If an electric blender is not available, pound the mixture together in a mixing bowl with the back of a wooden spoon.

Add pepper to taste and spoon the mixture into one serving dish or four individual ones. Pour the melted butter over the top. Place the dish or dishes in the refrigerator for at least 2 hours before serving.

This pâté will keep in the refrigerator for a few days.

Smoked Trout Pâté
6 servings

1kg (2lb) smoked trout, skinned, boned and flaked
125ml (4fl oz) single cream
125g (4oz) cream cheese

2 tablespoons horseradish sauce
2 tablespoons lemon juice
1 teaspoon black pepper
1 tablespoon chopped fresh parsley
3 thin lemon slices, halved

Place the fish and cream in the jar of an electric blender and blend at high speed until the mixture forms a purée. Alternatively, pound the fish with the cream, a little at a time, in a mortar with a pestle until the mixture forms a smooth paste.

Spoon the purée into a medium-sized mixing bowl. With a wooden spoon, beat in the cream cheese, horseradish sauce, lemon juice, pepper and parsley. Continue beating the mixture until it is smooth and creamy. Spoon the pâté into individual ramekin dishes. Smooth the tops down with the back of a spoon and garnish with the lemon half slices.

Place the dishes in the refrigerator to chill for 1 hour before serving.

Taramasalata

6 servings

450g (1lb) smoked cod's roe, skinned
4 slices white bread, crusts removed

and soaked in milk for 15 minutes
4 cloves of garlic, crushed
300ml (10fl oz) olive oil
4 tablespoons lemon juice
$\frac{1}{2}$ teaspoon freshly ground
black pepper
$\frac{1}{4}$ cucumber, thinly sliced
6 firm tomatoes, sliced
6 black olives

Place the cod's roe in a large mixing bowl and pound it with the end of a rolling pin, or use a pestle and mortar, until the gritty texture is eliminated.

Squeeze as much moisture out of the bread as possible and add it to the bowl, with the garlic. Continue pounding until the mixture is smooth.

Add the oil, a few drops at a time, pounding constantly and adding a little of the lemon juice from time to time. Continue pounding until the mixture forms a soft, smooth paste and is pale pink in colour.

Alternatively, place all the ingredients in an electric blender and blend at moderately high speed until a soft paste has formed.

Beat the pepper into the mixture and arrange equal quantities of it on six small serving plates. Surround the paste with the cucumber and tomato slices and top each portion with an olive. Serve immediately.

Taramasalata is one of the best known Greek dishes. Made from smoked cod's roe, cream and lemon juice, it is often served with hot 'pitta', the flat bread of the eastern Mediterranean.

Rollmops are salt herring fillets soused in flavoured vinegar and rolled round single pickled cucumbers. (See page 138.)

Rollmops
4-6 servings

10 salt herring fillets
350ml (12fl oz) white wine vinegar
350ml (12fl oz) water
6 black peppercorns
3 juniper berries
1 tablespoon mustard seed
3 whole allspice berries
1 bay leaf
2 tablespoons German mustard
1 tablespoon capers
10 pickled cucumbers
2 large Spanish onions, thinly sliced in rings
4 to 6 parsley sprigs

Place the herring fillets in a large bowl and cover with water. Place the bowl in the refrigerator to chill for 12 hours.

Drain the fillets and wash them with cold water. Pat dry with kitchen paper towels. Place on a wooden board and, using a sharp knife, carefully remove and discard any bones, making sure the fillets remain intact. Set aside.

Place the vinegar, water, peppercorns, juniper berries, mustard seed,

allspice berries and bay leaf in a large saucepan. Set the pan over high heat and bring the liquid to the boil. Reduce the heat to low and simmer, uncovered, for 10 minutes. Remove the pan from the heat and set aside to cool.

Lay the fillets out flat on the wooden board, skin side down. Spread a little of the mustard over each fillet and sprinkle with some of the capers. Place a cucumber at the wide end of each fillet, and roll up securing with a wooden cocktail stick. Set aside.

Lay one-third of the onion rings in

the bottom of a large, deep glass dish. Arrange half of the rollmops over the top. Continue making layers until all the ingredients are used up, ending with a layer of onion rings.

Pour the vinegar mixture through a fine strainer over the rollmops and onions. Cover the dish with aluminium foil and place in the refrigerator. Leave for 1 week before serving.

Rollmop Hors d'Oeuvre
4-6 servings

450g (1lb) rollmops, drained and with 50ml (2fl oz) of the liquid and the onions reserved
2 hard-boiled eggs, separated
Juice of 1 lemon
35g (1½oz) fresh brown breadcrumbs

Place the rollmops on a wooden board. Using a sharp knife, gently ease off the skin. Chop the rollmops finely with the knife and transfer them to a medium-sized mixing bowl. Chop the egg whites and reserved onions finely. Add them to the rollmops.

Stir in the reserved liquid, the lemon juice and the breadcrumbs until all the ingredients form a smooth paste.

Spoon the mixture into a serving dish. Rub the hard-boiled egg yolks through a strainer on to the fish mixture. Serve at once, or cover with aluminium foil and place the dish in the refrigerator to chill until required.

Super Kedgeree
8 servings

225g (8oz) long grain rice
450g (1lb) smoked haddock fillets
4 eggs
2 large onions
175g (6oz) butter
1 tablespoon capers
4 tablespoons chopped parsley
100g (4oz) cooked, peeled prawns or shrimps
Salt and pepper

Rinse the rice and cook it in boiling water for 10-12 minutes. Rinse in plenty of cold water to separate the grains.

Cook the fish gently in water for about 10-12 minutes. Strain, remove the skin and any bones. Flake the meat with a fork. Hard-boil the eggs, remove

Below: Super Kedgeree is perfect served at a Sunday 'brunch' party. For a simple, more economical breakfast or supper dish omit the prawns and use only smoked haddock flakes poached gently in milk (left).

their shells and chop roughly. Chop the onions and fry until soft in 25g (1oz) of the butter. Melt the rest of the butter and add the cooked fish and rice. Add the chopped eggs, the onions, the capers, 3 tablespoons of the parsley and the prawns. Mix carefully and season with salt and freshly ground pepper. Place in a hot dish and serve sprinkled with the rest of the parsley.

Kedgeree will not spoil if kept warm in a low oven – 120°C (250°F, Gas Mark ½) – for about half an hour. Cover the dish with buttered foil. For a more economical meal omit the prawns or shrimps.

Glazed Roast Ham
12 servings

1 × 4.50kg (10lb) ham, soaked
overnight in cold water
Bouquet garni, made with 4 parsley
sprigs, 2 thyme sprays and 2 bay
leaves tied together
1 onion, peeled and quartered
2 carrots, scraped and sliced
2 sticks celery, sliced
8 black peppercorns
225g (8oz) soft brown sugar
100g (4oz) clear honey
2 teaspoons dry mustard
125ml (4fl oz) Bourbon whisky
12 cloves
3 oranges, peeled, white pith
discarded and divided into segments

Remove the ham from the soaking water and rinse in fresh water. Place the ham in a large saucepan and add enough cold water to cover. Add the bouquet garni, vegetables and peppercorns. Bring the water to the boil, reduce the heat, cover the pan and simmer for 4-5 hours. Remove the pan from the heat and allow the ham to cool slightly in the liquid.

Preheat the oven to 180°C (350°F, Gas Mark 4).

Meanwhile prepare the glaze. Place the sugar, honey, mustard and 50ml (2fl oz) of the whisky in a mixing bowl and stir well to mix. Set aside. Remove the ham from the liquid and cut away the rind. Score the fat in a diamond pattern with the point of a knife.

Place the ham in a roasting tin and coat the fat with the remaining whisky. Spread the prepared glaze over the fat and insert the cloves into the ham to

make an attractive pattern. Arrange the orange segments on the top, securing each one with a cocktail stick.

Place the tin in the oven and roast the ham for 1 hour, basting occasionally, until the fat is golden brown. Serve immediately, with cider to drink.

Smoked Haddock Scramble
4 servings

8 eggs
2 tablespoons milk
¼ teaspoon salt
½ teaspoon black pepper
¼ teaspoon grated nutmeg
50g (2oz) butter
450g (1lb) cooked smoked haddock
skinned, boned and flaked
2 drops Tabasco sauce
8 slices hot buttered toast
4 parsley sprigs

Place the eggs, milk, salt, pepper and nutmeg in a medium-sized mixing bowl and beat the mixture with a wire whisk or rotary beater until it is frothy.

In a medium-sized saucepan, melt the butter over moderate heat. When the foam subsides, add the egg mixture. Reduce the heat to low and cook, stirring constantly, until the eggs have thickened slightly.

Stir in the flaked haddock and the Tabasco sauce and continue cooking, stirring constantly for 2 minutes.

Meanwhile, place the toast on warmed individual serving dishes. Remove the pan from the heat. Carefully pile the mixture on to the toast.

Garnish with the parsley sprigs and serve immediately, as a light supper or breakfast dish.

A piece of home-cured ham can be prepared in many ways, to eat hot or cold. Here, the ham is combined with sauerkraut. When preparing ham for roasting or baking, boil it first with the skin still on, then remove it before placing the meat in the oven.

Ham Baked with Sauerkraut
6-8 servings

½ smoked ham, about 2.75-3kg
(6-7lb), soaked overnight
6 peppercorns
12 juniper berries (optional)

5 tablespoons vegetable oil
2 medium-sized onions, thinly sliced
3 carrots, thinly sliced
1 garlic clove, crushed
1kg (2lb 2oz) sauerkraut, drained
300ml (10fl oz) dry white wine
300ml (10fl oz) chicken stock
1 tablespoon butter

Place the ham in a large saucepan and

*Right: Spiced Salt Beef is a tasty
way to prepare the more economical
cuts of beef like topside, silverside,
brisket or flank. The leftover stock is
a good basis for clear beef broth.
Below: Peanut Biscuits add a
touch of variety to the tea table.*

half fill it with water. Add the peppercorns and juniper berries, if used. Place over moderately high heat and bring to the boil. Reduce the heat to low and simmer for about 2 hours, allowing 20 minutes for every 450g (1lb) plus 20 minutes over. Add more boiling water when necessary. Remove the pan from the heat and cool the ham in the cooking liquid.

In a large saucepan, heat the oil over moderate heat. Add the onions, carrots and garlic and cook, stirring occasionally, until the onions are soft and translucent but not brown. Stir in the sauerkraut, then pour in the wine and stock. Increase the heat to moderately high and bring the liquid to the boil. Remove the pan from the heat.

Preheat the oven to 180°C (350°F, Gas Mark 4).

When the ham is cool remove it from the cooking liquid and peel off the skin. Place it in a deep roasting tin and dot the butter on top. Spoon the sauerkraut mixture around the ham, and bake for about an hour, allowing 10 minutes to every 450g (1lb), plus 10 minutes over.

Remove the tin from the oven and transfer the ham to a large serving dish. Heap the sauerkraut around the ham and serve at once.

Spiced Salt Beef
6-8 servings

1 × 2.25kg (5lb) piece of beef (topside, silverside or brisket)
2 tablespoons sea salt
2 tablesppons black pepper
2 tablespoons crushed bay leaves
2 tablespoons ground cloves
2 tablespoons mixed spice
Butter and oil for frying
2 onions
3 sticks celery
3 carrots
Water

Place the beef in brine, (see page 213), cover and leave in the refrigerator for 24 hours.

Remove it and rub in the salt, crushed bay leaves, black pepper and ground cloves.

Return the meat to the brine and continue the process for 4 to 5 days. After this time, remove the beef from the brine, rinse it in cold water and drain it well. Sprinkle it with the two tablespoons of mixed spice.

Fry the beef in a little butter and oil until brown. Chop the onions, celery and carrots.

In a large saucepan, fry the onions, celery and carrots (or other vegetables as preferred) in butter and oil. Place the meat on top of the vegetables and add sufficient water to come half way up the saucepan. Bring to to the boil and remove any scum from the surface. Reduce the heat to low, cover the pan and simmer for 3-4 hours until it is tender. Serve hot or cold with pease pudding (see page 194).

Peanut Biscuits
About 30 biscuits

225g (8oz) flour
1 tablespoon sugar
$\frac{1}{4}$ teaspoon ground allspice
125g (4oz) butter
60g (1$\frac{1}{2}$oz) vegetable fat
4 to 5 tablespoons water
2 tablespoons finely chopped salted peanuts
3 tablespoons salted peanuts

Sift the flour, sugar and allspice into a medium-sized mixing bowl. Add the butter and vegetable fat and cut them into small pieces with a table knife. With your fingertips, rub the fats into the flour mixture until it resembles coarse breadcrumbs. Add 4 tablespoons of the water and the finely chopped peanuts and mix them into the flour mixture with the knife. With your hands, mix and knead the dough until it forms a ball. Add the remaining water if the dough is too dry.

Cover the dough and chill it in the refrigerator for 30 minutes.

Preheat the oven to 190°C (375°F Gas Mark 5).

Remove the dough from the refrigerator and roll it out on a lightly floured surface to 5mm ($\frac{1}{4}$in) thick. Cut the dough into about 30 'fingers' and place them on two large baking sheets.

Divide the nuts among the dough fingers, pressing them into the dough with your fingertips.

Place the baking sheets in the oven and bake for 15 minutes or until the pastry is lightly browned at the edges. Remove the baking sheets from the oven and allow the biscuits to cool for 5 minutes. Transfer to a wire rack to cool completely before serving.

Short-term preserving

In these busy days everyone has to prepare and cook meals at some time so it is a good idea to make something extra to use in a few days time while you are in the kitchen, especially if the electric mixer is in use or the oven already turned on. Alternatively you may just feel you would like to make something different! It also saves time to make some extras that will help when entertaining or be useful for quick snacks, and it is nice to know that home-made biscuits or fruit cakes are at the ready to serve with a cup of tea or coffee when friends call in unexpectedly. For inexpensive gifts sweets and candies packed in attractive boxes are always acceptable. The following recipes are some suggestions for items which will keep for a fortnight or even longer – why wait until the week before Christmas to make the cake, as it will taste much nicer if made two or three months in advance!

Left: Home-made sweets and candies keep for several weeks if stored properly in airtight containers, and they are always firm favourites as gifts. Recipes for Vanilla Fudge and Peppermint Creams are given on page 240 and 241. Below: Newcastle Potted Salmon (see page 231) is one of the delicious fish recipes which keep for a few days in the refrigerator if completely sealed in clarified butter.

Short-term preserves

This is a general title to cover all those useful 'standards' which may keep for a little as two or three days or as much as three months. As with many of the other recipes in the different sections, a number of these could make use of ingredients you have already preserved yourself – for instance, the Christmas cake could use home dried or candied fruit, the herbs needed for pâtés could be your own, or you might even salt your own pig's head for brawn!

Bloater Paste

100g (4oz) fresh white breadcrumbs
175ml (6fl oz) water
4 bloaters, cooked, skinned, filleted and flaked
1 clove of garlic, crushed
50g (2oz) butter, melted
Juice of ½ lemon
½ teaspoon black pepper
½ teaspoon cayenne pepper

Place the breadcrumbs in a mixing bowl with the water. When the breadcrumbs are thoroughly soaked, squeeze out all the excess water. Place the breadcrumbs, bloaters, garlic, butter, lemon juice, pepper and cayenne in a mortar and pound them with a pestle until they form a smooth paste. Alternatively, blend all the ingredients in an electric blender until the paste is smooth.

Spoon the paste into small pots. Cover with aluminium foil and place in the refrigerator until required. This paste will keep for 2-3 days.

Potted Shrimps
4 servings

125g (5oz) butter
1 teaspoon mixed spice
½ teaspoon grated nutmeg
Pinch of cayenne pepper
1 teaspoon black pepper
450g (1lb) peeled shrimps
100g (4oz) clarified butter (see method)

Melt the butter in a saucepan and stir in the mixed spice, nutmeg, cayenne and black pepper. Add the shrimps and mix well until blended.

Spoon into individual pots and set aside. To clarify the butter, place in a small saucepan with 2 tablespoons of water. Bring to the boil then leave to cool and drain off the liquid. Melt the

Below: Bloater Paste uses the famous Yarmouth bloaters (see page 204) or their equivalent as its base, and is equally tasty served as a dinner party 'starter' with slices of lemon and toast, or as a sandwich filler.

Like Newcastle Potted Salmon, Potted Shrimps are sealed in clarified butter. Serve them in individual ramekins, or for an attractive display, in small tumblers, accompanied by buttered fresh brown bread with the crusts removed and rolled.

butter and pour over the shrimps. Cool, cover with aluminium foil and keep in the refrigerator for up to a week.

Newcastle Potted Salmon

450g (1lb) fresh salmon
1½ teaspoons salt
1½ teaspoons black pepper
½ teaspoon ground mace
¼ teaspoon ground cloves
150g (5oz) butter
4 peppercorns
2 bay leaves

Preheat the oven to moderate 180°C (350°F, Gas Mark 4). Season the salmon well with half the salt and pepper and the mace and cloves. Place the fish in a small casserole and dot it with 25g (1oz) of the butter, cut into small pieces. Sprinkle the peppercorns over the fish and lay the two bay leaves on top.

Place the casserole in the centre of the oven and bake for 30 to 40 minutes, or until the fish flakes easily when tested with a fork. Remove the casserole from the oven. Take the fish from the casserole and discard the skin and bones. Strain the cooking liquid and reserve.

Place the fish in a mortar with 50g (2oz) of the remaining butter and pound it with a pestle. Add a little of the strained cooking liquid to make the pounding easier. Alternatively, put the fish, butter and cooking liquid in an electric blender and blend until smooth. Mix in the remaining salt and pepper. Pack the fish into three small pots, leaving a 5mm (¼in) space at the top. Set aside to cool.

In a small saucepan melt the remaining butter over low heat. Remove the pan from the heat and set aside to cool for 5 minutes.

Pour one-third of the melted butter into each pot. Cover the pots with aluminium foil. Potted salmon will keep for several days if stored in the refrigerator.

Note: Trout or carp could be potted in the same way.

Chicken Liver Pâté
4-6 servings

100g (4oz) butter
450g (1lb) chicken livers, chopped
1 onion, peeled and finely chopped
1 clove of garlic, crushed
½ teaspoon mixed spice
1 teaspoon dry mustard
2 tablespoons brandy
Salt and pepper to taste
Stuffed green olives, sliced

Melt the butter and fry the chicken livers until cooked and brown. Transfer to a mixing bowl. Fry the onion and garlic until soft and add to the chicken livers with any remaining butter.

If a smooth pâté is preferred, put the liver and onion mixture through a mincer or an electric blender.

Stir in the mixed spice, mustard, brandy and salt and pepper. Spoon the mixture into a serving dish, garnish with the olives, cover and chill in the refrigerator.

This pâté will keep in the refrigerator for up to a week.

Preserved Goose
4-6 servings

1 × 4kg (8lb) goose
100g (4oz) salt
Lard (see method)
2 bouquets garnis
3 large cloves of garlic
8 cloves
8 peppercorns

Divide the goose into four pieces. Do not remove any carcass bones adhering to the flesh as they help hold the meat in shape during cooking. Remove all fat from the inside of the goose and render it down in a large heavy pan or casserole. Cool and store in a refrigerator or cool, dry place.

Rub the pieces of goose thoroughly with the salt, transfer to an earthenware pot or bowl and leave covered in a cool place for 48 hours.

Weigh the rendered-down goosefat. There should be at least 1.35kg (3lb); if not, add sufficient lard to make up to this weight. Then heat the fat in a large heavy pan or casserole. Dust the salt from the goose, wiping each piece with a cloth, and place in the fat. Tie the bouquets garnis and other seasonings in a piece of muslin and add them to the pan. Place a lid on the pan and cook over low heat for at least 2½ hours. Pierce the meat with a skewer or knitting needle. When the juices run absolutely clear the goose is cooked.

Drain the goose from the fat and carefully remove the carcass bones. Discard the herb bag and strain half the cooking fat into a sterilized glass or stoneware jar. Add the goose meat, then pour the remainder of the strained fat over and around the meat, completely filling the jar. If the contents does not reach the brim add extra melted lard as necessary. Leave

Garlic is a store-cupboard essential which is used in thousands of recipes. In the markets of Europe it is possible to buy large strings of garlic which, hung in a cool dry place, will last several months.

Above: Chicken Liver Pâté is cheap and easy to make. It is a useful standby when weekend guests are expected, as it can be served as a first course or used in sandwiches, perhaps for a picnic. Serve with wafer thin pieces of toast and curls of butter. Left: Preserved Goose is cooked initially with two bouquets garnis. These could use dried herbs (see page 187) or fresh ones. A typical fresh bouquet garni consists of a sprig of parsley and thyme and a bay leaf. These can be tied together and discarded at the end of the cooking time.

233

uncovered in a cold, dry place until the fat has solidified. Then press a piece of greaseproof or waxed paper well down on to the fat and seal the container with a tight-fitting lid. Store in the refrigerator. It will keep for about a month.

Confit d'oie is delicious re-heated in some of its fat and served with a potato purée, salad or fresh peas.

Pâté de Campagne
6-8 servings

350g (12oz) thin streaky bacon
rashers, rinds removed
450g (1lb) minced lean pork
225g (8oz) minced lean veal
350g (12oz) calf's liver, finely
chopped
2 cloves of garlic, crushed
$\frac{1}{2}$ teaspoon dried sage
1 teaspoon dried rosemary
100g (4oz) butter, melted
150ml (5fl oz) brandy
Salt and pepper to taste
6 bay leaves

Line the base of a 1 litre (2 pint) terrine or soufflé dish with half of the bacon rashers.

Preheat the oven to 180°C (350°F, Gas Mark 4).

Mix the minced pork, veal and calf's liver together in a mixing bowl. Stir in the garlic, herbs, butter and enough brandy to give a firm consistency. Add salt and pepper.

Spoon the mixture into the prepared dish. Place the remaining bacon on top, then the bay leaves. Cover the dish with foil.

Place the dish in a roasting tin and pour in enough water to come half way up the side of the tin. Bake for 2-2$\frac{1}{2}$ hours. Add more hot water to the pan if necessary.

Cool, cover with a clean piece of foil and chill. Providing it is kept in the refrigerator the pâté will keep up to two weeks.

Brawn
6 servings

1 salted pig's head
10 peppercorns
2 teaspoons salt
2 bay leaves
2 teaspoons dried marjoram

Pâté de Campagne is a good dinner party 'starter' which is best served with hot toast and butter. This pâté can be stored in the freezer for up to three months. Cook it in an aluminium foil container so that it can be covered, labelled and frozen as soon as it has cooled.

234

Succulent pieces of pork set in their own jelly, brawn is traditionally made with the meat from a salted pig's head. If this proves too daunting, you could use another cheap cut such as belly or hand and spring. Add pig's trotters to ensure a good set to the jelly.

1 carrot, scraped and chopped
1 small turnip, peeled and diced
1 large onion, sliced
1 hard-boiled egg, sliced

Wash the head thoroughly in cold water. Cut off the ears and cook them in boiling water for 1 minute, then scrape them free of hair.

Place the ears in a large pan with the head, peppercorns, salt, bay leaves, marjoram, carrot, turnip and onion. Add enough cold water to cover. Bring the water to the boil over high heat. Remove any scum which rises to the surface with a slotted spoon.

Reduce the heat to low, cover the pan and simmer for 2½-3 hours, or until the meat is tender.

Strain and reserve the liquid. Discard the vegetables and flavourings. Remove the meat from the head and cut it into small pieces, removing any fat or gristle. Cut the ears into strips. Arrange the slices of egg in the bottom of a large mould. Press the meat tightly on top of the egg.

Return the liquid to the saucepan with the head bones and bring to the boil over high heat. Skim off any fat that rises to the surface. Lower the heat to moderate and continue boiling until the liquid is reduced by half.

Pour enough of the liquid over the meat in the mould to come just level with the top of the meat. Place a weighted plate on the mould and leave until the next day, when the brawn will be set.

To turn the brawn out, dip the mould into hot water and turn it upside-down on to a serving plate.

Baked Meat Loaf

4-6 servings
6 large white slices white bread, crusts removed
150ml (5fl oz) hot milk
450g (1lb) best quality minced beef
225g (8oz) pork sausage meat
1 onion, peeled and finely chopped
2 tablespoons chopped fresh parsley
½ teaspoon grated nutmeg
1 egg, lightly beaten
Salt and pepper to taste
2 hard-boiled eggs

Grease a 900g (2lb) loaf tin. Preheat the oven to 170°C (325°F, Gas Mark 3).

Soak the bread in the milk then beat

For picnics, cold buffets and informal lunches or suppers, Meat Loaf is a useful standby. If you only need to use part of the loaf, wrap the remainder in aluminium foil and store it in the refrigerator.

with a fork until smooth. Pour into a large mixing bowl and add the remaining ingredients except the hard-boiled eggs. Stir the mixture well until all the ingredients are mixed together.

Spoon half of the mixture into the prepared tin and smooth it level with the back of the spoon. Place the hard-boiled eggs in the centre and spoon over the remaining meat mixture.

Cover the tin with foil and place in a roasting tin with a little water in it.

Bake for 1½-2 hours or until the loaf is firm in the centre and begins to come away from the sides of the tin.

Leave to cool in the tin, then turn out on to a large piece of aluminium foil. Wrap this loosely around the meat loaf and chill in the refrigerator.

The meat loaf will keep in the refrigerator for 2 to 3 days.

Christmas Cake

1.15kg (2½lb) raisins
450g (1lb) currants
175g (6oz) chopped candied peel
100g (4oz) glacé cherries
50g (2oz) crystallized ginger, chopped

175g (6oz) slivered almonds
450g (1lb) flour
1 teaspoon salt
1 teaspoon grated nutmeg
1 teaspoon ground allspice
1 teaspoon ground cinnamon
350g (12oz) butter
400g (14oz) soft brown sugar
8 large eggs, lightly beaten
2 tablespoons black treacle
50ml (2fl oz) brandy

Grease and line a 25cm (10in) round or 23cm (9in) square cake tin with greaseproof paper. Tie a double thickness of brown paper around the outside of the tin. Place the tin on a baking sheet with a double thickness piece of brown paper under the tin.

Preheat the oven to 150°C (300°F, Gas Mark 2).

Place all the fruit and almonds in a large mixing bowl and stir in a few tablespoons of the flour, just enough to lightly coat the fruit.

Sift the remaining flour, salt and spices into another bowl.

In another large mixing bowl cream the butter and sugar together until they are light and fluffy.

Beat in half of the eggs until well blended, then gradually beat in the

remaining eggs. (If the mixture starts to separate add a little of the flour mixture.) Stir in the treacle.

Gradually stir in the flour mixture and when combined stir in the fruit and brandy. Stir well until all the ingredients are well mixed.

Spoon the mixture into the prepared cake tin and smooth the top with the back of the spoon. This will prevent the cake from rising too much in the middle.

Place the cake tin on the baking sheet on a shelf just below the centre of the oven.

Bake for 1 hour. Then lower the temperature to 140°C (275°F, Gas Mark 1) and bake for a further hour. Check the cake and if the top is beginning to brown too much place a piece of aluminium foil over the top. Continue baking for a further 3 hours.

To test if the cake is cooked, insert a metal skewer into the centre – if it comes out dry and clean the cake is cooked.

Allow the cake to cool in the tin for 2 hours, then turn it out on to a wire rack. When the cake is cold remove the greaseproof paper. Set the cake aside for at least 12 hours.

Wrap the cake firmly in a double thickness of aluminium foil and store in an airtight tin.

As this cake improves with keeping it should be made 2 or 3 months in advance. The cake will be greatly improved if every few weeks during storage it is unwrapped and the top pierced with a skewer and 2 tablespoons of brandy are sprinkled over the top. Rewrap and return to the tin. Cover with marzipan at the end of storage time and ice a week later.

Top: All the delicious ingredients that go into rich fruity Christmas Cake. Above: Icing the cake. Roll out 450g (1lb) marzipan or almond paste to 15mm (¾in) thick and cut a strip as wide as the cake's side; then roll it round the cake. Roll another 450g (1lb) marzipan into a circle slightly bigger than the circumference of the cake. Place the cake on it and trim off the excess, pressing it down firmly. Wrap the cake in greaseproof paper and leave for a week to dry out. Then ice with frosted icing and set aside for a couple of days in a cool place to harden the icing.

Gingerbread is a popular teatime treat which has the advantage of keeping for several weeks in an airtight tin. It is equally good served plain or spread with a little butter.

Gingerbread

175g (6oz) butter
225g (8oz) soft brown sugar
175g (6oz) golden syrup
175g (6oz) black treacle
450g (1lb) flour
1 teaspoon salt
1 tablespoon ground ginger
2 teaspoons baking powder
1 egg, lightly beaten
300ml (10fl oz) milk
50g (2oz) crystallized ginger, chopped

Grease and line a 900g (2lb) loaf tin. Preheat the oven to 170°C (325°F, Gas Mark 3).

Place the butter, sugar, syrup and treacle in a saucepan, place over low heat and stir frequently until the sugar has dissolved. Set aside to cool.

Sift the flour, salt, ground ginger and baking powder into a mixing bowl. Make a well in the centre and pour in the melted sugar mixture, egg and milk. Stir gently to combine the flour and liquid, then beat well until a smooth consistency is formed. Stir in the crystallized ginger.

Pour the mixture into the prepared tin and bake for $1\frac{1}{4}$ to $1\frac{1}{2}$ hours or until a skewer inserted in the centre comes out dry.

Leave to cool slightly in the tin then turn out on to a wire rack. When cold wrap in aluminium foil and place in an airtight tin.

This gingerbread will be improved by keeping for at least a week.

Shortbread

200g (8oz) flour
100g (4oz) rice flour
200g (8oz) butter
100-125g (4-5oz) castor sugar

Grease a baking sheet with a little butter or sprinkle a shortbread mould with flour.

Mix the flour and rice flour together in a mixing bowl. Rub the butter into the flour mixture until it resembles coarse breadcrumbs. Add the sugar.

Knead the mixture gently until it forms a stiff, smooth dough.

Turn the dough out on to a floured board and divide in half. Form each piece into a round about 10mm ($\frac{1}{2}$in) thick and 15cm (6in) diameter. Place the dough rounds on the baking sheet or press them into the moulds; (if only one mould is available wrap the other half of dough in greaseproof paper and

Shortbread is as Scottish as whisky and together they are traditionally served on New Year's Eve, with Black Bun – a rich, dark fruit cake in a pastry case. If shortbread fingers are preferred, shape the dough into a rectangle, prick the top all over with a fork, then score the top with a knife lightly to indicate the size of the fingers. When the shortbread is cooked, partially cut into the lines while still warm, but do not separate completely until cold.

keep it in the refrigerator until the first shortbread is cooked).

Crimp the edges of the dough rounds on the baking sheet and place either baking sheet or mould in the refrigerator for 20 minutes.

Preheat the oven to 180°C (350°F, Gas Mark 4). Bake the shortbread for 10 minutes then reduce the temperature to 150°C (300°F, Gas Mark 2) and continue baking for 30-40 minutes until crisp and lightly browned.

Cut the shortbread rounds into triangles and sprinkle with a little castor sugar. Cool on a wire rack and when cold store in an airtight tin.

Providing the tin is really airtight the shortbread will keep for 2 to 3 weeks. If it softens slightly during this time it can be crisped in the oven for a few minutes before serving.

Vanilla Fudge

250ml (8fl oz) canned evaporated milk
50ml (2fl oz) water
450g (1lb) soft brown sugar
50g (2oz) butter
½ teaspoon vanilla essence

Grease an 20cm (8in) square baking tin with a little butter.

Place the evaporated milk, water and sugar in a medium-size saucepan.

Far right: Vanilla flavouring is obtained from the fruit of the vanilla plant, a kind of orchid, and can be bought in pods or as liquid essence. Right: Vanilla essence is often more convenient in cooking, but vanilla sugar, made by inserting a couple of pods into a container of castor sugar, can add a delicious flavour to desserts and sweets.
Centre: The recipe for vanilla fudge, given here, can be varied in many ways. Pieces of hazelnut or almond, crushed between pieces of greaseproof paper with a rolling pin, melted dark chocolate, raisins (preferable soaked in rum), or chopped dates could all be added to the basic recipe. Chocolate should be added with the sugar; nuts or dried fruit should be stirred in once the sugar has dissolved, removing the pan from the heat to do so.

240

Above: Refreshing peppermint creams are ideal for serving with after-dinner coffee. They can be cut in simple rounds, but it is more interesting to use shaped cutters – hearts, stars or geometric shapes. The addition of green food colouring makes an attractive variation.
Right: The peppermint cream mixture should be turned out on a board, dusted with icing sugar, then kneaded lightly for a few minutes.
Far right: If you are adding food colouring you can work it in with your fingers at this stage.

Place over low heat to dissolve the sugar, stirring frequently. Add the butter, in small pieces, and simmer until all the butter has been absorbed.

Increase the heat and boil the mixture, stirring occasionally, until it is fairly thick. Test by dropping a small spoonful into cold water: if it forms a soft ball it is cooked. Alternatively, a sugar thermometer should register 115°C (240°F).

Reduce the heat, add the vanilla and cook, stirring frequently, until the mixture is smooth and thick.

Pour the fudge into the prepared tin and when it is almost cold cut into pieces. Chill in the refrigerator then place each piece in small waxed sweet cases or wrap in greaseproof paper.

The fudge will keep up to 3 months if kept in an airtight tin in a cool dry place.

Peppermint Creams

450g (1lb) icing sugar
2 teaspoons lemon juice
1 egg white
$\frac{1}{2}$ teaspoon peppermint essence
2-3 drops green food colouring (optional)

Place all the ingredients except the green food colouring in a mixing bowl. Beat well until smooth. If you prefer, add the green food colouring to give a pale green colour.

Turn the mixture out on to a board or working surface and sprinkle with icing sugar. Knead the mixture gently and divide into small walnut-sized pieces. Form into flat round shapes and place on a taking sheet. Chill in the refrigerator for 24 hours.

Pack into a covered container with the layers interleaved with greaseproof paper. Store in a cool dark place for up to 1 month.

Chocolate Rum Truffles

125g (4oz) dark cooking chocolate, broken into pieces
3 tablespoons dark rum
50g (2oz) butter
75g (3oz) icing sugar
75g (3oz) ground almonds
2 tablespoons chocolate nibs

Melt the chocolate with the rum in a small mixing bowl placed over a saucepan of water, or in the top of a double boiler. When the chocolate has melted, remove the bowl or top of the double boiler from the heat.

Add the butter, sugar and ground almonds, stirring all the time, until the mixture is smooth and thick. Set aside to cool, then chill in the refrigerator for 30 minutes.

Divide the mixture into 25 to 30 small pieces and form into balls. Dip each ball into the chocolate nibs and press firmly.

Chill again then pack into containers or gift boxes, layered with wax paper, and cover. Store in a cool, dark place for up to two months.

Brandy Butter

100g (4oz) butter
100g (4oz) castor sugar
4 tablespoons brandy

Cream the butter and sugar together in a mixing bowl until light and fluffy. Beat in the brandy a little at a time and spoon the mixture into a small serving dish. Cover with aluminium foil and chill in the refrigerator for up to 2

weeks before serving.

Brandy butter is the traditional British accompaniment to Christmas pudding but is also good if served with other hot fruit puddings.

Cumberland Rum Butter

100g (4oz) butter
100g (4oz) soft brown sugar
1 teaspoon finely grated zest of orange
1 tablespoon lemon juice
75ml (3fl oz) dark rum

Cream the butter and sugar together in a mixing bowl until light and fluffy. Beat in the zest of orange, lemon juice and rum. Spoon into small jars and cover with lids or aluminium foil. Chill in the refrigerator.

This butter will keep in the refrigerator for about a fortnight. Like Brandy Butter, Cumberland Rum Butter is excellent served with Christmas pudding or mince pies.

Chocolate rum truffles can be finished in a variety of ways, apart from dipping them in chocolate nibs as suggested in this recipe.
Overleaf: Certain preserves are particularly associated with the festive season; originally they were meant to last through the dark days of winter. Cumberland Rum or Brandy Butter, worked into balls, are delicious with hot mince pies, preferably made with home-made mincemeat (page 94), and other warming preserves such as Peaches in Brandy (page 35) or home-made liqueurs (page 56) help to cheer a Christmas gathering.

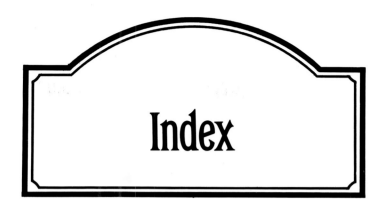

Index

Capitalized entries denote recipes

Pictures supplied by

A-Z Botanical Collection: 84(r), 227(t)
Bryce Attwell: 102(r), 170, 223
Alcan Polyfoil: 152/3
B. Alfieri: 79(1), 120(1)
Rex Bamber: 2, 133(1)
Barnabys: 32(1), 134(1), 136(1)
Bejam News: 155
C. Bevilacqua: 40
Steve Bicknell: 113, 187
Anthony Blake/Fotogram: 4/5, 212/3
R. Boston & Sons: 202, 203
Michael Boys: 114/5
British Tourist Authority: 200
B. Bullough: 12, 53
Camera Press: 166, 207
Eric Carter: 135(t)
Cent Idées No. 13: 6/7, No. 12: 184, No. 23: 215
Patrick Cockburn: 79(r)
R. J. Corbin: 56(1), 70(1), 77(b)
Delu/Paf International: 190, 199, 243
J. Downward: 177(b)
Alan Duns: 10/11, 14, 18, 32(r), 37, 44/5, 46/7, 50, 51, 54(r), 56(r), 77, 85, 86(r), 89, 92/3, 107, 111, 117, 118, 126/7, 128(r), 132, 137, 142(1), 142/3, 143(r), 145(t), 148, 149(b), 154, 156, 166/7, 168(1), 174/5, 178, 188/9, 189, 196(1), 197, 206, 216, 217(t), 218/9, 219(r), 222(t), 225, 233(b), 237(b), 242(t)
V. Finnis: 94(1), 196(r)
B. Furner: 25(r), 133(r), 144
Melvin Grey: 52(t), 64, 100, 110, 136(r), 177, 186(r), 228, 241, 244
Jerry Harpur: 171
HMSO: 66
John Hovell: 20(1), 63, 112
P. Hunt: 84(1), 175(t)
G. Hyde: 34(b), 38(t), 57(1), 83, 86(1), 87(b), 98(1), 121(t), 138(b), 183
Paul Kemp: 27, 34(t), 39, 42/3, 105, 176, 191(t), 192

Don Last: 146/7, 152, 173(b)
Mike Leale: 232/3
David Levin: 54(1), 55, 62, 74/5
Max Logan: 80, 119, 194
Mansell: 33(t), 48, 93, 104, 129, 193, 235(r)
David Meldrum: 24(r), 30, 30/1, 70/1, 134(r), 135(b), 185, 186(1)
National Trust: 147(t)
M. Nimmo: 106
Roger Phillips: 13, 16/7, 19, 21, 33(b), 35, 36, 38(b), 42, 43(b), 46(1), 47, 58, 59, 65, 67, 72, 76, 80/1, 82, 87, 88/9, 94/5, 96/7, 101, 102(1), 103, 108, 109(1), 121(b), 128(1), 130, 131, 139(1), 140/1, 144/5, 150, 150/1, 156/7, 162, 164(t), 164/5, 168/9, 204/5, 208/9, 214, 221, 222(b), 224, 226(1), 226/7, 229, 230, 231(tr, b), 232(1), 234, 235(1), 236, 237(t), 238(1), 238/9, 240, 240/1
Picturepoint: 81(t), 114(1), 121(1)
Prestige Group Ltd: 20(r)
Radio Times Hulton Picture Library: 147
Iain Reed: 22/3, 41, 44(1), 49, 139(r), 242(b)
George Rodger – Magnum: 181
Schwenkfelder Library, Pennsylvania: 99(b)
D. Smith: 24(1), 52(b), 73, 74(r), 98(r), 109(r), 120(r), 124/5, 220, 231(tl)
H. Smith: 25(1), 74(1), 78, 99(t), 138(t), 173(t), 217(b)
Syndication International: 61, 116
Tubby: 90/1, 122/3, 210
Tupperware: 149(t)
Zefa: 180

Acknowledgements

p.90/1 Craftsmen Potter Shop – pottery cups, plates etc.
Heals – Coffee pot, napkins
p.96/7 Heals – sieve